NB 2016

A GREAT JOB HAZEL. JT 2016

D Edwards

Des Edwards "Good Dancer"

HURRICANE
HAZEL

HURRICANE HAZEL

A LIFE WITH PURPOSE

HAZEL McCALLION

with Robert Brehl

HarperCollins*PublishersLtd*

Published by HarperCollins Publishers Ltd

First edition

HarperCollins Publishers Ltd
2 Bloor Street East, 20th Floor
Toronto, Ontario, Canada
M4W 1A8

www.harpercollins.ca

Library and Archives Canada Cataloguing in Publication
information is available upon request

ISBN 978-1-44343-471-3

Printed and bound in the United States of America
RRD 9 8 7 6 5 4 3 2 1

This book is dedicated in loving memory to my mother, whose unconditional love, strength and optimism were an inspiration and whose example of how to live a life of grace will forever remain with me; and to my beloved husband and best friend, Sam, whose support and encouragement taught me the meaning of true love. —HM

To Cobi, once (and always) a girl from Streetsville; now a wonderful wife, mother and manuscript reader with a keen eye and a sharp pencil. —RB

Contents

Prologue

It was October 1954, and a long work week was over. Among the projects I was juggling was leading a team in building a facility in Alberta that would be the first to experiment with extracting oil from the tar sands. My political life was more than a decade away.

I was employed in the private sector for an engineering company called Kellogg Canada Co. Ltd., a firm that had had many successes. Perhaps most notable for Kellogg—and for me personally—was that it built Canada's first synthetic rubber plant in Sarnia, Ontario, during World War II when rubber supplies dried up for the Allies as the Japanese military swept across the Far East.

After the war, Kellogg was building power plants and oil refineries—important things to help Canada grow in the post-war years. Though the hours were long, it was exciting work. The economy was booming and we were building and looking ahead. Always building.

There was nothing especially memorable about this particular work week, but the weekend would most definitely be extraordinary. It was a time I will never forget, and no one else who was there then will either. Little did I know that this event would also be linked to me throughout my career.

After work on Friday, October 15, 1954, I locked up the Kellogg office at the intersection of Yonge and Bloor Streets in Toronto and waited for my husband, Sam, to pick me up for the drive home.

Having married three years earlier, Sam and I both worked in Toronto, but we lived in a picturesque town twenty miles (30 km) northwest of the city, called Streetsville. My job was office manager at Canadian Kellogg, and Sam worked in production at Canada Ink; both companies have long since disappeared. Although today the roads and highways around the Greater Toronto Area are choked with hundreds of thousands of cars, back in 1954 it was not common to commute so far between home and work. With money tight, we often carpooled with another couple named the Bishops, who also lived in Streetsville.

As I got into the car, I noticed how dark it was and how the wind was picking up. There was rain, but it was certainly not a driving rain. We headed west and drove out along Dundas Street. As we made our way through the city, I noticed the branches of trees swaying and leaves blowing across lawns and onto the road. The four of us talked with the swish of the windshield wipers in the background. I don't remember being particularly concerned by this storm as we drove. We all needed groceries, so we stopped at the Dixie Plaza to shop. Though we were only about halfway home, this was the most convenient place for groceries. Unlike today with supermarkets in abundance across urban centres, there were few back then in what was mostly farmland in Toronto Township, as it was called. If we'd had any real concern about the storm, I am sure we would have continued straight on home. Our one-year-old son, Peter, was there with our nanny and we would have rushed to get to him if we'd thought there was any danger.

Our groceries bagged, we went out to the car and felt that the wind was noticeably stronger. We continued along Dundas and turned right on Mississauga Road to head north to Streetsville. A short while later, Sam slammed on the brakes because trees were down and blocking the road. This was around where the campus of University of Toronto at Mississauga (UTM) now sits. Sam turned the car around and headed back to Dundas. We jigged around and found a north-south township line that was clear of debris and we successfully made our way home. I turned the radio on and it sounded as if we were in for some rain and wind, but I still didn't get the impression there was any danger. I don't recall anyone on the radio issuing any warnings or emergency procedure orders.

Sam and I had dinner, played with our baby and hunkered down for the night. I could hear the rain and the wind whipping outside, but the three of us were warm and dry in our house, located on high ground not far from the Credit River.

The next morning, it was still raining, but not nearly as windy. Sam had promised his mother that he would bring the baby to her in Toronto's west end for a visit. After breakfast, they headed out to the car and off they went.

Like working mothers today, I tried to catch up on my housework on Saturday mornings. In the kitchen, I turned on the radio and got the shock of my life. Bridges were out or said to be unsafe. Homes were destroyed. Lives were lost. Hurricane Hazel had struck Toronto overnight with all its force, but thankfully we were spared the brunt of it in Streetsville, although one bridge was damaged beyond repair and had to be replaced.

After listening to the first radio report, I ran to the door to try to catch Sam, but the car was gone. There was no way to reach him. Fear set in as the man on the radio talked about this bridge or that bridge being washed out and police urging people to stay away from all bridges and rivers.

I phoned Sam's mother. She was fine and, like me, somewhat in the dark about the storm. Now she was worried, too, but what could I do? This was long before cellphones, and there was no way to reach Sam in the car. In time—it felt like hours, but it was only minutes—Sam called to let me know he and the baby were safe, and that the drive in wasn't all that adventurous. He later took the same route home and returned safely without incident.

Looking back, I often wonder why we weren't more worried that night. But years later I read the final official forecast of the storm from the Dominion Weather Office. It was issued at 9:30 p.m. on October 15, 1954. It reads:

> *The intensity of this storm has decreased to the point where it should no longer be classified as a hurricane. This weakening storm will continue northward, passing east of Toronto before midnight. The main rainfall associated with it should end shortly thereafter, with occasional light rain occurring throughout the night. Winds will increase slightly to 45 to 50 mph [72 to 80 km/h] until midnight, then slowly decrease throughout the remainder of the night.*

Someone at the weather office failed to do his homework. Or maybe it was simply Mother Nature telling us who is boss.

Instead of dissipating, Hurricane Hazel pounded Southern Ontario throughout the night with the fury of winds of sixty-eight miles per hour (110 km/h) and dumped almost a foot (300 mm) of rain on the Toronto region. Thousands of people were left homeless as torrents of water hurled through flood plains heading to Lake Ontario, taking homes, cars, trailers, anything in the path of the water.

All told, eighty-one people died around Toronto—almost as many as the hundred deaths in the United States, despite the hurricane having hit land with full force in North Carolina, where you'd think it would have been strongest, and making its way through Virginia, Maryland, Pennsylvania and New York. Could some of these Canadian deaths have been prevented had the hurricane been treated like the emergency it was? Would people have evacuated homes located in flood plains before surging storm water tore them apart?

Who knows? But one thing is certain: when another emergency struck the region twenty-five years later and I was mayor of Mississauga, I was sure not to repeat mistakes from Hurricane Hazel when it came to alerting the public, telling the truth, making tough decisions on evacuations and public safety. We'll get to the details of the Mississauga train derailment in a later chapter, but it is safe to say Hurricane Hazel taught me a lot about protecting public safety.

There was some good to come out of the storm. Laws were enacted preventing homes from being built on flood plains all across Canada. Water-diversion systems and engineering became top of mind when planning new urban developments. As pavement rolls out it covers earth that used to absorb water, and when there's a storm the water has to go somewhere, as Hurricane Hazel taught us, so diversion became even more important. The Toronto and Region Conservation Authority (TRCA) was created and flood warning systems were improved, too. And with great foresight, homes on flood plains were expropriated and a beautiful parks system was expanded and enhanced for all citizens to enjoy.

Back in 1954, little did I know this event would be forever linked to me. Heck, I had no idea I would have my health into my nineties and that I would carve out a fifty-year career in politics. Over the years, headline after headline would refer to me as "Hurricane Hazel" because I have always believed in being decisive and putting the best interests of the community ahead of all else.

I've been called other things, too, and some of them uncomplimentary and sexist, like the "Queen of Sprawl," "Attila the Hen," "The Mom Who Runs Mississauga" and the "Mississauga Rattler," so it's little wonder that my favourite nickname is Hurricane Hazel. I even named the most beloved dog I ever owned and my first female German shepherd "Hurricane."

Premiers and prime ministers have called me Hurricane Hazel for sweeping into their offices demanding they do things to help Mississaugans. Former Ontario premier David Peterson once famously called me "a terror to any premier in Ontario. Don't mess with her. She's the only person in the world I'm frightened of." At just five feet two inches tall, I doubt I really frightened David, but it was a compliment if he meant I would tenaciously do anything in my power to help my people.

And yet, in many ways, I am no hurricane. A hurricane destroys; it batters communities, ravages cities and towns. I consider myself a builder who has been so fortunate to be at the helm as Mississauga transformed farmland and a collection of villages into Canada's sixth-largest city, with a population of 750,000. A hurricane also comes and goes quickly; after blowing through it eventually peters out, leaving only its destruction. And that's certainly not me. At age ninety-three, I decided to retire but after twelve consecutive mayoral election victories (the most in Canadian history)—no one could describe me as coming and going quickly!

For years, people have been after me to write a book about my life. People like businessmen Avie Bennett, Harold Shipp, Walter Oster, Ralph Hunter, Ron Lenyk, Iggy Kaneff, Gerry Townsend, Ron Duquette, Elliott Kerr and others have urged me to tell my story, my way. And so, what follows is a book about one woman's life—a very long and full life.

It's worth mentioning that my account is not so long as to prevent it from being read. I want people to read about my accomplishments—and my failures—so that they see that women can be leaders or hockey players; that seniors need not be put out to pasture simply because of their age; and that hard work truly does pay off.

By keeping the book to a readable length, I may be accused of missing this or skipping over that part of the story. But in no way is that my intention. This story will not ignore important, and sometimes painful, events, such as the public inquiry that cost $7.5 million of taxpayers' money. If not for my faith and the faith in me of so many supporters, those dark days would have been far worse.

You bet I want to tell my side of that painful story, but I will not dwell on it, even the part about how I was personally in debt hundreds of thousands of dollars in legal bills over a civil suit that never should have gotten to court. (Fortunately for me, Peel Region voted in 2014 to reimburse me for the legal fees.) Besides, for anyone wishing to find out more about that inquiry, there is a 386-page report that is on the public record.

Instead, I wish to tell my story in the hope that it will inspire young people, perhaps even into considering a life of public service, or that it might help a family dealing with the pain of seeing a loved one with the insidious Alzheimer's disease, or drill home how essential it is to "do your homework" and be prepared for every important decision in life.

I've been called a pioneer among women in politics, and for working women in general. I don't know about that, but I have had important female role models in my life: specifically, my mother; former Ottawa mayor Charlotte Whitton, who in 1951 became the first female mayor of a big city in Canada; and Margaret Thatcher, Britain's first female prime minister.

Along the way, we'll delve into my views about women in politics and business, sharing a few of my personal experiences and insights. Perhaps I can inspire some young women and show them anything is possible, even if the playing field remains tilted towards men. I still chuckle at Whitton's famous quote: "Whatever women do they must do twice as well as men to be thought half as good. Luckily, this is not difficult." Margaret Thatcher said something similar: "If you want something said, ask a man. If you want something done, ask a woman."

I also hope that young men will enjoy this story. Over the last several decades I have been blessed with so much affection from young people. It is difficult to explain; I must remind them of their grandmothers—everyone loves their grandmother. I receive so many heartwarming gestures from young people, like letters and cards, and I am delighted by lineups of kids wanting to have their picture taken with me. Their energy and affection make me feel young.

There is also something in this book for seniors. Too often, we allow society to push us aside as we grow older. That's just plain wrong! I've been to China more than ten times, and it is a country that respects its elders, their experience and their wisdom. I wish seniors in Western society were treated better.

I've been blessed with good health and not everyone is as lucky. And I am not saying all seniors should be running a city or running a business, but I am saying seniors are good for a lot more than simply running a bath, baking cookies or babysitting grandchildren.

When I was eighty-two, I was struck by a pickup truck while crossing a pedestrian walkway. I was out of the hospital and back at work before the Chevy Silverado was out of the repair shop. There's a lot of luck and good genes involved when you live a long life, but feistiness plays a role, too. Ageism is a real form of discrimination, and I think seniors, whenever possible, should stand up and be counted more often instead of passively allowing society to shuffle us off somewhere. As Bette Davis said, "Old age is no place for sissies."

This book is not so much about the political battles of the day as it is about a life lived with purpose. A by-product of that purpose was being part of a team that built a great city from farmland and villages over the course of only forty years. When I was first elected mayor of Mississauga in 1978, I remember looking out of my office window at the old civic centre and seeing cattle and horses grazing across the street. Imagine that.

Today those farm animals have been replaced with things like the curvaceous "Marilyn Monroe" condo towers that have won international awards for their stunning design. The *Globe and Mail* calls Mississauga "The City That Hazel Built" and

Toronto Life says it's "as if she waved a wand and a city was built." That is flattering, but it has been a team effort, with councillors, city staff and residents all having input into building a city where so many different peoples and cultures can live in safety and harmony.

I have made both mistakes and political enemies along the way. But as Winston Churchill said, it is good to make enemies because "that means you've stood up for something, sometime in your life." And I have always stood up for my constituents, whether in the small town of Streetsville in the 1960s and early '70s, or in Mississauga after it was created in 1974 with the amalgamation of the Town of Mississauga (formerly Toronto Township), Port Credit and Streetsville.

They say politics makes strange bedfellows, but it can also build lifetime friendships. It was former Ontario premier Bill Davis who created Mississauga and it was me, then mayor of Streetsville, who fought him tooth and nail, inch by inch, on his plan. Now, Bill teases me regularly, and usually in public, that if not for his creating the City of Mississauga in the first place, I never would be where I am today. It is worth noting that it was also Bill who phoned me on a regular basis during the inquiry in 2010 with the same message: "Stay calm and don't let them get to you."

Another friend, Don Cherry, said much the same thing. After a tough day at the inquiry I came home one night, picked up my phone messages and there was Don's booming voice saying: "Don't let the bastards get to you." That really lifted my spirits. A few nights later, he said much the same thing on national television during "Coach's Corner" on CBC's *Hockey Night in Canada* when his partner Ron MacLean mentioned me on air.

When your spirits are down, is there anything better than having foul-weather friends who know you and stand by you?

The first mayor of Mississauga, Dr. Martin Dobkin, wrote in the *Mississauga News* in 2011 that I am "probably the most unique politician Canada has ever produced." The same year, the *Globe and Mail* said: "Hazel McCallion has been the subject of a political personality cult that dwarfs nearly any other in Canadian history." Former prime minister Jean Chrétien once joked that he thought his winning three consecutive majority governments was impressive until he looked at my record of consecutive mayoral wins dating back to 1978.

As I reflect back over a life that is almost a century long, one thing stands out and that is the people. I have been so lucky to meet people of every age, every ethnic background, every walk of life and every viewpoint. I've been invited to dozens of countries. I've travelled through the Holy Land, walked on the Great Wall of China and received the highest civilian honours from the German and Japanese governments. And yet, it's the people, especially the people of Mississauga, but people everywhere, who have added so much to my life. Some people have charmed me, some have inspired me, some have amused me and some have vexed me.

Looking back, I am not sure there is much I would change. Of course, if it were in my power, I would not have allowed my husband, Sam, to slip into the grip of Alzheimer's. But that, of course, was beyond my control. As for my careers and my decisions along the way, there is not much I would change.

I have enjoyed my life immensely and thank God every day that he blessed me with good health. At ninety-three, I am still not taking any daily medication, other than a baby Aspirin, and the only times I have been overnight in a hospital were after the births of my three children and when that truck hit me in 2003. I'm also still playing with a full deck. I just shuffle a little slower now.

To have lived this long and to have had a job I still love makes me think of that old adage, "Of whom much is given, much is expected." I have sincerely tried to do the most with what I have been given.

Now, let's head back to the Gaspé Peninsula in the early 1920s.

CHAPTER I

Early Years

I was born Hazel Mary Muriel Journeaux on February 14, 1921, in the family farmhouse, behind the wood-burning stove, in Port Daniel, a tiny community on the picturesque east coast of the Gaspé Peninsula in Quebec. Port Daniel is on the Gulf of St. Lawrence side of the Gaspé and if you draw a line due south, you pretty much hit Moncton, New Brunswick, and a line straight east will take you to Sydney, Nova Scotia. Valentine's Day 1921 was a little warmer than usual for February with a high of minus 4 degrees Celsius and a low of minus 18. Unusual, too, was that there had been no snow for more than a week. (It is amazing what you can find on the Internet. These facts come directly from a Government of Canada climate website.)

I remember winters being harsh and the snow plentiful, although much of it drifting due to ocean winds. Summers were lovely, attracting tourists from Montreal, Toronto and the United States. But winters made life on the Gaspé feel ever more remote.

Though our family didn't have a lot, we were never hungry, even during the Great Depression of the 1930s. My only toys during childhood were a doll and a plush bunny, but I can honestly say I was spoiled. I was the youngest child of five, almost fourteen years younger than the eldest. I'll return to my family, but first a bit about beautiful Port Daniel.

French explorer Jacques Cartier stopped in Port Daniel in 1534 on his first voyage to Canada in search of the Orient. On the voyage, Cartier landed in Newfoundland first, and looking around at the barrenness, his first impression was: "I am rather inclined to believe that this is the land God gave to Cain." After Newfoundland, Cartier stopped in Prince Edward Island, where he was impressed by the fertile land and the abundance of birds. From there, he landed in what would become my birthplace. Legend has it that one of Cartier's officers was named Daniel and that the captain barked out these orders after spying a safe harbour: "Let's go to port, Daniel." Some think it is actually named for merchant Charles Daniel from Dieppe, France, who captained several voyages to New France about one hundred years after Cartier.

Considering Cartier and his men stayed but eight days in July 1534 before pulling up anchor to make their way around the Gaspé Peninsula and up the St. Lawrence River, it is more plausible it was named for Charles Daniel after a settlement was established. But who knows? I certainly prefer the more colourful Cartier legend.

By the time I was born, Port Daniel's population was about 1,500 and pretty evenly split between French and English. The French tended to live on the east side with its Catholic church and magnificent spire, and the English were in Port Daniel West, centred on St. James Anglican Church. Today, the language is almost exclusively French, but back then many of those of French descent spoke only English.

Though our family name is Journeaux, we all spoke English and, I say with some regret, I never did learn French. My great-great-grandfather, Francis Journeaux, arrived in Port Daniel not long after the War of 1812. He was of French Huguenot extraction from Jersey Island, off the coast of England. I have a hunch speaking French in the Journeaux family was lost over generations on Jersey Island, but I can't say for sure whether Francis Journeaux was bilingual.

Due to religious persecution, hundreds of thousands of Protestant Huguenots fled France after King Louis XIV revoked the Edict of Nantes in 1685. It had been in place for one hundred years to stop the bloodshed and promote religious tolerance. The Edict of Nantes had given Protestants freedom of religion in Catholic-dominated France and allowed them to work freely in any profession, and even for the government.

But Louis XIV changed all that and the Huguenot exodus began, along with more bloodshed. Many Huguenots went to Protestant England and its Channel Islands like Jersey. Numerous well-known North American politicians can trace their lineage to the Huguenots, including George Washington, Teddy Roosevelt and Franklin Roosevelt.

Born on Jersey Island in 1795, my great-great-grandfather, Francis, left Jersey to build a life in Port Daniel centred on fishing and family. Unfortunately, he died in a fishing accident on August 6, 1827, when his youngest child, John Francis Journeaux (my great-grandfather), was only three and a half months old.

John Francis grew up and married a woman named Elizabeth Hall, who was eighteen months older, on September 8, 1851. I mention this for two reasons. First, it was almost exactly 100 years before my marriage to Sam McCallion on September 29, 1951. Second, in a family oddity, it was the first in consecutive Journeaux marriages where the bride was older than the groom. A rarity, for sure, for the husband to be younger, especially 160 years ago, yet my great-grandfather, my grandfather and my father were all younger than their wives. Coincidentally, Sam McCallion was younger than me, too. I am not sure it means anything, but it struck me as unusual when I put it all together while working on this book. Perhaps strong leadership stock comes down through the women on my father's side of the family.

In 1906, my father, Herbert Journeaux, married my mother, Amanda Maude Travers, herself strong of both mind and body. Mother always told me we were related to Lieutenant Colonel John McCrae, the Guelph, Ontario, doctor who wrote the famous World War I poem "In Flanders Fields." The family connection apparently comes through my maternal grandmother, who was named Margaret Ann McCrae.

When they married, Mom and Dad were certainly not young for the times: Dad was twenty-seven and Mother was thirty. Part of the reason was that Mother went to Montreal General Hospital to train to be a nurse and graduated in 1901; she would be the first formally trained nurse in the Gaspé. Interestingly, Sam and I were the exact same ages when we married in 1951.

My brother Lorne was born first in 1907, then Lockhart in 1909, followed by Linda in 1911 and Gwen in 1915, and then finally me in 1921. My mother was about to turn forty-five when I was born but I never, ever was given the feeling that my birth was an "accident." If anything, it was the opposite and I was made to feel special all the time.

Dad owned and operated a fish processing plant and a general store. Mom looked after the home and small farm. We would eat fish at least five times a week, and our big meal was always in the afternoon, not evening, which is common in rural and Maritime communities. Sunday dinner was either beef or chicken, rarely fish. We had plenty of homegrown vegetables from our small farm.

The freshness of the food, combined with a pure, pollution-free environment, made for a very healthy way to grow up. I never had any of the childhood diseases like mumps, measles and chicken pox, and can't even recall being sick with the flu or colds, although I must have been at some point. Maybe this freshness has had something to do with my long, healthy life, too.

Genes obviously play a big part in longevity and Mother's family, the Traverses of Scottish extraction, were incredibly hearty and long-lived. My grandfather Travers, for example, died when I was two years old in 1923 but he was eighty-nine years old, which was an extremely long life for a man back then. God graced me with good genes on the Journeaux side, too. Grandpa Journeaux was eighty-five when he died in 1937.

It was a rural and remote life on the Gaspé. The first train service to Port Daniel began in the summer of 1911, less than ten years before I was born. They hammered the last spike in British Columbia to reach the Pacific Ocean and completed the transcontinental railway in 1885, but it took more than a quarter century after that historic event to link up the isolated Gaspé in eastern Canada to the nation's ribbon of steel.

In a case of poor planning or forward-thinking, depending on your perspective, the Port Daniel train station was built in 1908—three years before the first train would arrive on July 17, 1911. Much of the delay was because the blasting of a tunnel near Port Daniel, one of the few rail tunnels in eastern

Canada, took longer than expected and went over budget, not something I would have had much patience with, had I been around then.

Once rail service came to Port Daniel most supplies came by train, and no longer by boat, and I remember wooden crates were unloaded and simply left at the little train station. It was up to the person or business whose name was on the box to come and fetch their things because there were no railway employees or agents delivering directly to stores or homes. It was not an easy life and Kevin Dea captures that in his recent self-published book about the community, called *Port-Daniel West and the Golden Land.* "There was very little money and most families in those days had to make their own garden and grow vegetables for the long, cold winter," he writes.

"They also made their own bread. Some kept a cow or two and maybe even a pig to kill for their winter's meat. They always kept a few hens for their eggs. There was no running water so most families got their water from a nearby spring or if they were lucky, some families had an outdoor [hand] pump."

Sometimes, when I look at the glistening towers in today's Mississauga, or at the Civic Centre or Living Arts Centre, or the vast neighbourhoods filled with beautiful homes to raise families with all the amenities—almost everything having been built in the last forty-five years—I think back to days in Port Daniel when life was in many ways harder, but also much simpler.

Both Mom and Dad were churchgoers who instilled in all of us that we must live our lives with purpose and help others. Dad was an incredibly hard worker. If he wasn't running the little plant and buying fish off the boats and selling salmon, halibut, cod and lobsters to customers in Montreal and Toronto, he was working in the store.

My mother was a tremendous role model for me. Being a nurse, she really looked after us. The closest hospital was 100 miles (160 km) away and, when I was young, the town's doctor (who was also the dentist) was said to be quite a tippler. Mother wasn't keen on us seeing him unless there was no choice. So, she was a jack-of-all-trades when it came to the family's health concerns.

Mother, who went by her second name of Maude, was also the church organist at St. James Anglican Church. She played the piano and had a beautiful singing voice, too, and she was often asked to sing on the radio at the station in New Carlisle, a town about twenty miles (30 km) south of Port Daniel. I can still hear her singing "Danny Boy." I love that song still and I fondly remember her singing it in a hauntingly beautiful way.

Many evenings, Mother would fill our one-and-a-half-storey farmhouse with song. Sometimes I would listen intently, other times I would sit at the table and listen to Dad and Lockhart talk politics. I would just soak up the political talk with Mother's melodies in the background.

I grew up in a Conservative family, so the talk could be about anything from how R.B. Bennett was being treated unfairly in the early days of the Great Depression to how cagey William Lyon Mackenzie King could be. (Don't get the impression I am a dyed-in-the-wool Conservative. I will get to that topic later.) Indeed, there is a personal Journeaux anecdote that came out of the famous King-Byng Affair of 1926.

Anyone can read about the details of the King-Byng Affair in the history books or through a Google search. In a nutshell, it turned into a constitutional crisis when Governor General Lord Byng stood up to Prime Minister King and refused his attempt to call a snap general election because of a verbal agreement between the two men months earlier. Instead, Byng invited Conservative Arthur Meighen to form a government.

It was such a political firestorm that our family actually named a dog Byng in honour of the governor general for taking King down a peg, if only temporarily. And this dog, a black-and-white mutt, was one of the smartest dogs I've ever seen in my life.

In 1930, when I was nine years old, my sister Linda got her first teaching job in Bridgeville, sixty miles (100 km) up the coast. She asked if she could take Byng with her to keep her company. None of us wanted to let Byng go, but Linda promised she'd take good care of him.

Reluctantly, we all agreed. I was very sad to see both my dear big sister Linda and my cherished little friend Byng get on the train and head north to Bridgeville. He was a cute little dog and well-behaved, but he still had to ride in the baggage car away from Linda while she sat in the coach. Off they went.

Some weeks later, Linda's landlady let Byng out and forgot about him. When Linda got home from school, she couldn't find poor Byng. She went trudging through the snow in Bridgeville looking for him. No luck. The next day, my brother Lockhart was playing hockey in a town called Chandler, almost halfway to Bridgeville. Lockhart was an exceptional hockey player who I think could have made it to the NHL if he hadn't been needed to work for the family during the Depression.

At this point, Linda was the only person who knew Byng was missing. Lockhart had no idea. He was standing at the train station and he noticed a dog walking along the tracks due south in the direction of Port Daniel. It was Byng. Another animal had attacked him and he had a wound on his side, but he was bound and determined to get home and he was smart enough to follow the railway tracks. He'd made it thirty-seven miles (60 km) towards Port Daniel, and who knows how long he'd been wounded.

Lockhart brought him home and Mother tended to his wound. It took about six months, but he finally was healthy enough to run and play. I love dogs and have had dogs my entire life, especially German shepherds because they are so smart. But Byng might have been the smartest of all and he will always have a special place in my heart.

To close the loop on that story, Lockhart became a politician, too. He was elected Port Daniel West mayor in 1945 and served for almost a decade before returning to the fish business full-time. Then in 1963, the political bug bit him again and he returned to the mayor's chair until his death in a tragic accident near Port Daniel after he lost control of his car on an icy road in 1964. They took him to hospital in Quebec City, where he passed.

Coincidentally, my other brother, Lorne, also died in a separate car accident in Montreal a few years after Lockhart died. Lockhart's son, Hughie, and his family live in our old family home in Port Daniel and he carried on the fish business until retiring and selling it a few years ago.

When it came to politics, Lockhart taught me the importance of fighting for your constituents. He was on hand for many infrastructure improvements, like roads and bridges, and he got some of them by telling Quebec Premier Maurice Duplessis that he would run against his Union Nationale candidate in our region unless Port Daniel got some provincial money. Lockhart was so popular locally that the premier, known for his strong-arm tactics, preferred giving Lockhart what he needed to help the people of Port Daniel to seeing his name on the ballot.

My sister Linda, who died in 2004 at age ninety-three, once modestly claimed that Lockhart and I had the brains in the family and like moths drawn to the flame we both loved the give-and-take of politics. "It didn't surprise us when Hazel went into politics," Linda said in a 2001 film for my eightieth birthday, produced by my friend Ron Duquette.

When I was ten years old, Dad asked me to help in the store. What a thrill! I would keep records of what customers bought, like flour, molasses and other goods, so Dad could collect the money at the end of the month. I loved working with my dad. He was tops in my eyes and he sure was good to me. Dad called me "Dubs" and, for the life of me, I don't know the significance. I know that when a king or queen bestows honours on loyal subjects they lightly tap the recipient's shoulder and "dub" the honour upon them. Maybe "Dubs" was his way of calling me his princess or something, but I don't really know.

My big sisters, Linda and Gwen, were well aware he and I had a special relationship but I don't think they were ever jealous. Instead, they'd work it to their advantage. For example, whenever they wanted a little pocket money they'd have me ask Dad for them and usually it would work because he couldn't say no to me. As I've said, because I was so much younger than the rest of the family, everybody spoiled me.

One of the most memorable examples of this was the Christmas of 1926, when I was five years old and Lockhart bought me my first pair of hockey skates. What a gift for a little mite like me. Even though I was pretty spoiled with love, I had only two toys to play with and when I opened the box and saw those skates, my eyes must have been the size of saucers. "Okay, Hazel, let's go take them for a spin," Lockhart said, and out we went to the pond.

There were no outdoor hockey pads in the Gaspé then, let alone indoor hockey rinks. (Lockhart would build Port Daniel's first outdoor hockey pad a few years later.) He laced the boots up for me and I got on the ice and immediately warbled and wobbled until I fell and hit the back of my head on the ice.

I was about to cry when Lockhart said: "That's not going to happen again, Hazel. We're going to teach you to skate properly." Then he paused and added, "Hold your head up when you're falling so that other parts of your body hit the ice first." That was a good lesson that I've never forgotten.

He then placed his hands under my armpits and worked with me, telling me to push my legs out and glide and push again and glide, until I was ready to go solo. In no time he had me skating on my own. Memories are funny things and I have this image of me skating like a pro when I was probably barely staying upright. But I would one day play professional hockey, and it started here with Lockhart.

For some reason, I was closer to Lockhart than to my other brother, Lorne, maybe because Lorne was that much older. He was fourteen years older than me, and Lockhart was twelve years older. Lockhart used to take me everywhere. When he would go fix a boat or a truck, he'd bring me along and ask me to pass him this tool or that tool as he worked.

When he would drive up and down the coast selling fish from the back of his truck, often he'd ask me to come to help out, maybe just for company. I even remember Lockhart taking me out for ice cream and being late for dates with girls because he and I would just sit and talk. He was wonderful to me.

I have so many fond memories of my childhood but, to be honest, I could be full of mischief. Two stories prove this out.

When I was five years old, in the summer of 1926, I saw a big pile of grass behind our farmhouse. I don't know why, but I got the bright idea to burn it. So, I pulled a chair over to the fireplace mantel where Mom and Dad kept the oil lamps and the matches. Climbing up on the chair, I grabbed the box of matches. I went outside and lit the dried grass and watched it burn. Problem was the wind came up and pushed the flames along the ground towards the nearby field of oats, which was covered in dry stubble. It looked like in the movies when you see someone lighting a long fuse that burns like a sparkler towards the explosives. The big problem was that when it got to the field of oats the fire grew and grew, and the wind was now taking it towards the woods about a half mile away. Well, somebody saw the fire and sounded the alarm, so to speak. Dad came running from the fish plant and saw the danger of a possible forest fire. He told all his employees to stop working and get shovels, brooms and any other tool to help stop the fire spreading to the woods. The only other significant employer in town then was Mr. Charles Nadeau's lumber mill and he closed it down, too, and had his men scurrying to help put out the fire.

Seeing all this commotion, I knew I was in trouble so I ran and hid in the tiny space between our house and the ice house where my father stored the ice in summer. Thankfully, all the men worked and worked and got the fire out before it could reach the woods.

Once it was out, I could hear them talking about me and wondering where I was. I stayed put. Then they started calling my name; yelling it, actually. Finally, one of the men found me tucked away and pulled me out. Dad was so happy to see me unhurt that he just hugged me. I didn't get a strapping, just a good talking-to about how worried he was that something had happened to me.

The other story happened the next summer, 1927, around the time Babe Ruth was tearing it up for the most famous New York Yankees baseball team of all time and Charles Lindbergh had just completed his famous transatlantic solo flight in May.

As a six-year-old, I was oblivious to these great events, when one day Mother asked me to go down to Dad's store to fetch a bucket of molasses. The store had big barrels of molasses from Barbados and customers would bring their buckets in and open the spigot to fill them.

On arriving at the store, I placed my bucket on the floor and pulled at the spigot, which was sticky, as one might expect when it comes to molasses. Finally, getting the spigot to turn, I watched the molasses flow from the barrel and I couldn't believe how slowly it was coming out and how long I would have to wait. Anxious and impatient, I figured that while the bucket was filling, I would go down to the beach outside the store and play, maybe look for seashells. By the time I came back, the molasses had overflowed my bucket and was oozing all over the wooden floor.

My dad, who was such a mild man, didn't even spank me. He didn't give me a spanking even once in my life, though heaven knows I deserved a few. When he saw what I'd done, he shrugged and muttered an exasperated "Oh, Hazel!" and set about cleaning up the mess.

I wasn't always a scallywag, but I was a bit of a tomboy. To help make ends meet, Mom would take in American tourists in the summer and I would help with chores and cleaning. But whenever I could, I would play with friends, scamper along the rugged coastline and make silly dares. I remember we'd often tell ghost stories and tall tales about pirates and buried treasure.

In winter any free time was hockey time, good old pond hockey. I remember being the organizer of teams, and when my sisters were still both in Port Daniel I'd be on their team. They played defence and I played centre. I was small, but I could skate pretty fast. Hockey, especially women's hockey, has been such a big part of my life as a player, organizer and fan.

Our school was a typical two-room schoolhouse; lower and upper rooms with wood-burning stoves for heat and one teacher for each floor. The winters were sometimes really rough and the ocean winds often whipped snow drifts so high I couldn't get over them. One time I remember Dad having to open the upstairs window at our home to get us out because snow drifts blocked the doors. What an adventure, getting out of the house from upstairs and sliding down the snow drift.

The little school in Port Daniel went to grade 9 and no further. For me to continue my education, I had to leave home at sixteen. There would be a bit of a soft landing because I'd live with my big sister Linda for the first year, near Montreal. But it was still a big adjustment, a very big adjustment, for a teenage girl from the Gaspé way back in 1937. Had I known then that it would also mark the end of my living in the Gaspé, except for holidays and visits, it would have been even more difficult to leave.

CHAPTER 2

Goodbye Gaspé

I said goodbye to the Gaspé Peninsula at age sixteen in 1937. Though sixteen years is a relatively brief period over a life now at ninety-three years, my Gaspé years were formative and they engrained certain core values: the importance of hard work, of being actively part of a strong community and of living life with a purpose.

Though these seeds were planted, there was still so much to learn, and the next ten years were the most intense learning period of any single decade on so many different levels: education, work and awakening my spiritual side. It was also during these years that I would first meet Sam McCallion, my partner in marriage but also my best political advisor and sounding board.

But this portion of my life began with anxiety and nervousness. I had never been away from home. I was a girl from the Gaspé suddenly on a train headed to Montreal. Thankfully, I was with Linda, who had taken a teaching job in what we called St. John, Quebec (Saint-Jean-sur-Richelieu), twenty-five miles (40 km) south of Montreal. In St. John, I lived with Linda in a boarding house and was enrolled in grade 10 at a nearby English high school. Linda, who was twenty-six, helped me not only to adjust to leaving Gaspé, but also to get over my homesickness.

Although still two years from the beginning of World War II, we couldn't help but be reminded that the winds of war in Europe were beginning to swirl. St. John was the base of the famous Royal Canadian Dragoons, a highly decorated cavalry regiment that was converting to armour as the war approached. The Dragoons are still loyally serving Canada today, as they have done since 1883, but their former base in St. John is now the Royal Military College Saint-Jean, where Canadian Forces officer cadets are trained.

The son of the Dragoons base commander was in my grade 10 class, and Adolf Hitler and the Nazis' pre-war moves in the Rhine Valley, Austria and the Sudetenland were most certainly regular topics of conversation, even if we truly didn't grasp the ramifications of what lay ahead.

That grade 10 school year can be summed up quickly: the teacher was an entertainer, not an educator. He was highly intelligent and knew a lot, but he spent most of the time telling us stories, interesting stories. Problem was that he didn't keep our noses to the grindstone and he didn't really teach us much. Come exam time, we simply weren't prepared. In the class of ten students, only two passed: me and the son of the military base commander. If it hadn't been for Linda tutoring me in the evenings, I don't think I would have passed, either. Even with Linda's help, this distracting grade 10 year would hurt me the following year because I lacked the proper foundation for grade 11.

The next year, Linda moved on to a new job and I went to Quebec City to take my grade 11 at Commissioners' High School.

I can't say I was upset at leaving St. John, but now I was totally on my own, and lonely at times.

I boarded with the Sisters of St. John the Divine, an Anglican nunnery in Quebec City that ran an orphanage and took in boarders to help offset costs. Linda and my other sister, Gwen, paid my boarding fees. There were about eight or ten boarders attending Commissioners' High School. In today's world it may be difficult to imagine, but Commissioners' was an all-English high school in the middle of Quebec City.

That year was a wonderful experience, but I was homesick at times and that often brought out the shyness in me—if you can believe that I was ever shy.

The yearbook editors wrote this about me: "Hazel came to us in September, a stranger from the Gaspé coast. Quiet, industrious and adjustable, she quickly identified herself with all our interests. Although we don't hear much from her, she is certainly an asset to our class." No doubt many people, including former Ontario premiers Bill Davis, David Peterson, Bob Rae, Mike Harris and Dalton McGuinty, will see the irony of the words "we don't hear much from her" in reference to Hazel Journeaux, the future Hazel McCallion.

Luckily, a good friend from Port Daniel was also at Commissioners' that year and in my class. Her name was Barbara Rowe and her father had been the Anglican priest in Port Daniel. A couple years before, her father had been transferred to Sillery, then a small town just outside the walls of old Quebec City.

The Rowes, originally from Newfoundland, were most hospitable and had me stay at their home most weekends, where Barbara would help me with homework. Barbara was perhaps the smartest in the class and she had a flair for writing, especially poetry. (I still exchange Christmas cards with Barbara, whose married name is Gordon. She now lives in Bloomington, Indiana. We've both been blessed with long lives.) If it weren't for Barbara, I might not have graduated that year. The yearbook editors said this about Barbara, with an indirect reference to me: "Barbara joined us two years ago and has since distinguished herself as a very promising student. Her literary mind and poetic talent are a constant source of inspiration to her less gifted classmates." That was the first public jab at me in print and it still makes me chuckle.

One of the highlights of my year at Commissioners' occurred when King George VI and Queen Elizabeth (later the Queen Mother) kicked off their royal tour of Canada in Quebec City in May 1939. It was on this royal tour that the couple officially opened a new road in southern Ontario called the Queen Elizabeth Way that would become so important to the future development of the City of Mississauga.

As I watched them on the podium in Quebec City that spring day, along with throngs of people, I had no thoughts of the QEW or that I would later meet the Queen Mother, her two daughters and her grandchildren on numerous occasions. (One of her grandsons, Prince Andrew, would open Mississauga's brand new Civic Centre in 1987 and be quite amused, perhaps even befuddled, by the design.)

After grade 11, Dad wanted me to go on to university, study economics and business, and eventually come home and help him run the business. By this point, his health was starting to deteriorate. Unfortunately, the family simply didn't have the money for my university education. Instead, I headed back to Montreal, where I enrolled in a secretarial school run by the Catholic nuns of the Sisterhood of Notre Dame. The school was located on Atwater Avenue in Westmount, and is now the site of Dawson College.

Here again, Linda and Gwen helped me so much. Every family has challenges, I know that, but what a wonderful family I grew up in. Linda paid all my tuition and Gwen gave me money to pay my room and board while at school. Many weeks I would have to go to Gwen and get the money. I remember this so vividly seventy-five years later because she worked at the Verdun Protestant Hospital for the Insane and I had to walk up a long, tree-lined laneway to the front door. It spooked me every time. Even though I wasn't much of a moviegoer, I could imagine Alfred Hitchcock using this long, lonely walk up to the psychiatric hospital in one of his horror movies.

My time with the nuns of Notre Dame coincided with the so-called "phony war," when the world held its breath waiting for Hitler to make his next move after the invasion of Poland, in September 1939, and the beginning of the brutal occupation of that country. It wasn't until May 1940 that Hitler threw the might of the Third Reich against the Allies by launching his blitzkrieg through the Netherlands, Belgium and France that led to the capitulation of the French generals and that country's surrender in June.

In my view, one of the greatest displays of political leadership in history happened when Winston Churchill became British prime minister on May 10, 1940. The newsreels showed Churchill everywhere: flying to meet French Allies again and again before their surrender, inspecting home defence and dashing through the streets meeting ordinary British people.

I would never compare myself to the great Churchill, but I will say that his stalwart presence during such difficult times made a strong impression on my teenage mind, even if back then I had no idea I would be a politician one day. Years later, whether during the emergency of the Mississauga train derailment or simply during day-to-day events, like opening a new restaurant, store or building in Mississauga, I loved being with the people and hearing their ideas and concerns.

In the spring of 1940, I was finishing up my secretarial school training. I was very good at shorthand and I won the top award in the class with a speed of 120 words per minute. Typing was altogether another matter. I just couldn't seem to get the hang of it and was at the bottom of the class, typing only forty-two words per minute while the top girls were at about sixty-five words.

Linda and Gwen continued to help with my room and board, which was eight dollars a week at the home of a widow named Mrs. Lucy Wilson. Knowing money was scarce for me, Mrs. Wilson insisted I come home for lunch each day, at no charge. So, I was getting a bed and three meals a day for eight bucks a week. I've been lucky all my life, with people like Mrs. Wilson giving me just a little bit of extra help. Sometimes a *lot* of help.

After I got two of my bottom teeth almost knocked out in a hockey game, Mrs. Wilson sent me to her dentist. The teeth were beyond repair and had to be pulled. The dentist put a bridge in the front, and these are the only teeth I am missing after all these years. (I still have my wisdom teeth, for goodness' sake.) It cost sixty dollars for the dental work and Mrs. Wilson paid it all. I paid her back a little bit at a time, and I've never forgotten her generosity.

I even found out Mrs. Wilson was giving me a financial break on room and board when one of the male boarders told me what he was paying. Interestingly, this information came from Charlotte Whitton's brother, Steve, who was living at the house and working in Montreal. It is funny how small the world can be! I was living at the same rooming house with the brother of the woman who would one day be a role model for my political career. In a little over ten years, Charlotte Whitton in Ottawa would become the first woman mayor of a big city in Canada.

Upon completing secretarial school, I went home for a brief holiday in the summer before starting a new job in Montreal. It was a lovely trip, during which something quite bizarre occurred, reminding me that an ocean separated us from the war, but it was closer than I sometimes realized.

One early summer evening, Dad was sitting on the front porch in a rocking chair smoking his pipe. He loved to watch the comings and goings on the road, just down the hill from our house. I went out and joined him for a chat. Soon after I sat down, a smartly dressed man came walking up the path and struck up a conversation with Dad.

We had many strangers in town during the summer tourist season, mostly visitors from the United States or Toronto and Montreal. But this man was not Canadian and he had a slight accent, but his English was flawless. He was pleasant and he asked Dad lots of questions about the area. Both Dad and I thought nothing of it, other than that he was a traveller who seemed interested in Port Daniel and the Gaspé coast. Two days later, we heard the very same man was arrested as a German spy in New Carlisle, a few miles down the coast. Imagine that. We were talking to a Nazi spy!

Returning to Montreal, I began my new job at the Louis Rolland Paper Company in the summer of 1940 and I worked there until autumn 1941. (During this time I started my professional hockey career.) Mr. Rolland was a distributor of redwood lumber and the company was basically him and me. He did sales and made business deals, and I did all the paperwork: placing orders, accounting, delivery schedules and anything else to keep the office running. Just like Mrs. Wilson, he took an interest in me and was generous with his time in teaching me the business. I was only nineteen when I started working for him but he gave me a lot of responsibility.

At the time, all three Journeaux girls were working in Montreal: Gwen was a nursing aide at Verdun Protestant Hospital; Linda was teaching; and I was running Mr. Rolland's office. One sad day later in 1940, all three of us boarded a train for Port Daniel. We had gotten word that Dad had died, probably from cancer, but in those days doctors often didn't really know or tell you definitively the cause of death. Mother had taken him to the nearest hospital in the town of Campbellton, New Brunswick, about a hundred miles (160 km) from home. Having been told there was nothing the doctors could do, Mother brought him home.

He died in our family home at age sixty and only three years after his father died at eighty-five. There was no funeral parlour in Port Daniel, so the doctor prepared the body and there Dad lay in our living room for the wake before his funeral at St. James Anglican Church.

I was only nineteen when Dad died, and it was the first time I said goodbye to someone so close to me. It was difficult, especially knowing that my future children would never know this wonderful man. And that Dad would not know what I would make of my life. He and Mother are both buried in the little cemetery beside the church. Besides a grave marker, in 2007 I donated new gates to the church and cemetery, with a little plaque in my parents' and Journeaux grandparents' honour.

After Dad's funeral, Linda, Gwen and I returned to Montreal and it was back to work. Dad had instilled in each of us to live life with purpose and I was determined to do just that. I didn't know exactly where I'd end up, but I just knew I wouldn't give up trying to do my best.

Mr. Rolland was wonderful, but the problem was he couldn't afford to pay me more than twelve dollars a week and I was paying eight dollars for room and board and reimbursing Mrs. Wilson two dollars a week for the dental bill, leaving only two bucks for expenses and a little saving. When I saw an advertisement for a higher-paying position to run the office of the Quebec North Shore Paper Company in Shelter Bay, up the north coast of the St. Lawrence River near Labrador, I applied. I got the job; given the remote location, I may have been the only applicant.

When I arrived in Shelter Bay, a tough industrial town and nothing more, my immediate thought was: "Oh, my! What have I done?" I thought the Gaspé was rural but this place made Port Daniel look sophisticated. And it was no place for a young woman, either. No place at all. I am no quitter, as my record proves, but I got out of that town in less than a month and returned to Montreal.

Mrs. Wilson welcomed me back and still had my room available. Sister St. Catherine of Palma, head of the secretarial school, was another matter. She sat me down and scolded me for taking a job up on the North Shore without talking to her beforehand. After she was finished and my contrition was clear, she picked up the phone and made a call that would launch my future business career, just as Canada and its Allies were plunged into the darkest days of World War II.

CHAPTER 3

Business Unusual

Sitting behind her desk, cradling the telephone receiver between her shoulder and ear, Sister St. Catherine scribbled on a piece of paper, thanked the person on the other end of the line and hung up.

"Hazel," said the head of the Montreal secretarial school, "you have a meeting with this man. He has something available and it's a fine opportunity for you."

Sister St. Catherine had many contacts of various stripes in the business world. She was tough and not in the least subservient to these businessmen; indeed, she trained valuable resources for them—hard-working, capable young women, especially prized because there was a labour shortage with men off at war—and she negotiated hard to make sure her girls received the right placements in good working conditions.

She pushed the piece of paper across her desk towards me with an address a few blocks away in downtown Montreal. The name on the paper was "Mr. Robert Stiles. Canadian Kellogg."

For years, when explaining this part of my life, I always prefaced any story with "Kellogg, the engineering firm, not

37

the cereal maker." I have a story related to mixing up the two different companies named Kellogg. It is about an old, torn and yellowed typewritten letter that I received from someone named R.B. Lloyd in Middlechurch, Manitoba, near Winnipeg, and dated August 23, 1958. Let me quote parts of the letter.

The Kellogg Co. Ltd. Toronto.

Dear Gentlemen

I am now well past 90, in rugger health and active. I bowl, curl, golf and walk about five miles every day. However, I have one complaint. I am at times costive.

I have a daughter, a registered nurse in the hospital in Saskatoon. She is now on visit to Winnipeg and knowing of my failure tells me of a new pill that they find very good with older patients. A pill at bed time [that] insures a complete evacuation the next morning. This sounded good to me.

The other evening I bowled and arrived home at 11 p.m. I felt a bit hungry [and] I had a package of All-Bran and concluded that in lou [sic] of something else I would try that and found it very easy to take and very satisfying…I slept well, awoke…and went through my regular setting up exercises and took a mile walk before breakfast. Just a little while after breakfast, there was a complete evacuation. I have followed this same technique eating a bowl of All-Bran at bed time and have been equally successful ever since.

I have the pleasure of telling my daughter how potent her pills are. I have had them five days now and had five successful operations and have not touched a pill. I give All-Bran, together with my technique, all the credit.

Sincerely Yours, R.B. Lloyd.

Why I kept this letter, I don't know. But it still gives me a chuckle reading it today. It's interesting to think that Mr. R.B. Lloyd, given his admission of his age, was born around 1867, the year Canada became a country. Maybe that's why I hung on to the letter for all these years, or maybe it's simply because his writing me about his evacuations gave me a good laugh.

Kellogg Canadian was the Canadian subsidiary of M.W. Kellogg Co., a New York engineering firm that started out building industrial chimneys and expanded to designing and constructing petrochemical plants and other business complexes. In Canada, Kellogg built the chimneys at International Nickel Co. Ltd. in Sudbury, Gaspé Copper Mines Ltd. in Murdochville, Quebec, and St. Lawrence Cement Inc. in Clarkson, now the southwest part of Mississauga. During World War II, M.W. Kellogg was also part of many top secret projects, including early research on the Manhattan Project, which led to the atom bomb.

Founded in 1901 in New York by a young entrepreneur named Morris Woodruff Kellogg with an initial investment of only $2,750, M.W. Kellogg Co. recorded a net profit (and hefty return on investment) of $16,201 in its first year of operation.

Success continued through the years and the company expanded during the Depression to the United Kingdom and Canada, no doubt in part due to government public works projects and inexpensive labour. Regardless, the founder had instilled a corporate culture of getting things done quickly and properly. Mr. Kellogg was a visionary whose motto was "Show me something new." This was the type of company for me.

At age twenty, I arrived at Mr. Stiles's Montreal office with some trepidation. It was 1941 and dark days for Britain and its Allies like Canada. The United States would not enter the fray until after the Japanese attacked Pearl Harbor on December 7 of that year. But when I stepped into his office, Mr. Stiles immediately put me at ease.

He was a tall, strapping, handsome man from San Antonio, Texas. (If anyone thinks it sexist of me to describe him physically, too bad. Men routinely describe women's appearances without a second thought.) Mr. Stiles instantly impressed me as a man with confidence, with no airs about him. He was a professional engineer and chartered accountant with university degrees in both. He was highly intelligent.

I figured the job would be some sort of secretarial role, assisting him with letter writing, appointments, taking dictation, things like that. But he had something far more interesting in mind.

"I want you to run the office," he said, adding that he would concentrate on getting work contracts by meeting business leaders and, increasingly, talking to officials in the war government of Mackenzie King's Liberals. The office consisted of me and Mr. Stiles and people we would hire for specific projects as needed. The Depression was over and with men off to war there was a labour shortage, but I didn't expect this job at such a tender age, barely out of my teenage years.

Mr. Stiles was a patient man who taught me so much, including what would become my lifelong mantra, something I would adhere to and pass along to others for more than seventy years. "Hazel," he said, "you must *always* do your homework. When we have a meeting, say a budget meeting for a project, where you have to come in and justify things to me, I want you to take some time beforehand and think.

"Think about what are the sorts of questions I will ask, and then you must come up with the answers and have them ready.

You likely won't think of every question, but you'll come up with most. There is nothing more important than doing your homework," he said.

What an incredible piece of simple advice. If young people take away only one thing from reading this book, I hope it is that. It is so important to *do your homework* every day of your career; every time you have a big decision in your personal life, too. Mr. Stiles's advice has stood me well my entire life.

As it rolled into 1942 and Canada and its Allies were suffering one defeat after another, I developed the feeling that I should be doing more for the war effort. The work was fascinating and fast-paced at Kellogg, but I still wondered. My sister Linda had joined the Wrens (Women's Royal Canadian Naval Service), a new branch of the Royal Canadian Navy. In a bid to free up more men for combat, the Wrens were trained in non-combat roles such as radar operators, switchboard operators and teletype operators. I thought enlisting sounded like a great idea so I went down to their Toronto office and volunteered. (By war's end around seven thousand Wrens like Linda had served.)

When Mr. Stiles found out, he called his government contacts in Ottawa and just like that, the very next day, I was told by the Wrens that I could not join because I was needed for "essential wartime work" at Kellogg. I was in the navy only one day and I was disappointed, but at the same time I felt rather proud that my boss thought enough of me and my work to do that.

And a good thing because, within weeks, Kellogg was awarded the Canadian government contract to design and build Canada's first synthetic rubber plant.

More than 90 per cent of the world's natural rubber supply came from plantations in the Far East when war broke out.

Japanese aggression in the region cut the supply to a trickle before stopping it altogether after the attack on Pearl Harbor.

Scientists had experimented with synthetic rubber formulas for two decades in Germany, Russia and the United States. Ironically, it was a German formula held by an American licensee that would be used in Canada to make synthetic rubber to aid the Allied war effort. C.D. Howe, colloquially known as Canada's wartime "Minister of Everything," and his team convinced the Americans to share the formula so that a Crown corporation called Polymer Corp. could build a plant in Sarnia, Ontario, to produce synthetic rubber.

It was our job at Kellogg to design and build the plant. The engineering was done in New York and the Canadian office would coordinate the various teams of construction workers and find and requisition all the necessary materials to build the plant. My role was to use the designs from Kellogg engineers to get it built on time and on budget. For a young woman in her early twenties, I can tell you it meant long hours, more than one hundred per week.

In his book, *Profiting the Crown: Canada's Polymer Corporation 1942–1990*, author Matthew J. Bellamy calls the synthetic rubber plant one of Howe's greatest projects during the war: "Rubber was indispensable to modern warfare and wartime industry: most military items used it in one form or another because its malleable properties minimized mechanical wear and tear. Without an alternative source, the Allied war machine would have come to a grinding halt."

As part of our government contract, Kellogg had to move its Canadian head office to Toronto and that is how I ended up in Ontario in 1942. (I was later given a choice by Kellogg to move back to Montreal, but decided to stay in Toronto.) We had ultimate authority to get this synthetic rubber plant built. We could go into any plant and commandeer anything we needed—materials or workers—all in the name of the war effort.

With each day, I seemed to be making more and more decisions and Mr. Stiles seemed pleased. We worked well together. He had hired me as a secretary, but like any good boss, he mentored me and increased my responsibilities as I proved I could handle more. Before long, I was office manager. (Late in the war, I believe it was in 1944, Mr. Stiles was transferred to England to head up operations in Kellogg's London office.)

The Polymer plant was up and running in less than two years after we won the contract. I visited it a few times on the shores of the majestic St. Clair River, but most of my time was spent at the Canadian Kellogg office, then at 34 Adelaide Street West, in Toronto's financial district. I was hiring people and tracking down needed materials for construction.

Polymer produced five thousand tonnes of synthetic rubber every month for everything from tires to airplane parts. I've read estimates that that one plant was producing 90 per cent of Canada's rubber by the last year of the war. The plant was so efficient that extra rubber was even sent to the U.S. as part of the common war effort.

Mr. Stiles's departure added stress to my job but we just kept moving forward as a team. It was a lesson I would not soon forget. When everyone has their oar in the water and is pulling together, incredible things can be achieved.

As construction was nearing completion, my role was to wind down Kellogg's involvement, and make sure the operator understood all parts of the specs and drawings. Kellogg's role during construction was essential and it was personally one of the highlights of my private-sector career. (To mark the importance

of that plant, in 1971 the Government of Canada formally recognized Polymer's contribution to the war effort by putting the
plant on the back of the ten-dollar bill for several years.)

My new boss was sent up to Canada from the United States.
His name was Hank Wurdemann, and he was another person I
would learn a lot from and the only other boss I had at Kellogg.

Shortly after the war, Mr. Wurdemann sent me to Kellogg's
New York head office for budget meetings. I was only twenty-
five years old so it was quite a compliment that he would entrust
me to handle this job on my own. I remember him dropping me
off at Union Station in Toronto to catch the train to New York.
"You'll do fine, Hazel," he said. I was a little nervous heading to
New York on my own, but I kept reminding myself that I had
done my homework and I was ready for this.

After a long journey, I arrived at Grand Central Station in
Manhattan. As I made my way off the train and towards the
concourse, I was struck by so many things. The crowds were
enormous, far bigger than in Montreal or Toronto and almost
overwhelming for a kid from the Gaspé coast. Believe it or not,
there were 123 tracks going into and out of Grand Central, so
no wonder there was a crush of people. The light was remarkable. I remember bright sunshine streaming in like huge spot
beams. On my first trip to the Big Apple, it is safe to say Grand
Central made a huge impression.

It was a short cab ride, about ten minutes down Broadway, to
Kellogg's office in the famed Woolworth Building in the financial district at 225 Broadway in Lower Manhattan. The building
was constructed in 1927 and designed in the Art Deco style,
with a masonry exterior and capped with a pyramid-shaped
copper roof. Intricate detailing surrounded the entry doorway,
as was common in Manhattan skyscrapers of that era.

I remember meeting with a Kellogg vice-president and his staff for about half the day. Nothing particular stands out in my mind, but I obviously made an impression based on something Mr. Wurdemann said years later in a video commemorating my eightieth birthday: "I sent her down with these papers and she had to see the chap to whom I reported in the U.S. company. And he called me right after she left his office and said, 'Where the hell did you find her? She thinks like a man!'"

After the meeting, I had half a day to be a tourist in New York before taking the train back to Toronto the next morning. The streets were busy. I had never seen so many people all walking together on sidewalks and crossing streets in unison. I visited Times Square and I went up to the top of the Empire State Building, made famous a few years earlier in the movie *King Kong* with the giant ape climbing the outside of it while carrying Canadian actress Fay Wray to stardom. It was a fun trip but it was short.

The first ten to fifteen years after the war were exciting at Kellogg because the economy was expanding and Canada was growing and prospering. We were part of this big growth push. Even if it couldn't match the excitement of the war years and building a synthetic rubber plant at near-lightning speed, Kellogg was still a fun place to work and learn.

Mr. Wurdemann, an American who became a Canadian citizen and ended up living in Mississauga most of his later years, was the driving force behind building several oil refineries, including Imperial Oil's in Halifax and British Petroleum's in Port Moody, B.C., and another in Clarkson, now the southwest part of Mississauga.

Our Toronto office had grown to thirty people, and we moved north out of the city's financial district to a space above the Laing Galleries at 194 Bloor Street West, just west of Avenue Road, until finding a permanent location above the subway at Yonge and Bloor streets. The engineering was done in New York, but the purchasers of material, construction supervisors and inspectors were part of the Canadian office.

With each building contract, the staff would swell or contract depending on the work involved. And I was in charge of hiring. It was then that my boss suggested I join Toronto's personnel and office management organizations. I was turned down by both because no women were allowed to join back then.

Kellogg didn't care if you were a man or a woman, just whether you could do the job. And since I didn't know any different, I was shocked when the reality of the outside business world slapped me in the face and I was refused because I was a woman. Oh well, I thought. There are more ways to skin a cat, so I started up similar networking organizations for women, my first foray into pioneering for women in business without even realizing that was what I was doing.

Meanwhile, at Kellogg we were also building power plants like the "Four Sisters" coal-fired hydro generating station in Port Credit. The four smokestacks dominated the skyline of southern Mississauga until 2006, when I presided over their demolition as mayor. I helped build it, and ironically I was asked to push the button to destroy it fifty years later when other technologies replaced it.

In the 1950s, we also built a laboratory for a pilot project in Fort McMurray to test the feasibility of extracting oil from the tar sands. M.W. Kellogg in New York came up with an idea to unlock the oil from the tar sands. It was our office's job to get the materials and to build the facility for the pilot in Fort McMurray.

After the pilot project was running, I made a trip to Fort McMurray and I still remember seeing a huge bulldozer the size of my house shovelling through the tar sands and moving vast amounts of earth. The tires on this thing must have been ten feet (3 m) high.

Kellogg's tar sands process was too expensive for its time, but years later others, like Suncor, came in with even more modern ways. Kellogg was, by then, a footnote in the history books.

I left Kellogg in 1963 to help my husband, Sam, with his growing printing business in Streetsville. And Kellogg's Canadian operations were later sold to TransCanada PipeLines.

During my twenty-two years at Kellogg, I learned so many things. First, under the tutelage of Mr. Stiles and Mr. Wurdemann, I developed a "small-c" fiscal conservatism approach that I practised over my entire political career. Related to that, I came to appreciate the importance of project management, keeping a close eye on things, and the need to get the job done on time and on budget. Sometimes unforeseen events occur, but you should always keep your eye on the ball. I've always believed you should run a city like a business and my business training came at Kellogg.

Second, I learned the need to be decisive. Mr. Stiles said: "You're paid to make decisions, not waffle. Even if you make the wrong decision, you're paid to make that decision and learn from the mistake." Oftentimes, the worst mistake is delaying and postponing making a decision.

Third, because I was working and dealing with men all the time, I learned to work well with them. I didn't rant and rave or use tears to achieve my goals. I simply did my homework and tried to get the job done. It was much the same when in 1978 I was elected mayor of Mississauga and all the councillors—except

Margaret Marland—were men. It didn't faze me in the least that nine councillors were men.

I don't recall episodes of being treated as an inferior at Kellogg because I was a woman in a man's world. Although I am sure there must have been some men who didn't like dealing with a woman, especially if I was telling them what needed to be done. And, of course, there were those misogynist outside organizations that would not let me join because I was a woman.

Fourth, I learned to be flexible and adaptable to change. It was an inability to adapt that ultimately led to Kellogg's demise in Canada. Oil companies got bigger and started designing and building their own plants. Even though we were the first engineering firm in Canada to build oil refineries and power plants, competitors came in and undercut us on tenders. Kellogg simply didn't adapt quickly enough to changing times.

Fifth, I learned I didn't have all the answers but if I wasn't too proud, I could get the answers easily enough. There are always people who know things you don't, and if you ask politely and sincerely, they'll help you, I've learned over the years. This lesson has been extremely important to me as mayor because I can't be expected to understand every detail or drawing in the numerous plans that come through council.

And lastly, I learned to do my homework, perhaps the greatest gift I received from Kellogg; that, and the $85-a-month Kellogg pension I've been receiving since 1986 when I turned sixty-five!

After the Kellogg experience, I had the business training to move forward in a new profession: politics and public service. But before getting to that, it's worth mentioning a few important things that happened to me in my personal life during those Kellogg years.

CHAPTER 4

Beyond Work

In this secular day and age, it is not always popular to talk about one's faith, particularly if you are a politician. But it is impossible for me to tell my story without touching upon it. My faith is that important to me and has been since I was a little girl.

I promise not to go on at length, but feel free to flip to the next chapter if religious matters do not particularly interest you. Atheism seems to be very much in vogue these days, but there is something I have discovered about atheists: though they don't believe in God, many are open-minded and interested in why others believe in a Creator, whether they be Christian, Jewish, Muslim or any other religious faith.

I am Christian, an Anglican to be precise. But I don't believe in proselytizing or "getting in your face" with my beliefs. Faith is a very personal thing and I respect that in everyone. I happen to believe that society is better off with people belonging to various religious groups. The fellowship, the discipline and commitment involved, and the humility of knowing there is a God make for a better world, in my opinion.

49

And I am not about to get into that age-old, dog-chasing-his-tail argument about one God versus another God. The head of the Catholic Church, Pope Francis, says it best: "I believe in God, not a Catholic God." I agree with the Pontiff that God is not Catholic, Anglican, Jewish, Muslim or whatever. He is God. And I believe, like Pope Francis, that Jesus Christ is God's incarnation.

I was born and raised Anglican and the first church I attended was St. James Anglican Church in Port Daniel, Quebec. My mother was the church organist, and she and my father both instilled in all their children the importance of having God in our lives and of doing God's work by helping others.

As a young person, not unlike young people today, I found some of the messages each Sunday would go in one ear and out the other. But the seed was planted. While living in Montreal, I attended church regularly but didn't get involved in any of its organizations.

By the time I was living in Toronto, the seeds Mom and Dad planted took root and flowered. I was boarding in the home of a lovely couple named Mr. and Mrs. Clark at 523 Oakwood Avenue in Toronto's west end on the border with the Borough of York. I happened upon the Clarks' home because their daughter was living at Mrs. Wilson's boarding house the same time as I was in Montreal. She told me to call her parents because with an empty nest, they would certainly have me stay for a short while. As it turned out, the Clarks became second parents to me and I stayed with them almost ten years until I was married.

The Clarks were members of the United Church, but knowing I was Anglican they suggested I join St. Michael and All Angels Church on St. Clair Avenue, just west of Bathurst. Here, while still working long hours at Kellogg, I immediately got involved with the Anglican Young People's Association (AYPA), a dynamic group whose four pillars were "worship, work, fellowship and edification."

St. Michael and All Angels was led by a priest named George Boyd Snell, who was in his late thirties; old enough to supply a guiding hand for our youthful exuberance, but young enough to be progressive and understanding of a new world emerging from World War II. Reverend Snell, who would live to ninety-nine and serve as the eighth bishop of Toronto from 1966 to 1972, was an extrovert, highly intelligent, scholarly, compassionate and pastoral. These are prized characteristics for a leader of a congregation, or any leader, for that matter. Finding them packaged together in one person is not common, but Reverend Snell had them all in spades.

Like me, he was also an avid stamp collector and we would talk about stamps for hours and hours. Philately is a hobby that has been a lifelong passion for me, as it is for millions and millions of people around the world. There are many famous stamp collectors, from Franklin Roosevelt and King George V to Charlie Chaplin and John Lennon. I find stamp collecting so relaxing, and I have literally thousands of stamps to organize and catalogue in my retirement years.

Reverend Snell and his wife, Esther, understood youth and encouraged us to develop a contemporary worldview based on the Christian tenets of comforting the afflicted and, when needed, afflicting the comfortable. They would have us over to their home Sunday evenings, where we'd have lively discussions on anything from interpreting Bible stories to the role of youth in the postwar era.

It was this strong Anglican community that kept me in

Toronto after the war. I was given a choice by my employer Canadian Kellogg to move back to Montreal or stay, and I simply couldn't imagine leaving my friends at St. Michael and All Angels and the AYPA in Toronto.

It was around this time that I got to know another active member of the AYPA named Samuel Robert McCallion. I was by now the national vice-president of the AYPA and Sam was chair of the literature committee, overseeing much of the literature and communications sent to the eight thousand or so members across Canada. We worked closely and a friendship developed into something more.

Indeed, Sam, who was already working hard at photography, which would be a lifelong passion, sold me one of his cameras for my trip to Oslo, Norway, for the Second World Conference of Christian Youth in July 1947. It was a Kodak 35 camera and I paid Sam twenty-five dollars for it. I used to enjoy teasing him that he "re-owned" the camera after we married so he should have simply loaned it to me in the first place.

These were exciting days to be a young Anglican, even if the *Anglican Journal* called them "turbulent times" because the Church was transforming from an ancient worldview to a contemporary one.

With George Snell's encouragement (and possibly Sam's, too), I wrote my first letter to a Canadian prime minister in 1947. (There would be many more over the years.) I asked Prime Minister King to look into the unjust internment of Japanese Canadians during World War II with an eye towards compensation to the wronged. "I trust I will be able to advise the Conference Delegates [in Oslo] of the fair treatment accorded to Japanese Canadians by the Government of Canada," I wrote a few weeks before leaving for Norway.

Unfortunately, I did not receive assurances from the prime minister that I could pass along to the 1,200 delegates from seventy countries. And it would be four decades before another prime minister, Brian Mulroney, would apologize on behalf of the Canadian government for forcibly evacuating 22,000 Japanese Canadians from their homes and imprisoning them during World War II.

Still, that conference in Oslo was one of the highlights of my young life. I was one of only five delegates from the Anglican Church in Canada, which was an honour in itself. It was also the first time I had ever been in an airplane. It was a long transatlantic flight in a noisy Trans-Canada Air Lines (the forerunner of Air Canada) propeller plane called a North Star. The Canadair-built plane was so noisy it took two days before my ears would stop buzzing. We flew non-stop across the Atlantic to Prestwick airport, near Glasgow, Scotland. I took a train east to Newcastle in northern England, where I was to catch a ship to Norway.

While billeted overnight in a family home in Newcastle, I witnessed and experienced something special. The family was middle class and they served me two eggs and two strips of bacon for breakfast—and that was their breakfast ration for the month. Even two years after the war, they were still on government rations. I felt so guilty, but they insisted that as a guest in their home I must eat it all up. I tried to share my food with them, but they would have none of that. Just recalling that story almost seventy years later brings back tinges of guilt, but also thanks and warm admiration.

In Norway, we landed in port at Bergen and hopped on a train east to Oslo. We passed through more than one hundred tunnels, and by the time we arrived most of us were filthy from soot that came in through the open windows. Then we found out that the building we were staying in had only one bathroom for twenty-two people. Two solid days of travel, much of it alone, and what an adventure even before the week-long conference started!

The conference was an eye-opening experience, meeting people from around the world, from all sorts of different cultures, but all with a commonality of our faith and a belief that our generation must do whatever possible to prevent the world from ever again plunging into another abyss like World War II.

Perhaps we were naïve and idealistic, but we meant it when we passed resolutions urging Christians to seek public office in the postwar world and to adhere to Christian principles to fight racial discrimination, poverty, social inequity and more. Just because the forces of evil, Nazism and fascism, were defeated it did not mean we could toss away our belief in what Jesus taught us about peace and love. Even before the end of the war, young Anglican groups like our AYPA issued resolutions that stressed love and compassion above military might when dictating terms to defeated countries and peoples.

I wanted to see a bit of Europe before going home. Another delegate, Hazel Greenwood from Vancouver, and I travelled to Amsterdam, Paris and London. Beyond the Champs-Élysées, Eiffel Tower, Big Ben and Buckingham Palace, what I remember so clearly all these years later is our first breakfast in Amsterdam. The conference food had been dreadful, mainly canned food without fruits and vegetables. So when we got to Amsterdam we ordered a huge breakfast platter with omelettes, bacon and fresh fruits. That may have been the best-tasting breakfast of my entire life.

Upon returning home, I continued my leave of absence

from Canadian Kellogg and toured much of Canada to report to various chapters of the AYPA what happened at the conference and the resolutions we drafted. Less than two years later, this experience led to my appointment as Dominion president of the AYPA for a two-year term beginning in June 1949. It also gave me my first taste of politics and serving constituents.

Over the years, I have often been asked how I reconcile my belief in Christian charity with the slings and arrows of politics. It's not an easy question, but I honestly believe that without my strong faith, I don't know where I'd be in politics because it allows me to put things in proper perspective.

I've said many times that you can't be namby-pamby in politics, but that doesn't mean you have to yell and scream and treat people with disrespect. I believe in telling people the truth. Sometimes they don't like what I have to say, but they know where I stand. And sometimes they take what I say, go away, come up with a better plan and return with a solution that works better for everyone.

I feel it is spiritually healthy to have one's faith tested once in a while, whether as a result of life's trials and tribulations or through interaction with others, like political opponents. If not tested, we run the risk of becoming complacent and taking our faith for granted. It is easy to be a person of faith if our faith is never challenged.

Fortunately, during my entire career I have never had to make a decision that compromised my Christian faith. But I have had my faith tested many times by political enemies. There's an old saying about laying a strong foundation with the bricks that others throw. Despite this, I encourage people of faith, any and all faiths, to enter politics and use their faith to raise the bar of public service.

Too often in this secular world people of faith feel pressure to hide their faith as if it were something to be ashamed of, but it's not. Compassion and giving voice to those less fortunate are part of what makes for terrific public service. Truly, I believe my faith helps me deal with real issues. It is why I lend my name and give time to help so many splendid charities, like World Vision in its battle against HIV/AIDS in countries like Tanzania in Africa. Faith helps make me conscious of people's needs and concerns locally, too. There are a lot of lonely people and you have to give them the opportunity to discuss things with you. You can't always help them, even as mayor, but at least you can listen and maybe offer suggestions as to how they might find help.

But compassion does not extend to suffering fools or patting folks on the head nicely when they don't do their homework. That only encourages mediocrity, or worse. Bluntness and truth ultimately lead to better people and better communities.

Each day at 5:30 a.m., after stretching and getting my blood flowing, I open a Joyce Meyer book of inspirational quotes and read one as my daily affirmation. Ms. Meyer is a charismatic Christian from St. Louis, Missouri, who gives me something to ponder each morning before I dig into the newspapers, city reports and other work for the day.

I am also a regular churchgoer and have been a member of the Trinity Anglican Church in Streetsville for more than sixty years. We started at the church even before it had indoor plumbing. Like so many others, I sadly witnessed its destruction in 1998 after a malicious teenager set it ablaze, but I was happily part of the fundraising and rebuilding of the church, too.

Up until his death in 1997, Sam was very active in the church as a lay reader and communion assistant who would also lead services, when needed, not only at Trinity but also at smaller congregations in the surrounding rural areas. Our shared faith was a cornerstone of our marriage.

And speaking of our marriage, our wedding day was September 29, 1951, the feast day of Saint Michael and All Angels, with the ceremony at the church in Toronto of the same name. It was a cool day with a high of thirteen degrees Celsius, with evening temperatures dipping down near freezing. And after close to a decade, the day also marked the end of my time living in Toronto.

CHAPTER 5

Streetsville

Sam's dad had a tradition of giving each of his four children one thousand dollars when they married. We used our money in 1951 towards a down payment on a house and five-acre (2 ha) property northwest of Toronto near the village of Streetsville. My father-in-law thought I was crazy dragging Sam out of Toronto, where he had been born and raised, and into the country.

And, make no mistake, this was the country even if the postwar rush to the suburbs was under way around Toronto in places like Scarborough, North York and Etobicoke. Our property was on Britannia Road, which was then a dirt road, not the four-lane paved street it is today with big-box stores, restaurants and outlet shopping. Our little white home of 1,200 square feet (110 m²) was cozy, albeit drafty in winter and not the sturdiest structure. It cost us $15,000, which was a lot of money to us in those days.

Before our wedding, we spent summer weekends driving in the country looking at homes and communities. After almost fifteen years living in the big cities of Montreal and Toronto, I yearned for the rural life that I loved from my early years on the Gaspé. But the reality was that both Sam and I worked in Toronto so we had to be near enough to the city. Once we found Streetsville, we immediately knew it was the place for us.

Though our property was technically in the Township of Toronto (it would not be renamed Mississauga until 1968) on the east side of the Credit River, we most certainly considered ourselves part of the Village of Streetsville. It was literally a two-minute drive into town, where we did our shopping, socializing and churchgoing at Trinity Anglican Church on Queen Street.

We were drawn to Streetsville for practical reasons and for its idyllic beauty along the banks of the Credit River. Indeed, for years from Victorian times to post–World War II, many Canadian artists and writers visited Streetsville and neighbouring communities of Meadowvale and Churchville to draw inspiration from their rustic charm.

It is funny how life works, though. Without even really knowing the history of Streetsville at the time, it was almost as if an unseen force from the village's past was attracting me to the place. As I was to find out through the years, its history is laced with some of the things I cherish: independent spirit, feistiness, strong community involvement, volunteerism, even a love of sports. The culture of this village was a perfect fit for me and Sam.

We arrived in Streetsville about one hundred years after the death of its founder, Timothy Street, a United Empire Loyalist and entrepreneur who established the town from government land grants for survey work he had done in the area. With five mill sites on the Credit River, Streetsville was a bustling place for its first forty years, up to the 1860s.

Beyond Timothy Street, there were many well-known

people building Streetsville and adding to the rich colour of the place. Except to historians and some local citizens, their names have faded into obscurity. One remains prominent, however, and he wasn't even a full-time resident. That man was William Lyon Mackenzie, the grandfather of Canada's longest-serving prime minister, the aforementioned Mackenzie King.

In the late 1820s and 1830s, reformer William Lyon Mackenzie used Streetsville as one of his strongest bases of operation in his fight against the corrupt Family Compact that controlled Upper Canada (Ontario) politics. In fact, two days after the famous battle at Montgomery's Tavern in Toronto during the 1837 Rebellion, Mackenzie was hiding out in Streetsville with a one-thousand-pound reward hanging over his head. He narrowly escaped capture and made his way to temporary exile in the United States. Streetsville mill owner William Comfort was arrested and imprisoned for giving shelter to his friend Mackenzie, who would eventually go on to be the first mayor of Toronto.

Streetsville grew to 1,500 people by 1857, and it broke free from Toronto Township and became an incorporated village on July 24, 1858, with John Street, Timothy's son, the first reeve. (Reeve is a title used by some towns and villages for the leader of council.) It was thriving as both an industrial and cultural centre with five mills, six hotels and, believe it or not, seven liquor stores.

This new, independent village campaigned vigorously to be named the seat of county government. Streetsville lost the battle to Brampton, but Streetsville resident Dr. John Barnhart was given the honour of being the county's first warden (the equivalent to a mayor or regional chairman nowadays) when Peel County was established in 1866.

History would repeat itself more than a century later when Streetsville fought like a lion for its independence and against amalgamation with Mississauga in the early 1970s, only to lose that battle, too. And, although a Streetsville resident didn't become the *first mayor* of the new City of Mississauga as Dr. Barnhart had done in Peel County, someone from Streetsville most certainly did eventually become mayor.

The 1860s and 1870s were challenging for Streetsville. Besides losing the county seat battle, the village was also bypassed by the railway and its two best hotels, the Telegraph and the Globe, both burned to the ground. The village's population plummeted to about seven hundred, a level where it would remain for almost a century before Sam and I moved there in 1951.

With only the stagecoach delivering visitors to Streetsville in 1873, the village decided to "go all in" and build its own railway, the Credit Valley Railway. "Streetsville's characteristic independent spirit asserted itself," John and Sandra Emerson write in *Mississauga: The First 10,000 Years*.

The railway's somewhat dubious business plan was based on transporting Chisholm sandstone from the Credit River Valley to Toronto for the construction of brownstone buildings like the Ontario Legislature, Toronto's Old City Hall and numerous mansions in Rosedale and the Annex neighbourhoods. The line opened in 1879 but the sandstone shipments were not enough to keep the independent company going and it was absorbed by Canadian Pacific Railway in 1883. Despite the disappointment of losing the railway's independence, there was now a railway station in Streetsville that would be essential to its future. The CPR would also play a significant role in Mississauga's history one hundred years later with a derailment in 1979.

Around the time of the Credit Valley Railway construction came a man who would also leave his mark on Streetsville. His name was William Couse and he gave an economic lift to the local farming community. "He established a beekeeping operation, producing world-famous honey, then expanded his business to include the processing and export of locally grown clover seed," write the Emersons. (I own the Couse family wagon, which we have at the McCallion farm near Guelph, where my daughter, Linda, lives. I have donated it to the Streetsville Historical Society.)

Together with the mills producing flour for bread, Couse launched the honey business so closely associated with Streetsville. For decades, live honey bees would be mailed from the Streetsville post office to beekeepers across North America. And when Mississauga swallowed up Streetsville, it would be Sam who would come up with the idea to create the Bread and Honey Festival as a way to preserve some of Streetsville's history and independence. The festival, started as a one-time farewell party or wake, just kept on going and has run annually for more than forty years.

Streetsville's other great attraction for me was its residents' love of sports. Streetsville was one of the first towns in Ontario to organize baseball games, in the mid-1800s. Hotel owners in the nineteenth century staged horse races on Queen Street right in front of their establishments. In the first half of the twentieth century, sulky races took place in Streetsville Park, on the flats of the Credit River. Lawn bowling was popular throughout the nineteenth and twentieth centuries. (Lawn bowling would lead to one of my more acrimonious, yet humorous, political battles.)

In the 1890s, the Streetsville Thistles won many regional and provincial championships and were one of the strongest lacrosse teams in Canada. Hockey also has a rich history in the village, dating back to the days of playing on the frozen Credit River, and today the community is the only one in all of Mississauga operating its own hockey arena and children's leagues, instead of being under the city's control.

There definitely was a lot about Streetsville's past that tugged at me to say, "This is the place to build your future."

Not long after we arrived in Streetsville, our first child, Peter, was born, in 1953, followed by Linda in 1958 and Paul in 1964. (I have one beloved grandchild, Peter's daughter, Erika, born in 1991.)

Our first home in Streetsville was small, but it was great for raising a family. The five acres was enough space to have horses, chickens and all sorts of other animals, including dogs, of course. The kids loved the horses, especially Linda, who today raises horses on the family farm near Guelph.

In 1955, Sam gave up his Toronto job and started a printing business in our garage called Unique Printing. Ever industrious and hard-working, Sam was also doing some commercial photography like weddings and portraits, operating a laundry business and acting as the local Streetsville representative for a moving company called M. Rawlinson Ltd. of Toronto. Within a short while, his printing business grew and he moved his press out of our garage and into a building on Falconer Avenue in Streetsville.

While this was all going on with Sam, I was doing his book-keeping and still working in Toronto at Canadian Kellogg. I was driving into work on my own by then. I've always loved to drive and still do. Over the years, I've been encouraged to get a driver but I just love the independence of driving myself and I am always cognizant of how I use taxpayers' money.

It was quite unusual for a woman in those days to be commuting into work alone, not to mention managing an office. And I never could have done that without the incredible support from our nanny, a woman from Streetsville named Annie Karl. Her family had escaped the ravages of Europe and came to Canada after World War II. She worked for us for fifteen years or so, and she was like a second mother to our kids, who all dearly loved her and still do to this day. While Annie was single she lived with us during the week and spent weekends at her family home. When she married Henry Zysk, she would come each morning and leave around dinnertime. I always tried to make dinner for Sam and the kids, especially after leaving my job at Canadian Kellogg in 1963.

I'd been at Kellogg for twenty-two years and it was time to leave. Not only was Kellogg's engineering business slowing, but Sam's Unique Printing was getting really busy and I wanted to help him manage it and be closer to home and the children. Beyond commercial printing, Sam was now publishing a community newspaper called *Plaza News*, which would be renamed the *Streetsville Shopping News* and then the *Streetsville Booster*, and finally the *Mississauga Booster*. (We sold it after Sam's death.)

In the early days, I acted as editor and business manager of the *Booster*. I always got a kick out of selling ads and continued doing that for years, even after giving up the other posts to concentrate on politics. The goal of the *Booster* was to report good news and give a boost to the local community. As publisher, Sam figured there was so much bad news reported in other newspapers that there was a market for giving people in Streetsville a lift. He was right.

In 1964, I joined the Streetsville Chamber of Commerce (of which Sam had been a founder), figuring my business experience from Kellogg could be an asset to the organization. I was named president in 1966.

As an advocate of volunteerism, I was also volunteering my time with the Girl Guides of Canada as the division Girl Guide commissioner in Peel County from 1963 to 1966. In 1964, when the Girl Guides were planning to build Camp Wyoka in Huron County, I signed the loan guarantee with the Canadian Imperial Bank of Commerce for five thousand dollars. "I don't think we need to tell you how very much we appreciated your faith and confidence in us," wrote G.L. Moore, executive secretary of White Oaks Area, the local division of Girl Guides. It was a lot of money to guarantee, but I knew the Girl Guides were committed to building the camp and raising the money, and I was right. Thousands upon thousands of girls over the years have spent many, many happy camping experiences at Camp Wyoka.

The more Sam and I became enmeshed in Streetsville, the more I began to think its political leadership was slipping into complacency. There seemed to be the feeling of an old boys' network and that things were done certain ways simply because that's the way they'd always been done. This frustrated me and I made overtures to join the Planning Board.

Streetsville mayor John Fulton appointed me to the Planning Board in 1964, and when I started sinking my teeth into its procedures and its reports, I quickly realized things were worse than I thought. There was no official plan, although they were working on developing one. Still, no one seemed to know exactly where everything the town owned was located; for example, the sewers. In one case, we found that a sewer was located on private property owned by my church, Trinity Anglican. Buildings were going up without permits. There was a fundamental lack of regulations. The town was a mess in this respect.

The more questions I asked, the fewer proper answers I got. At least, initially. I quickly developed a reputation as a renegade when really all I was doing was trying to clean up things that should have been done years earlier. In 1966, I was named chair of the Streetsville Planning Board.

The mayor was a scholarly man named Bill Tolton who had a degree in agricultural science. Maybe it was because I was a woman or perhaps because my schooling ended at grade 11 versus his university education, but the mayor didn't take too kindly to my questions about modern planning and the lack of consultation with the public.

I locked horns with him at many public meetings, particularly when it came to two seven-storey apartment buildings he was backing in the centre of Streetsville. They got built and remain eyesores today because they stick out in the heart of the quaint village.

I am proud to say that when I was chair of the Streetsville Planning Board we did draft a comprehensive official plan that included a temporary freeze on development in the downtown, and new parks and other amenities, including identifiable sewers under town-owned lands.

By late 1966, I was ready to take my first plunge into politics and I decided to run for deputy reeve of Streetsville. Unfortunately, I lost to a man named George Parker, then a manager at Streetsville's flour mill.

After twelve consecutive Mississauga mayoral wins and five

other victorious elections before that, I sometimes get teased that I have turned poor George Parker into the answer to a trivia question and made him into the Wally Pipp of politics. Wally Pipp was the New York Yankee first baseman whose headache one day in 1925 famously put a young Lou Gehrig into the lineup. I was a little girl and only four years old so I obviously don't recall it happening. But I do know the story that the Hall-of-Famer Gehrig would play every Yankee game at first base for the next fourteen years and set the "iron man" record of 2,130 consecutive games that lasted fifty years.

But even after all these years and all these successes, I am not going to lie. The loss to George Parker stung. And I believed some nasty tactics were used by my opponent's campaign, like my lawn signs mysteriously disappearing. But what was I going to do? Sulk and feel sorry for myself? No, sir. I was going to learn from it, get out and meet more people, find out more about their concerns, and return to the Planning Board and ask questions that the public wanted answers for. I also dedicated more time to volunteer work such as with the Streetsville Chamber of Commerce.

In December 1967, I again ran for deputy reeve and won this time. And Jack Graham, also known as a reformer, was elected mayor. Within six months, the reeve, Don Hewson, resigned because his law practice demanded more and more of his time, so I quickly moved up to reeve. (Since Streetsville council had a position called mayor, the reeve was de facto second-in-command. In other municipalities the reeve was the position in charge, but not in Streetsville.)

Jack Graham and I saw eye to eye on most things, but we had a falling-out about, of all things, lawn bowling. A land dispute arose between a well-to-do man who lived next to the lawn bowling club and the lawn bowlers. This rather curmudgeonly fellow, with a Dickensian name of House Brocklebank, claimed the bowling green was partially on his land. The bowling green was donated to the town in the 1890s on the condition it be kept for lawn bowling. I sided with the bowlers and Jack sided with the landowner. We won and it remained a lawn bowling green into the twenty-first century, until participation in the game dwindled. It has since been converted into a beautiful office for the Streetsville Business Improvement Association.

Things were never quite the same for the working relationship between me and Jack Graham. And then we tangled mightily on the single biggest issue in Streetsville—whether Streetsville would continue as its own independent municipality or be swallowed up.

On January 1, 1968, many Toronto Township communities (excluding Streetsville and Port Credit) amalgamated into the Town of Mississauga. Adding to the pressure against Streetsville (which was now entirely surrounded by Mississauga) was that the Progressive Conservative government at Queen's Park was in the middle of creating regional governments across Ontario. Our areas west of Toronto known as Peel and Halton counties were the last to be converted to regional government.

The intent of regional government was for cities and towns to share services like police, garbage and water to save money. I've always argued regional government in Peel actually causes duplications of services and costs taxpayers more money. Regardless, through the late 1960s and early 1970s no issue was more important to Streetsville than its independence.

In the mid-1960s, the Ontario government commissioned Judge Thomas J. Plunkett to look into municipal restructuring west of Toronto. The Plunkett Report called for a one-tier government of Mississauga. Initially, I supported this because I was, and still am, against regional government. Streetsville's mayor, Jack Graham, also supported the idea.

Queen's Park shelved the Plunkett Report, but the issue of regional government and amalgamation was snowballing. It became clear that the Town of Mississauga wanted to swallow Streetsville whole, and the people in Streetsville were dead set against that. Listening to the people made me change my mind and I was against any merger for Streetsville, whether like Plunkett's idea or full-blown regional government.

On council, I asked for a consultant's report to examine Streetsville's borders and look for other ideas. The experts came back with an idea to push Streetsville's borders west towards Oakville. We would ask for almost ten thousand acres (4,050 ha) of land under the jurisdiction of the Town of Mississauga (2,830 ha) and Oakville (1,215 ha) and create a much larger Streetsville, with us controlling growth and development of our independent municipality.

I loved the idea and fought hard for it. Jack Graham did not. I never fully understood why Jack didn't follow the people and their obvious desire to expand an independent Streetsville. He seemed resigned to the fact that Streetsville's dissolution as a municipality was inevitable and not worth fighting against. He was out of step with the people of Streetsville and decided to step aside in the next election. "I wouldn't be elected dog catcher," he is quoted as saying in the book *Farewell, Town of Streetsville* by Tom Urbaniak. "Not even my wife would have voted for me!"

Jack's decision led to my election as mayor of Streetsville. I beat former mayor Bill Tolton on a platform of "Planning for the People" and fighting for Streetsville's independence. I became mayor on January 1, 1970. Those were emotionally charged days around Streetsville and it is my belief that Jack Graham remained bitter over our falling-out for quite a while.

Interestingly, in December 2013, I was at the Christmas dinner of the Streetsville Business Improvement Association and the owner of the restaurant came over to me and said: "Madam Mayor, your predecessor is here this evening, too." I thought he was referring to one of the two Mississauga mayors before me. I looked around the room and saw neither of them, and then my eyes caught Jack Graham. The restaurateur was referring to my Streetsville mayoral predecessor, not my Mississauga predecessors! Now that is going back some years. Can you believe that?

I immediately went over to chat with Jack, who is a couple years younger than me. His first wife, whom everyone called "Bubbles" for her effervescent personality, had passed away years before and he told me his current wife was suffering from Alzheimer's disease, just as my Sam had. We shared stories and I offered some advice about dealing with Alzheimer's. So much water under the bridge. He was a perfect gentleman and I enjoyed catching up with him.

In 1969, I had a sneaking idea that not only was I the town's first woman mayor, but I could also be its last. I would never say that publicly back then, but I knew we were in for one tough fight to keep Streetsville intact. I didn't believe it inevitable that Streetsville would be swallowed up, but I wouldn't bet against it because the provincial government was hell-bent on creating regional governments across Ontario.

Where only a decade before a mood of complacency hung over Streetsville politics, now the citizens were charged up like never before. The Streetsville Citizens' Organization for

Retention and Expansion (SCORE) was formed and the majority of adults signed a petition to keep Streetsville. Local schools ran essay competitions on why Streetsville should survive. Citizens, young and old, were writing poems and letters to Queen's Park and newspapers urging Streetsville be kept independent.

And though our council held the line on tax increases and dealt with other issues, the town's very survival was the number one issue during my entire time as mayor. In fact, it was during this period that I began the "development must pay for growth" mantra that would mark my years as Mississauga mayor. But this was hardly noticed during the "fight to save Streetsville" years.

In 1971, William Davis became premier of Ontario, and we initially saw his election as good news because Streetsville was part of his riding of Peel North. Surely our elected MPP, now holding the highest office in the province, would come to our aid. But it was not to be, and the premier made it clear he would not stand in the way of so-called progress.

By 1973, it looked as if the government had made up its mind that it would create a new City of Mississauga by combining the Town of Mississauga with Streetsville and Port Credit to the south. All of our ideas and campaigns were dismissed. Streetsville council passed a resolution calling for the premier to come and face his constituents and justify why his government was doing this. For good measure, we suggested he resign his seat in Peel North if he chose to duck such a meeting.

I even wrote a letter to his minister of municipal affairs, John White: "It is unfortunate that our Member of [provincial] Parliament has forced us to pass such a resolution, as we had great confidence and faith in him—a faith which has been completely shaken."

To his credit, Bill Davis came to Streetsville on June 14, 1973, and faced more than five hundred people in the community hall. He was roundly booed and I noticed the newspaper reporters gleefully scribbling notes, knowing this story of the premier on the hot seat was only going to get better as the evening went along.

The premier knew it was going to be a tough night, but he was there and I think everyone respected him for that, even if we pretty much knew he had crossed the Rubicon. With his famed "Brampton Billy" folksy charm, the premier tried to win some audience support. "I am not saying for a moment there isn't some logic to the arguments of the town of Streetsville and the citizens there, heaven knows," he said.

The audience could tell that comment was one that had an unsaid *but* dangling at the end of it. And this followed from the premier: "It is just as difficult for us to make a determination that does upset a number of people in Streetsville as it would be to accede to their request, believing it, perhaps, in the long run not to be in the interest of the total community."

Though that statement was mixed with some of his best ambiguous language, it was clear his government had no intention of changing course, even if these people were voters in his riding. Indeed, in only two weeks the bill to create a new City of Mississauga and the dissolution of Streetsville and Port Credit municipalities would receive royal assent.

As I've said, Bill Davis loves to tease me that I fought him tooth and nail but if not for him, I wouldn't be where I am today. Yes, I love Mississauga and, I say humbly, my name is synonymous with the City of Mississauga. But had history been different and if Streetsville were given the opportunity to stay independent and grow to the west so that Streetsville,

Mississauga, Brampton and Oakville would all be roughly the same size, would that also not have been a good outcome? Sometimes cities and governments can grow so big that they are beyond the reach of the average person. I am not saying Mississauga is too big, but sometimes I wonder what could have been.

Regardless, the City of Mississauga became a reality on January 1, 1974, and we had a lot of work to do in Streetsville in our last six months as an independent municipality.

For one thing, council was determined to spend every last cent in the town's coffers on Streetsville instead of this money going into the larger pool that could be dispersed elsewhere in Mississauga. Ironically, much of this money came from the provincial government and its $80-million South Peel Water and Sewage System endeavour. This plan created a huge trunk sewer to carry waste to state-of-the-art water purification facilities on the shores of Lake Ontario. Under this proposal, the province paid $6.3 million to buy and mothball smaller sewage treatment facilities like those in Brampton and Clarkson and ours in Streetsville.

We used our share of the windfall to spruce up the downtown area with new sidewalks and light standards, and to bury hydro lines. Council also hosted a lavish banquet to thank several hundred volunteers in Streetsville. Wine flowed, toasts were made and each volunteer was given a silver plate engraved with the town's crest.

We were determined to give this grand old independent municipality with so much colourful history the send-off it deserved. One thing we couldn't do was keep our aerial ladder fire truck in Streetsville. Though we had a volunteer fire department, we had saved money for the aerial ladder truck in case there were any fires in the downtown Streetsville apartments that were occupied mostly by seniors. As soon as the Mississauga Fire Department took over in Streetsville, officials moved our aerial ladder truck down to Cooksville in the southern part of Mississauga, which had lots of apartments. That still rankles with long-time residents of Streetsville.

On December 31, 1973, at 7 p.m., we held our final Streetsville town council meeting. It was a sombre event, full of reflections and heartfelt speeches. As a municipality, Streetsville was a special place with so much community spirit woven into the fabric of life.

We took Streetsville into the City of Mississauga debt-free, with a needed aerial fire truck and a fifty-dollar utility levy on each new home built. This lot levy was precedent-setting for Mississauga and the money went towards hydro upgrades. These Streetsville achievements made all twelve thousand of us in town at the time proud.

And even though it is now part of a larger entity, Streetsville retains its spirit and its charm. Allow me to tell a brief story. A few years ago the hockey arenas in both Streetsville and Port Credit required multi-million-dollar renovations. The Streetsville community raised $1 million to offset some of the costs to Mississauga taxpayers. Now that's community spirit. Not a nickel was raised by the Port Credit community.

Before the autumn election in 1973, I was asked to run for the office of mayor of the soon-to-be City of Mississauga. I made the correct choice and decided against it. Though it wasn't a difficult decision, in hindsight it was one of my best. Instead, at age fifty-two, I ran for and won a seat on Mississauga council representing the voters of Streetsville. A new year. A new job. And many new challenges. I couldn't wait to get started.

CHAPTER 6

City of Mississauga

Not long after I decided I could not possibly run for mayor of the new City of Mississauga, which I had fought so hard against as Streetsville mayor, a stranger appeared at my office in the Streetsville Town Hall. "I'd like to talk to you about the mayoral election," he said.

"But I'm running for council to represent the people of Streetsville. I'm not running for mayor," I said.

"I am going to run for mayor and I am going to win," he said.

This self-assured young man was Martin Dobkin, a family physician who had recently been appointed coroner of Peel County, soon to be Peel Region. He was only thirty-one years old, with absolutely zero experience in politics. I had never heard of him before our meeting that day in 1973.

His attitude was striking. He was extremely confident. I asked him how he could be so sure of winning, and he talked about all sorts of hanky-panky that he'd uncovered between some of the old guard—the *ancien régime*—and developers in Mississauga. Things like fancy dinners and cases of liquor traded for access to officials, building permits and backroom deals.

I'd heard whispers of such things, but had seen no real proof, no smoking guns. I was in Streetsville, not the Town of Mississauga, and it was months before amalgamation would turn the area into the much larger City of Mississauga. Things were absolutely booming at the time with waves and waves of families coming from Toronto and buying single-family, afford-able dream homes.

And the Town of Mississauga, a Tory bastion and part of the old Big Blue Machine that ran Ontario for decades, oper-ated differently from Streetsville. For instance, there was no policy manual in Mississauga at the time. Such a document lays out rules for issuing permits, procedures for council and committees, hiring practices and so on—all sorts of simple but important things that most large organizations, public and pri-vate, usually follow. The Town of Streetsville had such a policy manual but the much larger Town of Mississauga did not, for goodness' sake.

I wasn't convinced Martin Dobkin had foolproof evi-dence against anyone, but I certainly agreed that the people of Mississauga deserved reform and I was impressed by his pas-sion. By the end of our meeting, I told the doctor as much and wished him luck in the campaign. As for me and my elec-tion campaign, the old guard had parachuted an opponent, Grant Clarkson, the reeve (or deputy mayor) of the Town of Mississauga, to run against me for the council seat of Streetsville.

The Mississauga old guard of Lou Parsons (then newly appointed by the province as chairman of the Region of Peel), Chic Murray (who was running for mayor of Mississauga against Dobkin) and the developers wanted me out of local politics before the new city got going. They mistakenly believed me to be anti-development and thought a serious challenge by Clarkson might be the ticket to push me aside. Over the years, I won them all over, especially the developers. Chic's son, Jim, a corporate real estate agent, has long been one of my biggest supporters and a close friend who heads one of my charitable foundations.

"Hazel, the reason the old guard was against you was because they viewed you as an interloper from Streetsville who would come in and take things over," Jim told me one time. "And they were right. That's what you did, but they eventually realized you taking over was the best thing that could happen to Mississauga."

In that first City of Mississauga election, despite Clarkson's challenge, I expected to win the Streetsville seat. And I promised Dobkin to do what I could to help his reform agenda should he win. As it turned out, this political novice needed no help during the campaign. Beholden to no one and with no political baggage or broken promises to defend, Dobkin hammered his opponent, Chic Murray, tying him to the old guard and the developers and their interests, not the people's real interests.

The voters ate it up. It had been fifteen years since tough-talking Mary Fix had taken on the developers, trying to reel in the rapid and oftentimes reckless growth that threatened the residential quality of life. Fix was the reeve of Toronto Township, which later became the Town of Mississauga. Since her departure, many residents felt that unrestrained development was out of control and they blamed the old guard for being too cozy with developers. Change was in the air.

Dobkin swept into office as the head of a "reform council." I won easily, with the Streetsville outsider Grant Clarkson getting only 24 per cent of the vote against me. Other reformers elected were Mary Helen Spence, David Culham and Caye Killaby, who lived near me just east of the Credit River.

The term of the first council was creative and productive. But I would also describe it as frustrating at times because the old guard was still around and not about to go away. Ron Searle, a councillor aligned with Chic Murray, Lou Parsons and the others, would battle constantly with the new mayor, creating a pall of negativity over council sessions. Along with Councillor Bud Gregory, Searle would attack Dobkin and call him things like an idealist with no experience in running a city.

As much as I liked Martin Dobkin, he added to the volatility. Maybe it was because of his lack of experience in politics, or maybe it was simply his personality. But he went after individuals without having the smoking guns. Even the night he was elected he made the mistake of telling the media he planned a housecleaning of staff at city hall. He named names, too, which was not wise.

During his tenure, many staff members departed, including city manager Dean Henderson, works commissioner William Anderson, clerk John Corney and solicitor Len Stewart. In one year, we lost seventy-five city staffers, and many headed to the Region of Peel where former Mississauga councillor and current regional chairman Lou Parsons was delighted to find them jobs and spread the word that Dobkin's city hall was in disarray. Others went to different municipalities or to developers like the McLaughlin Group. These defections opened areas for talented people I'd worked with in Streetsville to step up into City of Mississauga jobs to prove their mettle. But there is no denying, the atmosphere around city hall was less than ideal.

In an interview published in 2000, one gets a feel for Dobkin's style and what the atmosphere was like when he was mayor through his own words: "There was a perception in Mississauga that things were rotten," Dobkin told *Toronto Life*. "I called all the developers into my office and told them the way it was going to be . . . no monkey business. I mean, the first two months I was mayor, people were still coming up the city hall steps with cases of liquor for the building and planning department."

Believe me, there was no love lost between the developers and the mayor, either. "He was anti-development," said Bruce McLaughlin, the visionary developer who built the Square One shopping centre, in a video produced in 2001 for my eightieth birthday called *Hurricane Warning!* "He didn't think about what was good for the whole community."

The animosity between the mayor and the developers was so strong that Martin Dobkin called for a public inquiry in early 1975 to investigate possible improprieties swirling around and related to development in Mississauga. His critics called it a witch hunt. The inquiry was quashed because the courts said the city had no right to investigate other corporations such as the old Town of Mississauga and the hydro commission. Luckily, this aborted inquiry cost taxpayers only $300,000, unlike a future inquiry in Mississauga that would cost much more.

Even with these battle lines drawn between the old guard and reformers, the first Mississauga council under Martin Dobkin achieved many things. Perhaps the most important was the creation of a comprehensive official plan for the new city. This plan was the blueprint that led to the road map for large-scale development of Mississauga in the coming years that would eventually turn our city into the sixth-largest in Canada.

Dobkin also came up with a unique idea to start the Public Vehicle Advisory Board, which is an advisory committee of council, made up of members of the taxi and limousine industry, that makes recommendations on matters relating to the provision of taxicab, limousine and livery services in the city and at Pearson International Airport, which I sometimes like to call the Mississauga International Airport. Dobkin's public vehicle board has been emulated by many other cities.

The progressive moves didn't stop there. Properties were purchased to provide green space and parklands, including the Rattray Marsh, Adamson House, Cawthra-Elliot Estate, Jack Darling Park, Morning Dew Park, Cooksville Creek lands and the parkland at the mouth of the Credit River. We concentrated on protecting and preserving the Lake Ontario waterfront for Mississauga residents to enjoy. It was not lost on us how the City of Toronto missed its opportunities to create a spectacular waterfront accessible to all residents. We also built three libraries and two community centres which would foreshadow what was to come for the city.

It's worth singling out the Rattray Marsh, the last remaining lakefront marsh between Toronto and Burlington. This environmentally sensitive wetland was preserved as parkland and officially opened in October 1975. It offers a different experience for all nature lovers with its variety of wildlife and plants and spectacular bird-watching opportunities that change with the seasons. The marsh averages almost a thousand visitors every day of the year and it's not just Mississauga residents who come to walk the trails and enjoy it. People from across the Greater Toronto Area, including numerous school children on class trips, come to experience the tranquility, look for birds and fauna, and do science and geography projects.

Beyond its beauty, the eighty-nine-acre (36 ha) Rattray Marsh is important as a symbol of community involvement, volunteerism and the downright feistiness of residents who did not want to see it destroyed. It was saved from development by a pugnacious group who won government support by relentlessly doing their homework. A developer owned most of the land and was intent on filling in the marsh and building homes there. (It is surrounded by lovely, large homes and the plan was to build dozens more.)

On council, Mary Helen Spence played a pivotal role. She was not only a conservationist, but she represented the ward where the Rattray Marsh sits. The mayor and other councillors, including me, also supported the wetlands preservation. We were impressed by the residents who not only talked a good game, but put up their own money to save the Rattray Marsh.

In 1972, the residents bought twenty-five acres (10 ha) with the more than $200,000 they raised. The province designated the rest of the marsh as a significant wetland area, and the city and province bought the remaining land for $2.5 million in 1974 so that generations and generations could enjoy it, all thanks to passionate citizens who fought for sixteen years to prevent development of the land. Their legacy remains today through the Rattray Marsh Protection Association, a citizens' group of volunteers who work with the Credit Valley Conservation Authority to ensure the long-term protection and appreciation of the marsh.

Looking back, my support of the marsh is ironic, given that I come from the Gaspé coast and when I was growing up we hated marshes because of the smells, especially at low tide. Of course, we didn't know the value of wetlands to the environment back in those days.

Come the election in the fall of 1976, Martin Dobkin was defeated by Ron Searle, who ran on a platform of what he called "restoring the confidence of business in Mississauga." By lashing out at Dobkin's inexperience and perceived mistakes, Searle became Mississauga's second mayor, beating Dobkin by 3,500 votes, with Streetsville accountant and business-man Gerry Townsend finishing a respectable third just a few hundred votes behind Dobkin. (In the early and mid-2000s, Townsend helped the city by stopping the financial bleeding at the Mississauga Living Arts Centre.) I won my Streetsville council seat by acclamation in 1976.

But after that 1976 election, council was still divided and not very enjoyable to be part of, with more bickering than con-structive work being done to build our new city. I kept arguing for lot levies to ensure that growth would pay its way. The suc-cess of the fifty-dollar utility lot levies in Streetsville for capital cost expansion for hydro didn't seem to sway the pro-developer councillors that we should be tougher on getting growth to pay its way.

My view was and remains that existing residents should not be paying to build things like new libraries, community cen-tres, soccer fields, baseball diamonds and hockey arenas that are needed for new residents. Paying the operating costs is one thing, but the construction costs should come from developers who profit from buyers of their homes.

Lot levies are basically entrance fees into the city. They worked well in Streetsville and I knew they'd do the same in Mississauga. Today, this "growth must pay its way" strategy is commonplace across the country, even institutionalized under laws in many jurisdictions. But back then it was viewed as rather radical. Developers and the mayor of the day routinely fought me and other reform-minded councillors when it came to lot levies.

The fact is that we were building a city and you only get one chance to do that. And I was getting both tired and annoyed being critical all the time without the power to change things.

I sat on virtually every committee at both the Region of Peel and the City of Mississauga, so I was voicing my opinion and being heard during the years between 1974 and 1978. I just didn't feel like I was being listened to by the powers that be. I am a joiner, so serving on all these committees was no hardship for me, other than facing the constant roadblocks. Even still, I was getting valuable experience that would serve me well down the road, despite the fact it felt like I was sometimes banging my head against the wall.

The problem is, when you criticize and complain all the time without seeing tangible results, it is easy to become negative, very negative, and I am not by nature a negative person. It was at this point that I decided to run for mayor in the next election and either win or get out—or as my mantra became: "Go up or go out."

My platform was simple: Let's grow, but let's do it in an orderly, controlled way with the concerns of the people first. Growth must pay its way and the city must be run efficiently, like a business. I promised to be careful with voters' money, just as I am always careful spending my own money. As I often say to citizens, I spend the taxpayers' money the way I spend my own money, which is seldom and carefully.

I also advocated for more than single-family residential homes. Mississauga, I believed, had to develop an industrial and commercial base to create jobs so people could live, work and play close to home. It was never my intention to build Mississauga to be a "bedroom community" where people toddle off to work every morning to Toronto or elsewhere.

Today Mississauga has 54,000 registered businesses employing 413,000 people. We have the second-highest number of jobs in the Greater Toronto Area, behind only our colossus neighbour to the east, Canada's largest city. And Mississauga has 34,700 more people coming to work here every day than leaving to work elsewhere. Mississauga is also home to sixty-two Fortune 500 companies with a head office or major divisional head office here.

Think about that: here is a city that was little more than farmers' fields fifty years ago and now it is a net importer of thousands of jobs each and every day. As mayor, I remember sitting in my office back in 1978–79 and looking across the street and seeing cows and horses grazing in the field. In fact, today you could fill the Air Canada Centre for a Maple Leafs hockey game twice over with those thousands more people coming to Mississauga every day than leaving. This is something we should be very proud of in this city. We are a strong economic urban centre, not just a suburban adjunct to Toronto.

In 1978 did we know how things would unfold? Of course not. But it became clear to me that if we didn't do something about that bickering council, little of lasting economic value would be achieved. We needed to find compromises—bridges, if you will—between the anti-development people and the old guard.

All one had to do was look around and see two great advantages bestowed on Mississauga by others, not by the city council. First, the country's biggest and busiest airport sat in our city. Major international companies, whether American, British, German, Japanese or whatever, want to locate their Canadian operations near such an airport. Furthermore, all the big highways in Southern Ontario run through Mississauga, again helping businesses that want to locate here.

Second, back in the 1970s, Mississauga had three big developers who owned thousands and thousands of acres of farmland, and they were ready to build top-quality homes and communities with all the amenities. They weren't interested in willy-nilly development; they had big plans for neighbourhoods and large defined communities of thousands of people.

It was up to the political leaders elected by the people to ensure these communities were livable, and not just for ten or fifteen years but for generations and generations. As I said, you only get one chance to build a city from scratch. We also had several large (but not as big) builders tying their developments to the peripheries of those Big Three communities of Erindale, Meadowvale and the City Centre near the Square One shopping centre. From the perspective of planning, building infrastructure and creating a livable, modern city, this helped, too.

The benefit of the so-called "Big Three" developers—E.P. Taylor's Cadillac Fairview, Markborough Developments and Bruce McLaughlin's McLaughlin Group—cannot be overstated. Each had so much at stake and so much invested that they wanted to build high-quality and affordable dream homes for young families and good jobs in the community.

They built massive water diversion projects to prevent flooding. One of the biggest was started when I was mayor of Streetsville, called the Mullet Creek Diversion. It was controversial but it was necessary. Others followed in the City of Mississauga, after amalgamation. I can't help but think that had the old Town of Mississauga, or maybe even Toronto Township, as it was called until 1968, shown more foresight with storm management strategies, we wouldn't have the periodic flash floods from the Cooksville Creek. Given how these big developers operated, had they been told to divert the Cooksville Creek, they would have, without question.

The developers also built manmade lakes with water run-off that support fishing and other recreational uses. They built infrastructure, community centres, libraries, sports complexes that all added to the quality of life. They were not the enemy, as some thought, but they were also not elected by the people. Corporations put profits first. Elected officials must always put people first.

There had to be some give-and-take. We had many advantages in Mississauga, but all the squabbling during those early years was getting in the way of building the city. We had to put the people first, but we also had to be fair and reasonable to developers with transparent rules on how the city would unfold.

In the early years, the developers didn't see it the same way as I did and the old guard certainly were resistant. But I was convinced that if elected mayor, I would embrace controlled growth that would pay its way and Mississauga could grow into one of the biggest and best urban centres in Canada.

In 1978, I was fifty-seven years old, an age when many people start to slow down. But I was the opposite. I saw so much promise, so much opportunity to build a fantastic city that I was champing at the bit to lead. It was time to "go up or go out" and I was prepared to take that risk and run for mayor.

To be successful, I knew I had to run a grassroots campaign with a promise to be a "mayor for the people." The power brokers and the money would be behind my opponent, but I knew the people would be behind me if I effectively got my message out.

Our residential development had badly outstripped our commercial and industrial development, and darned if I wasn't going to change that ratio. No one, least of all me, wanted Mississauga to be a sleepy suburb in the shadow of Toronto, the self-proclaimed centre of the universe.

We needed more jobs in Mississauga. We needed more community facilities to keep residents working and spending at home, not having everyone travelling to Toronto to work. My plan was to cut red tape to attract new business so that I could eventually cut ribbons, more and more ribbons, to open new offices and plants in Mississauga with good-paying jobs for residents. Today, our property tax ratio is about 62 per cent residential and 38 per cent commercial/industrial, which indicates how strong our economic base is in Mississauga.

In my first mayoral election, I had a terrific campaign team, albeit somewhat unorthodox in those days because the three senior men were all from different political stripes. Finance Chairman Frank Walker was a Conservative; Campaign Manager Desmond Morton, a university professor at the Mississauga campus of the University of Toronto, was a New Democrat; and Doug McIntyre, who headed the Committee to Elect Hazel, was a diehard Liberal.

I remember having meetings at Doug's house on Princess Street in Streetsville and these three guys would get into it about the Liberals, Conservatives and NDP. The arguments could be about specific issues of the day or overall philosophies, but they were always spirited debates. At one meeting the three got into a heated discussion about one of the political parties, so I said, "Come on, guys, we're not here to talk politics. We're here to get me elected."

They all laughed. Throughout the campaign, I'd use that line on them every time they'd get into it. And every time they'd laugh, put their differences aside and come up with fresh ideas for the campaign. In many ways it was appropriate that I had a Conservative, Liberal and New Democrat working for me because I've always thought I have a part of each party in my politics: I'm a fiscal conservative and a populist liberal with a social conscience.

At our last meeting the night before the election, a great idea came to my son Peter, and we went to town on it. My opponent, the incumbent mayor, used the slogan "A Good Mayor." So we adopted "A Better Mayor." My husband, Sam, hurried off from the meeting to print up hundreds, maybe thousands, of "Hazel" sticky labels with the slogan on each reading: "A Better Mayor." Frank, Des and Doug and their teams then went around the city and plastered big "Hazel" signs all over Mississauga with "A Better Mayor" stickers to catch the eye of voters on election day.

I think that idea helped me get elected, but my opponent helped me even more. In politics, as in life, you don't look a gift horse in the mouth. And when he took a swipe at me for being a woman, I could hardly thank him enough.

CHAPTER 7

A Woman Mayor

My first Mississauga mayoral race was a tight contest. I was up against the incumbent mayor, Ron Searle, who was backed by developers and the old guard with a campaign war chest about five times bigger than my $12,000. I was certainly hoping for victory but as the underdog, I was well aware that a loss would put me out of politics for the first time in a decade.

What turned the tide in my favour, ironically, was something I had faced all my life: being a woman in a male-dominated world.

I am not one to dwell on the topic of male chauvinism, especially because things have improved so much over the last three or four decades. But it would be naïve to suggest that sexism has been eradicated from Canadian society.

After a debate in the 1978 campaign, Mayor Ron Searle told a reporter that having a challenger who was a woman required him to pull his political punches. "My instinct is to hammer the hell out of her," he said, "but I can't really do it. I'm really inhibited by the fact that she's a woman." When this quote appeared in the *Mississauga News*, it sure changed the campaign. It was so patronizing. And, believe me, I'm not the only woman who despises being patronized. The women of Mississauga were *furious* over his remarks. Ron's comment galvanized female voters' support behind me. Many, many women told me that they weren't initially going to vote for me, but now they would.

Ron and I had many differences, but even to this day, I can't get upset with him about those comments. He was a product of his times. Indeed, he was a Canadian war hero who volunteered for overseas action and was wounded storming the beaches of Normandy on June 6, 1944. We all owe men like Ron a debt of gratitude for their sacrifices. But, unfortunately, many men of his generation held the view that a woman's place was in the home. I am a mother, but I have never subscribed to that view and believe it is a woman's choice if she wishes a career in or outside the home.

Out on the campaign trail, I refused to get dragged into a discussion about my gender. I didn't want to target the women's vote because I wanted to be mayor of the city, not mayor of the women in the city. The self-inflicted damage was done by Ron, and I wanted to talk about Mississauga and its future. When the topic of gender came up, I would deflect it and try to talk about the issues facing Mississauga and the promises tossed out loosely by my opponent.

I got great mileage out of a fictional story about how Ron and I were forced to climb a ladder to Heaven and how we were told to write out all our broken promises as we ascended. By the fifth rung, my hand got stepped on. It was my opponent on his way back down to get a new box of chalk. Ron bristled every time I told that story.

On the night of November 13, 1978, I beat Ron by less than three thousand votes. I believe the sexist comments were a major contributor to my victory. And, as I had done whenever I faced gender discrimination, whether in business or politics, I didn't rant and rave and kick up a fuss to draw attention. I just worked harder and looked for ways to capitalize. It wasn't much different than in the 1940s in Toronto when I was told I could not join an organization of personnel professionals because I was a woman. Instead of crying bloody murder, I started another networking group that was more inclusive, and I worked hard at it for a decade or so.

Over the years, I've often been called a "pioneer" on women's issues when it comes to politics, business and home life. But I've never really cared for that description. First of all, the term "pioneer woman" brings to mind author Susanna Moodie, living in the backwoods of Canada and hauling water for the family. I loved my rural upbringing, but I view myself as living in a contemporary world and as someone who helped build a modern, world-class city. Second, it gives me the feeling that some people would like to slot me into a role as a feminist, which I am not. I believe in hard work to get ahead, not quotas. As I have told many women's groups: "Think like a man, act like a lady and work like a dog."

Don't misunderstand me: I do believe women's issues are incredibly important and I have faced (and done my best to overcome) sexism my entire life. If there were more women involved in federal and provincial politics in Canada, this country would be better off. I just don't believe in "pink quotas" or tokenism that so many in the feminist movement advocate. It doesn't matter if you are a man or a woman in this day and age. What really matters is how hard you work and how determined you are to reach your goals and fulfill your dreams.

Now, I am not saying the world is no longer tilted in men's favour and that sexism no longer exists because, in some ways, it still is and it does. Heck, in 2011 the *Mississauga News* was still referring to me as "Mother McCallion." The *Toronto Star*, the self-appointed arbiter of all things politically correct, has long taken a sexist slant against me, though the paper would chastise anyone else that acted in such a way. The *Star*'s gender-slapping goes back to January 1979, with a headline that screamed in huge type: "Mom Who Runs Mississauga." (The *Star* gleefully attacked me on the age front too, later in my career.)

In that 1979 *Star* article, I said something prophetic that is worth talking about. I wish the events that made it prophetic later had never happened, but they did. Here's what I said to the *Star* reporter, only ten months before the train derailment would make Mississauga famous: "In my term in office I want to make Mississauga's name known the world over. I think a sense of identity is a good thing, for people and for cities." Mississauga *did* become known the world over, and I would never have wished on my worst enemies what was about to befall us in Mississauga.

Can you imagine any newspaper calling the prime minister "Father Harper" or the "dad who runs the country"? I can't. Nevertheless, things are so much better than in the past; and each year the situation improves for women, particularly young women, in Canada. You just have to go back to the year I was born, 1921, when the first federal election that finally allowed women to vote and run for a seat in the House of Commons occurred. Can you believe that? Women couldn't vote in a federal election the first fifty-four years after Confederation in

1867. It sounds outrageous today. (Some provinces gave the vote to women earlier than 1921, some later, in provincial and municipal elections.)

Granted, God has blessed me with a long life, but it is ridiculous how many decades Canadian politics were so unequal that in my lifetime women were just beginning to be able to vote. In one woman's lifetime, Canadian women went from being denied voting rights (or even the ability to sell their own property without their husband's consent) to living in a country that embraces equality for the most part.

Today, women represent only a quarter of the elected representatives in the House of Commons. That's the bad news. The good news is that, despite similar imbalances in provincial legislatures, more women are becoming premiers and proving they're just as able to lead as men. At one point in 2013, the majority of Canadian premiers were women, leading provinces and territories representing more than three-quarters of the population of Canada. That tells me that, given the opportunity, talented and hard-working women rise to the top.

There are several Canadian women who blazed trails long before my arrival in politics, including three mayors in the Toronto area: Marie Curtis in Long Branch, True Davidson in East York and Mary Fix in Toronto Township. But two Canadian women politicians really stand out and have inspired me over the years. They are Canada's first female member of Parliament, Agnes Macphail, and the first woman to be elected a big-city mayor, Charlotte Whitton of Ottawa.

Macphail was elected in 1921 in the rural Ontario seat of Grey South East. Besides her rural background, like me she did not come from a wealthy family with political connections. And, most importantly, she never made a special play for the women's vote. She wanted to represent all her constituents, not just women.

Being a trailblazer, she faced many obstacles. On her first day in Ottawa, another member of Parliament played a prank on her by leaving flowers on her desk in the House of Commons. The bouquet was not meant to congratulate her; it was the consequence of an MP betting wrongly that she would not get elected. Cabinet ministers replied to her questions by referring to her as the first "lady" member of the House. She would routinely shoot back that she wanted to be addressed as the "member for Grey South East," in the same manner as the men were acknowledged.

She was feisty. "Whatever is dirty, it is women's job to clean up, or drive some man to clean up, and that goes for everything from cellar to Senate," Macphail said. And she was a visionary who fought her entire nineteen years in the House of Commons for things all Canadian women today should be thankful for: "I want for myself what I want for other women, absolute equality." We're not yet there, but we're a lot further along than in her day.

Macphail was also involved in a sexist incident that was all too common in her day. How she responded is the key to her character. As a long-time advocate for the humane treatment of prisoners, she went to Kingston Penitentiary to see the conditions for herself. When she arrived, a guard at the gate told her no ladies were allowed inside the prison. To which she replied: "I am no lady, I'm an MP." No fuss. No bother. Just determination. She was allowed in and was the first woman to tour the facility.

It is interesting that something similar happened to me decades later and I hope my response to the situation would have pleased Agnes Macphail, even if I did acknowledge that I was a lady! During the Mississauga train derailment in 1979, the world media were reporting on this near-catastrophe and the orderly emergency evacuation of 220,000 people from their homes. One day a BBC reporter called from England looking for an on-the-spot account. The phone was passed to me and this guy assumed he'd been handed off to a secretary. "I don't want to talk to another secretary. I want to talk to someone in charge," he said. To which I replied, "I am the mayor *and* I am a lady."

His assumption surprised me because only six months earlier Margaret Thatcher had been elected as the first woman prime minister of Great Britain. You'd think a British reporter would have been familiar with having a woman in charge. But I guess sexism dies hard.

Thatcher was also a hero to me. She too did not come from wealth. She grew up living atop the family grocery store. As prime minister, the "Iron Lady" spoke plainly and decisively. After years of economic decay in her country, she and her policies turned Britain around. She was an extraordinary leader. Though I've had the privilege to meet the Queen on many occasions, I never met Lady Thatcher but would have loved to sit down and talk to her.

Charlotte Whitton was another great trailblazer, becoming the first woman mayor of a major Canadian city in 1951. I loved her decisiveness and determination. "Action makes more fortune than caution," she said. And, "When one must, one can." The Ottawa mayor took office with a mandate to clean up the shenanigans going on in city hall and she called things as she saw them. She wasn't afraid to say no instead of deferring decisions or acting like so many politicians who say they'll look into something when they know it won't happen. She was a leader. She just happened to be a woman. She was a role model to me and many other women who simply want to be recognized for our work, not our gender.

Because my career has stretched back almost seventy-five years, most of it in politics but a big chunk in business, too, I am often asked what advice I have for women, particularly young women who want a career while still raising a family, as I did.

My first piece of advice is to find a partner who truly understands what you want and the sacrifices involved. Talk to your prospective partner honestly before marriage. Sam knew what I was about and vice versa and that's why our marriage worked so well. Second, do your homework. *Always do your homework.* I know I sound like a broken record, but it is so important to be prepared and understand what's around the corner and how to capitalize on opportunities. Third, work hard and accept disappointment and failure as challenges to overcome next time. Dismiss any "woe is me" affectations and move on and learn.

Fourth, try to use your work at home as a benefit to your career opportunities. Instead of begrudging the housework, embrace it as time to unwind or use it to think through problems. This might sound crazy, but I actually enjoy doing the dishes. (My kids bought me a dishwasher years ago, but living alone and being out at evening events many times per week, I don't use it all that often.) I get some of my best work ideas cleaning up dishes or vacuuming. Housework keeps me humble, too.

Some women view running a household and advancing in a career as a zero-sum game. This is often not the case. The two are not mutually exclusive. You can have a great family life and an exciting career. In fact, some of the work you do in the home will benefit you in a business or political career. For example, I think mothers make great mayors. In the home, we must make decisions based on the whole family, not solely on individual needs. We must be able to balance the budget and not spend money the family doesn't have. More politicians should realize they can't spend taxpayers' money they don't have. And mothers and mayors must have a feeling for the mood of the people and be available to hear complaints and entertain ideas for improving things. There are many similarities between the roles of mother and mayor.

The great Margaret Thatcher took it a step further. "Any woman who understands the problems of running a home will be nearer to understanding the problems of running a country," the Iron Lady once said. And she's right. The pragmatism and intuition so often found in women are valuable to a political leader, or any leader, for that matter.

After I was first elected mayor, women started applying for jobs as garbage collectors in Mississauga. This caused a real kerfuffle back in 1979. For some unexplained reason, a small but vocal group of people didn't want women garbage collectors. They came out to complain to Mississauga council.

Their argument was irrational. This was not women's work, they'd say. Women were not strong enough to do it, others would chime. Stuff like that.

After hearing one too many of these complaints, I asked, "Who do you think carries the garbage to the street in the first place?" That quieted the complainers and we moved on to more important business. As I said earlier, sometimes sexism dies hard. It has to be battled on all fronts, all the time, even if our world today is far more equal than it's ever been.

My last piece of advice is to get involved in your community. Volunteer your time. Start with your town or city—

important things close to home—and take part in municipal affairs, whether it be joining volunteer boards or helping on campaigns. I am a joiner and always have been. I can tell you it works. Over the years, I have learned so many things simply by joining and working with various organizations, from the Girl Guides of Canada to the Anglican Young People's Association to various municipal, provincial and federal government boards and commissions. Once you've got some experience, be bold and put your name forward. Or, as I used to say, "Stop licking envelopes for male candidates and run yourself." There are lots of talented women in politics today, and we need more, but I still prefer quality over quantity.

In municipal politics, women represent 16 per cent of mayors and 26 per cent of councillors, for an average of 24 per cent of municipal politicians across the country, according to the Federation of Canadian Municipalities, an organization that honoured me with a lifetime achievement award in 2008.

The United Nations defines 30 per cent as the bare minimum of women needed for government to truly reflect women's concerns. With that in mind, the Federation of Canadian Municipalities has a goal to reach 30 per cent by 2026. I think it will happen, especially when countries like Sweden (45 per cent), Finland (38 per cent), Spain (36 per cent) and New Zealand (32 per cent) are so far ahead of Canada. We can do better.

I am proud to say that of the twelve members on my final council seven were women, including me. The city and region hire senior staffers based on ability, not gender, with many of the most senior positions belonging to women, including City Manager Janice Baker, City Solicitor Mary Ellen Bench and Police Chief Jennifer Evans.

We no longer live in the days of Agnes Macphail or Charlotte

Whitton. We don't even live in the era of the groundbreaking days of the 1967 Royal Commission on the Status of Women. That commission found oodles and oodles of examples of sexual discrimination, particularly when it came to the gender wage gap. Men were being paid more for doing the same work as women, or women were being pigeonholed into lower-paying career paths. The commission found the average full-time salary for women was $2,522 compared to $4,172 for men. That means women were paid, on average, 60.5 per cent what men were paid in the late 1960s.

Things have improved, but not nearly to equal levels. Numerous studies today show the gender gap in Canada ranges from about 70 to 76 per cent. The World Economic Forum ranked Canada twentieth in the world with a gender gap of 74.2 per cent in 2013. And the gender gap in Canada is wider than in many countries like Belgium, France, Sweden, Germany and even Nicaragua and the Philippines, according to the World Economic Forum.

There are all sorts of theories as to why the gap exists: women pausing their careers for babies; women's careers negatively impacted because they do up to two hours more housework per day than their husbands; an old boys' network weakened but not broken; and women being more willing to trade work flexibility for less salary. No one knows for sure. But what is certain is that direct discrimination is illegal and yet the gender wage gap is real.

Canadian women are now close to half the entire labour force and they are more than half the graduates of universities, but "the wage gap has remained largely unchanged since the 1990s," states a 2010 Library of Parliament report entitled *Wage Gap Between Women and Men*.

After a long business and political career in which I have faced gender discrimination many times, I feel it is my obligation to talk about these issues. When Canadian families today rely on income from both parents to meet basic needs, we should not have wage disparity between genders. And when many single-parent families all too often rely on the women's employment as the main or only source of income to raise children, it becomes an important social issue.

While I do not support quotas and such, I do think the more we talk about these issues, the more answers we can find. The more educated we all get about the reasons, the better the chances the gender gap will dissolve. The more women leading major Canadian corporations or getting into politics of all levels, the better.

The Charlottetown Conference occurred when twenty-three Fathers of Confederation met in 1864 with a bold vision to create what would become Canada in 1867. As part of the 150th anniversary of the Charlottetown Conference, five Atlantic Canada women's groups have organized a conference for Canadian women leaders in 2014 to meet and exchange ideas for the next 150 years. I am honoured to be chosen as one of these twenty-three women leaders for the conference in Prince Edward Island—the so-called "Mothers of Re-Confederation." Canada and Canadian women have achieved so much over the last few decades, but we still have a ways to go before we reach what Agnes Macphail called "absolute equality."

CHAPTER 8

Derailment

It was around midnight when my then-teenage son, Paul, climbed up on the roof of our house on Britannia Road in the northern part of Mississauga after we heard a thunderous bang on November 10, 1979. "Mom," Paul screamed, his eyes focused southward, "I think city hall has blown up."

What he saw was a fire blasting its way a mile into the sky. The yellowish-orange torch lit up the autumn night in all directions and could be seen from Niagara Falls, Oshawa and even Peterborough.

Saturday night at 11:53 p.m. was the beginning of the longest week of my life and no doubt the same for thousands and thousands of people in Mississauga. My head would not hit a pillow for three days and I would sleep a total of fourteen hours during the entire week.

To paraphrase Charles Dickens, that week was the best of times and the worst of times. Over the course of what I call the "Mississauga Miracle," there was fear followed by relief, and relief followed by fear. There were shifting winds that helped and shifting winds that hurt. There were frayed nerves and

rising tempers and acts of great charity and incredible community. There were times of exhilaration and times of near
exhaustion. This was the world's largest peacetime evacuation
(to that point in history) and it went off without looting or
other acts of selfishness. And, most importantly, there were
countless examples of bravery and not one single loss of life.

Immediately after hearing Paul's screams from the rooftop,
I phoned police. City Hall had not blown up, I was told, but a
train had derailed and emergency crews from police and fire
departments were already on the scene with calls out for more
help. Shortly after, I received a call from Fire Chief Gordon
Bentley telling me this was extremely serious. I knew Gord
from Streetsville, where he had been our volunteer deputy fire
chief, and he was not a man to exaggerate.

First responders, who included a deputy fire chief in his
tuxedo from a wedding, certainly knew this was no ordinary
event: unidentified flammable liquids and vapours had caused
the massive explosion. The explosive catalysts would soon be
identified, but these valiant first responders were in the dark as
to what was in the tankers on the ground. Yet, none wavered;
all went straight into harm's way.

"I had my back to the wreck when she blew. My hair was
singed. I felt I was dead," says Bob Barridge, the first police
officer on the scene, as quoted on the Heritage Mississauga
website.

"We took a few seconds to assess the situation," says Dave
Ewing, one of the first three firefighters to reach the derailment. "It was just a wall of fire, as high as you could see. [The
first explosion] blew me down, simply threw me in a way I've
never felt before. As I lay there, the flames rolled out like a
mushroom and up over me. . . . It took a few seconds to get

myself together and I was up and doing the hundred-yard dash, and no one has ever gone quicker."

After the initial explosion, there was another, then another a few minutes later, then another. "The sky looked like the 'Tea Party' from Alice in Wonderland," says eyewitness Sue Zoerb on the Heritage Mississauga website. "The sky was rosy pink and in constant motion across the horizon."

Other witnesses thought initially it was a jumbo jet crash, or even a nuclear attack. "It was horrific," said John McGlashen, who lived three blocks away. "Our house shook. The windows rattled. The sky was bright orange, and when I saw the fireball, we were already running to the car, only with the clothes we had on, and on our way out of the city. We didn't even know where we were going."

Canadian Pacific Railway train 54 started on its infamous journey early in the afternoon of Saturday, November 10, 1979, from Windsor, Ontario, with a scheduled destination of Agincourt in the northeast part of Metropolitan Toronto. It was supposed to be a routine run. It stopped in Chatham, where it picked up cars from another train from Sarnia, home of Dow Chemical Co. After getting these cars all hooked up, the train left Chatham around 6 p.m. and would stop in London for a crew change. It was here that twenty-seven-year-old brakeman Larry Krupa boarded the train, a pivotal player in events about to unfold.

West of Mississauga, near Milton, is where trouble began, as investigators would later determine. A lack of lubrication in the journal box around an axle led to tremendous heat buildup. In the vernacular of the railway, the overheated journal box became a "hot box."

By the time the train moved into Mississauga at speeds

of up to fifty miles per hour (80 km/h), witnesses could see sparks and smoke coming from the middle section of the train. Immediately after passing a street-level crossing at Burnhamthorpe Road in the middle of Mississauga, the thirty-third car—the one with the hot box—lost one of its four axles and red-hot wheels. Mississauga resident Lynne Riddel saw the wheels crash into her backyard. The train didn't immediately derail and kept going for nearly two miles (3 km).

By now the train was approaching Mavis Road, just south of Burnhamthorpe. In 1979, this was a relatively isolated area between two neighbourhoods. If the derailment had happened just a half-mile farther down the track—either east or west—we could have seen thousands of people wiped out. It's a miracle it happened there.

In no time, twenty-four cars careened off the tracks, many smashing into each other in a twisted metal heap as the train ground to a halt. The first explosion occurred shortly after cars hit the ground. According to Heritage Mississauga historians, brakeman Larry Krupa yelled to the engineer, his father-in-law, Keith Pruss: "Oh, my God, we've got a tanker on fire."

Krupa jumped off the train and ran towards the flaming wreckage. There were twenty-seven cars, many with explosive and flammable contents, still upright on the track and between the three locomotives and the fire. (There were about fifty cars behind the wreck but nothing could be done about moving them immediately.)

Near the fire and in intense heat, Krupa uncoupled two tankers so that his father-in-law could drive those twenty-seven front cars still on the track eastward to safety and away from the searing heat and flames. For his bravery, Krupa was inducted into the North American Railway Hall of Fame. Who knows what might have happened if any or all of those cars at the front of the train had caught fire? (Krupa was also recommended for the Order of Canada for his bravery and, as a recipient myself, I would be delighted to see him receive it someday.)

Within minutes of the first explosion, emergency personnel arrived. A patrolling police officer was there in one minute and firefighters within three minutes. (In only a few hours there would be five hundred emergency workers on site.) Those firefighters on scene first were battling the blazes as best they could; police set up roadblocks and a command post. During that first hectic hour, there were a series of explosions, some tossing debris four hundred metres or farther, and witnesses reported seeing a green haze drifting in the air.

At first, emergency responders did not know exactly what they were dealing with; how could they have known there was a toxic stew of chemicals lying in the wreckage of tankers and that many, like propane, were highly explosive? We were so fortunate no one was killed during this early chaos.

"It was an incredible sight," said Deputy Fire Chief Art Warner, one of the first senior officers on site and the one who arrived in a tuxedo. The explosion "was like a thousand feet high by a thousand feet wide. . . . I will say this about the men, I am proud of them, there was no backing down off this fire, not once. Not one man shirked. When you asked someone to do it, he did it . . . regardless of the danger."

I cannot say enough about the heroism of these first responders, and all the emergency workers through those first critical hours.

An hour after the first explosion, emergency crews still didn't know exactly what they were dealing with, as police and fire could not get a full manifest of what the train was transporting. The manifest in the caboose was not legible enough to precisely ascertain what was in the tankers on the ground. (Readily accessible and legible manifests for trains and trucks carrying dangerous commodities would be one of the key safety regulations brought to bear after this accident.)

At home at my kitchen table, I was working the phones, alerting staff, looking for municipal buildings and schools we could use to house people should evacuations be necessary. As mayor, this was my city and these were my people living in homes near the disaster area. As we learned during Hurricane Hazel twenty-five years earlier, public safety and clear communication must be priorities during any emergency.

At 1:10 a.m., there was the first meeting at the police command post with Police Chief Douglas Burrows, Deputy Police Chief Bill Teggert, Deputy Fire Chief Art Warner, Chief Fire Inspector Cyril Hare, various CPR officials, two people from the Ministry of the Environment and several chemical experts. Various emergency plans were implemented, including the Peel Region Peacetime Emergency Plan, the Emergency Fire Services Plan and the Spill Control Contingency Plan.

At 1:30 a.m., CPR officials finally tracked down a legible manifest, and immediately after reading it Chief Burrows radioed police headquarters and instructed a senior officer to give me my first detailed briefing and alert me as to what was on the manifest. It was frightening news.

Of the twenty-four derailed cars, two were boxcars filled with insulation but all the others were tank cars filled with dangerous commodities: eleven were propane, four caustic soda, three styrene, three toluene (including car number 33 with the hot box that caused the accident) and one tank was filled with nearly ninety tonnes of chlorine.

Chlorine is used in the production of textiles, disinfectants, paper and petroleum products, medicines, insecticides, solvents, plastics and many other products. But when inhaled in concentrated doses, chlorine gas destroys the respiratory organs and leads to a slow death by asphyxiation. It was one of the most horrific killing weapons of World War I. Chlorine gas is heavier than air, so when it is released it lurks close to the ground as it moves and disperses.

We had to assume, for safety's sake, that the chlorine was leaking, because people had seen a floating green haze. Our assumption was proven correct when firefighters battling the blazes got close enough to the chlorine tanker to see a metre-wide hole in the tanker. But this confirmation did not come for several hours. (The puncture was caused by another tanker full of propane ramming into it during the collision as cars derailed.) Evacuations began hours before this confirmation.

The first evacuation order from Chief Burrows—one of thirteen over the next twenty hours—affected 3,500 people living less than a half-mile from the derailment, and it was issued at 1:47 a.m., followed soon after by another before 2 a.m. for a further eight thousand people to leave. Police drove around with loudspeakers and they banged on doors urging people to leave their homes immediately. Residents fled with nothing but the clothes on their backs.

I was still at home working the phones, trying to find out where evacuees could be housed. There needed to be systems in place to help family members locate loved ones if they got separated. We needed to find ways to get medical professionals to Mississauga as soon as possible. We needed to round up hundreds of volunteers to help out at temporary shelters.

I spoke with the Red Cross, the Salvation Army and many

other organizations dedicated to helping in an emergency. Their help and that of a legion of volunteers is impossible to exaggerate. In the first twenty hours after the evacuations began, they served 125,000 meals! Much of that food was donated by restaurants, grocery stores and private citizens.

Throughout that night, emergency procedures and plans continued as unfolding events dictated. For example, 139 ambulances arrived from all over Ontario, and buses from Toronto, Oakville, Brampton and elsewhere were shuttling evacuees to makeshift shelters, including the Square One shopping centre. Store owners opened their businesses to provide food, clothing, baby formula, prescription drugs, anything to help in the emergency. (Unfortunately, as the evacuation zone widened due to wind changes, Square One soon had to be evacuated, too.)

By 5 a.m. Sunday—even before firefighters saw the hole in the chlorine tanker—we determined we had no choice but to wake and alert Solicitor General Roy McMurtry (who was also attorney general). He was chairman of the emergency planning committee of the Ontario cabinet and the province's most senior person in a public emergency.

As mayor, I wanted to be as visible as possible. I can't recall exactly what time I jumped in my car and drove south from Streetsville, but it was dark outside. One of my first stops was Square One. It was important to be among the people, reassuring them everything that could be done was being done and to remain calm.

By 7:30 a.m., less than eight hours after the derailment, we had our first face-to-face meeting of the decision-making committee called the Emergency Operations Control Group (EOCG) at the command post near the derailment. The initial meeting was with Police Chief Burrows, Fire Chief Bentley,

Peel Region Chairman Frank Bean and me. Roy McMurtry arrived on site shortly after and was a key player in all other meetings of "the think tank," as the media began calling the EOCG. Besides the five of us, we'd call on senior officers from the Ontario Provincial Police, chemical engineers and other experts to offer valuable advice in making critical decisions during the emergency.

For six hours, we had been issuing one evacuation order after another and at 8:30 in the morning came a most important evacuation order: we had to empty the Mississauga Hospital (now called Trillium Hospital), southeast of the crash site. Two nearby nursing homes were also to be evacuated. It is one thing ordering people from their homes and it is quite another thing to move people from their hospital beds. I went down to the hospital and will never forget seeing patients, many with intravenous tubes, being moved out. It was incredibly calm given the circumstances, but I said a few prayers, nonetheless.

The hospital evacuation began at 10:06 a.m. and ended at 1:15 p.m. with patients in the intensive care units given priority. It was simply incredible. In all, 450 hospital patients and 539 nursing home residents were evacuated. Ambulances from all over Ontario were there to help. Everything came off without a hitch. Then at 3:40 p.m., 280 patients at the Queensway Hospital, just down the road in Toronto, were evacuated due to high readings of chlorine in the air. A hospital to the west in the town of Oakville was also evacuated, at 7 p.m.

After leaving the Mississauga Hospital, I visited shelters in schools and community centres. I talked to people lining up for shuttle rides out of evacuation zones. And I met with the media often to brief them on anything new. Dashing to one media briefing, without thinking it through, I tried to hop over a small ditch and ended up twisting my ankle. There were many pictures of burly police officers and firefighters carrying me into these press briefings. A little levity is good for cutting the tension.

Not only did we constantly feed the media with information but we had a team of people monitoring all media reports to ensure only correct information was getting out to the public. When a mistake was identified, the offending media were alerted and asked to clarify or correct the information. Luckily, this did not happen often, but it did occur.

For example, the national broadcaster, the CBC, reported that Etobicoke, a large borough of Metro Toronto to the east of Mississauga, was about to be evacuated, when in reality only a few neighbourhoods nearest Mississauga were to be evacuated. Other media reported erroneously that pockets of chlorine were found in the Credit River. Reports like these could spread panic needlessly so the mistakes were quickly rectified over the air.

That first night and the morning of November 11, as winds shifted, areas of evacuation were widened. Firefighters continued to spray water on the fires and the experts determined the best strategy would be to cool the cars and not extinguish the flames because this would allow for a controlled burn of escaping gases and cut down on the possibility of more explosions.

In addition to police and firefighters arriving from other jurisdictions came experts in the handling of dangerous goods, including a team from Dow Chemical in Sarnia, owners of the chlorine leaking from the tanker. My background in building petrochemical plants at Canadian Kellogg helped during these briefings from experts on the various dangers of these chemicals and the different scenarios that could play out.

By end of day Sunday, we had evacuated 218,000 people

who were then staying either with family and friends, at temporary shelters or in hotels outside the evacuation zones. At the time of the derailment, our population was 284,000 and we were the ninth-largest city in Canada. An incredible 77 per cent of Mississauga residents were evacuated in less than twenty-four hours.

Basically, the only people in Mississauga still in their homes were those living in the north end near Streetsville and Malton. I was so proud of thousands of residents in these areas who opened their homes to strangers. So many people throughout the city, and in the nearby western neighbourhoods of Metropolitan Toronto, had this great attitude of "What can I do to help?"

By now, the central and southern parts of Mississauga were a ghost town. The only thing missing was tumbleweeds. We sealed off the city by closing down the Queen Elizabeth Way, the major highway that runs through the southern part of Mississauga, and all east-west roads coming into and out of the city. There was only one way to get through Mississauga and that was along Highway 401 at the north end, and ramps were blocked so motorists could not enter Mississauga.

As the calendar flipped to Monday, at 12:30 a.m. I uttered to the media a line that would become synonymous with the crisis: "Mississauga is closed until further notice."

People needed clear and concise information. They didn't need "best-case scenarios," as in if everything works out perfectly you'll be home tomorrow. No, sir. I was not about to talk that way. That's not leadership. That's sugar-coating. Instead I said things like "If you think you'll be out of your home for two days, then plan on being out four days." People want the truth, not namby-pamby possibilities and what-ifs.

Another problem arose that, on the surface, may sound frivolous, but I can assure you it was not. Evacuees were becoming agitated about the pets left behind in their homes. People wanted to go get them but we couldn't allow that. The evacuated zones were sealed off for a reason. Besides, you couldn't have dogs and cats in the emergency shelters with families, so many of them with babies and very young children. But, on the other hand, we couldn't take needed emergency personnel in the restricted zones off their posts to go feed dogs and cats.

In the end, it got sorted out with teams of volunteers, under the guidance of police, going back into homes to provide food and water for pets. We had evacuees leave their house keys at city hall with their addresses and instructions for their pets.

By this point, the derailment/evacuation was no longer a local or national story, but a major international story. Hundreds of newspeople from all over the world were flying in, some from as far as South Africa and Europe. Acclaimed CBS news anchor Walter Cronkite was having difficulty *pronouncing* Mississauga and American reporters on the ground were dumbfounded that there was no looting to report, as there surely would have been in many American cities. That week, there were only two news stories on the world stage: Mississauga and the fifty-two U.S. hostages being held by extremists at the overrun American Embassy in Iran.

By mid-morning on Monday, work began on putting a metal patch on the chlorine tanker. I still had not slept a wink. My sixteen-year-old son, Paul, was so upset about me being away for so long that he came down to the site to see me, driving Sam's Chrysler New Yorker.

We remained in a state of emergency as propane fires continued, but things were starting to improve. We still didn't know how much chlorine remained in the tanker but air-quality samples were showing low levels of chlorine gas and it was restricted to low-lying areas near the crash site, not widely dispersed.

But as the ebb and flow of the crisis moved between relief and fear, we got some bad news. The metal patch for the tanker, which offered so much hope only hours earlier, was proving to be difficult because workers were hampered by another tanker blocking full access to the pierced chlorine tanker. They simply couldn't get a perfect seal on the patch all through Monday.

It wasn't until about 2:30 a.m. Tuesday that we could all breathe a huge sigh of relief when propane fires ceased and workers could concentrate solely on patching the chlorine tanker. The chances of more explosions were much, much lower now. It was at this time that I finally returned home for a few hours of sleep, my first in days. Our Streetsville home was outside the evacuation zone.

It is quite astonishing how in the time of crisis your adrenaline kicks in and gives you the energy to do things you simply would have thought impossible. It was now early Tuesday morning and I had been without sleep for more than ninety hours.

Heading home that Tuesday morning, November 13, I realized something: this was the first anniversary of my election as mayor of the City of Mississauga. But there was nothing to celebrate until after this crisis was over and all of my people were safely back in their homes.

Around dinnertime Tuesday, those evacuated from houses and apartments farthest from the derailment scene were allowed to return home. But the patch on the chlorine tanker still could not be sealed absolutely and chlorine was leaking, albeit in smaller quantities. For the public's safety, caution was still the watchword.

It was around this time that I started to think of the after-math and what we could do to make sure another one of these near-catastrophes didn't happen in this or any other urban area. I had remembered the manager of the Mississauga public utilities commission, Arthur Kennedy, warning about lax standards when it came to the transportation of dangerous commodities and how the senior governments should tighten regulations for the sake of the public. City staff found me some Mississauga and regional council resolutions criticizing the federal government for not doing more to protect citizens in these matters. While I had the media's attention, I wanted to point these things out to give Ottawa the chance to get off its collective duff and get to work to tighten regulations to help make sure things like this didn't happen in the future.

By Thursday, it was discovered there were seven to ten tonnes of chlorine remaining in the tanker that once held ninety tonnes. As luck would have it, much of the chlorine had been sucked up in the giant flames during the initial fireball explosions and the wind had carried it southward and harm-lessly dispersed it over Lake Ontario. Still, we could not allow everyone back in their nearby homes until the cleanup was complete and the chlorine threat totally eliminated.

That occurred Friday and all residents were allowed back in their homes by 7:45 Friday night. Mississauga was once again open for business. Only the derailment site remained out of bounds. By Monday, the chlorine tanker was completely emp-tied and site cleanup began.

Over the course of thirty-six years as mayor, I have had a number of successes, but none more significant than that week. It was a challenge second to none and it was my first year in office. It was an extraordinary team effort between police, fire, other emergency workers, medical professionals, scientists, chemical experts and political leaders like Solicitor General Roy McMurtry and Peel Region Chairman Frank Bean.

Many of the tactics and strategies we employed to get us through that crisis have been adopted by other municipalities and modelled into their own emergency plans. At the top of the list is the importance of clear communications, as I stated earlier. History has shown us, over and over, the importance of communicating effectively. To quote Napoleon: "The key to victory lies in the communications."

In the months after the derailment, we had visitors from agencies across the United States and Europe all come to Mississauga to collect first-hand information on how the emergency response was carried out so efficiently. Here are some of things we learned and passed along: Keep the size of the group making decisions manageable; leaders must get out there with the people, be seen to be doing things, and symbolic gestures mean something; keep calm; communicate abundantly and tell the truth, even if it's bad news; let the experts do their jobs; and give any and all people the opportunity to help, even in the smallest ways like serving juice at a shelter. We were all in this together and everyone felt they had a role.

Thanks to quick-thinking individuals, an unwavering spirit of co-operation and fearless emergency workers, we look back at the "Mississauga Miracle"—not the "Mississauga Disaster." And for that, everyone in Mississauga, and those in other parts of Canada who helped, should all be proud.

By working with industry and government authorities at all levels afterwards, we've also achieved many public safety initiatives that are commonplace today. I sat on the federal Transportation Goods Committee, representing the Federation of Canadian Municipalities. Things like tighter controls on the shipment of dangerous goods by land, air and sea, reduced speeds for trains in urban areas, better identification of dangerous goods that are being transported, "hot box" detectors that warn of problems before an emergency occurs and many other safety regulations. As we saw, tragically, in 2013 at Lac Mégantic, Quebec, we must continue to be vigilant and keep public safety the number one priority at all times.

Another important thing to come out of that week was that laws were changed to protect municipal officials from lawsuits following an emergency. Some may think this self-serving, but I can assure you it's not. The public does not want leaders to be thinking about whether their decisions during an emergency could one day land them in court. Such a legal chill is not in the public's interest by any stretch of the imagination. In times like this, the public needs their leaders to be thinking of one thing and one thing only: what is the best thing to do to ensure the public's safety.

Believe it or not, Canadian Pacific Railway sued me, the police chief and the fire chief because CP claimed some of their costs were our fault, like hotel accommodations and living expenses for people they felt didn't need to be evacuated for so long. Today, municipal officials who are acting in good faith on the behalf of the public in an emergency have stronger legislative protections.

Some have said that week made my political career, because I had initially been considered a "one-term mayor." There were plenty of very powerful people who were against me still, erroneously thinking I was going to hold back development. A psychic was even quoted in a newspaper predicting I would be defeated in the next election. So much for the tarot cards. One year after

Here I am, Hazel Journeaux, growing up on the eastern shores of the Gaspé Peninsula. I was born February 14, 1921, so this picture was taken in the mid-1920s.

That's me on the left (and a girl named Thursa Swinerton visiting from Toronto) cuddling up to Byng, perhaps the smartest dog I ever owned. Byng was named for Governor-General Lord Byng, who knocked Liberal prime minister Mackenzie King down a peg briefly during the constitutional crisis of 1926.

This family photo was taken in the summer of 1928 on the porch of our Port Daniel farmhouse. There's Dad with one hand in his pocket and the other hand holding his familiar pipe. Mom has her arms on my shoulders. My brother Lockhart is beside Dad, my sister Linda is beside Mom, and my other sister, Gwen, is holding something; I think it's a little dog. The other member of the family, Lorne, is not in this picture. The other people are tourists from the United States who my mom and dad took in to earn a few extra dollars.

On the beach in Port Daniel around the beginning of the Great Depression. Summers were spectacular in the Gaspé, and I remember playing with friends and telling tall tales about pirates and buried treasures.

Mother and me on one of my return trips to Gaspé after leaving for good in 1937 to get my high school education.

With big sister Linda in Montreal just before World War II. Linda was a teacher who tutored me and, along with our sister Gwen, helped me with tuition and room and board during my school years in Montreal and Quebec City.

My wedding day was September 29, 1951, the feast day of Saint Michael and All Angels. The ceremony was at the Toronto church of the same name. It was a cool day but my heart was warmed with Samuel Robert McCallion as my husband.

Here I am as a young mother in the early 1950s showing my first son, Peter, some chicks on a farm in Streetsville, northwest of Toronto. The area is all urban now and part of the City of Mississauga.

At my desk at Canadian Kellogg, where I was office manager.

On our five-acre property near Streetsville, which was big enough to have horses, chickens and all sorts of other animals. Sam and Peter are holding Centennial, and I am standing with Linda and Paul and Linda's prized pony Rinty, whom she loved so much.

In 1964, I joined the Streetsville Chamber of Commerce (of which Sam had been a founder), figuring my business experience from Kellogg could be an asset. I was named president of the organization in 1966.

Ever industrious and hard-working, Sam was a commercial photographer doing portraits like our family's self-portrait. He also operated a laundry and acted as the local Streetsville representative for a moving company called M. Rawlinson Ltd. of Toronto before concentrating on his printing business and publishing a local newspaper.

Mississauga's future city centre—the Square One shopping mall being the focal point—in late 1973, only weeks before Mississauga became a city on January 1, 1974.

My friend Ron Duquette took both pictures of the city centre from a helicopter. By 2006, you can see the buildings and homes replacing the farms. Look closely on the left and you'll see the Civic Centre, the Living Arts Centre and the Central Library.

Building Mississauga into Canada's sixth-largest city has been a team effort. My background at Canadian Kellogg, where we built petrochemical and other industrial plants, gave me an understanding of blueprints and planning documents.

With Mississauga's first mayor, Martin Dobkin (hands behind his back), cutting a ribbon to open another new business in Mississauga.

One of the few photos of my entire family at an official event. From left to right: Linda, Sam, me, Paul, Peter and our only grandchild, Erika.

With Erika, not long after her grandfather passed away.

With Paul, Linda and Peter at the opening of the Alzheimer Society's daycare centre in Peel, named for Sam shortly after his death. Friends donated more than $45,000 to this centre, where loved ones can go in safety while allowing caregivers needed breaks.

Sam and I heading out on one of our last vacations. Sam was a lot of things: devoted husband, loving father, businessman, neighbour and friend. One of the things he was most proud of was his community spirit, especially when it came to his beloved Streetsville.

Toronto Star

One year the *Toronto Star* did a Valentine's Day story about love in which I talked about my relationship with Sam. He was my best friend and the best political advisor I could ever have had.

I began fishing as a little girl on the Gaspé with a piece of wood, string and hook. Since then, I've landed many whoppers, including two coho salmon, thirty-two pounds and twenty-eight pounds, that hung on my office wall for years.

I began playing hockey when I was five years old and played in a women's professional league in Montreal in the early 1940s for five dollars a game. I laced up the skates at times during my years as mayor and still do periodically.

This shot is from one of my dozen trips to China. I love China and its people, not to mention the pandas! It's a country that respects its elders, their experience and their wisdom. I wish seniors in Western society were treated more like that.

the Mississauga Miracle, I was acclaimed in the 1980 election, and I was re-elected in every election thereafter until my retirement in 2014, usually with 90 per cent of the vote or more.

I really don't think one week can make or break a career. But what that week did show, under intense media scrutiny, was that I always work for the people and the City of Mississauga. My election campaign runs every day. I show up for work every day, doing my best for the people of Mississauga, always trying to deliver value for their tax dollars and putting people first.

In the months and years afterwards, there was lots of work involved in helping prevent similar dangers to the public, from the federal government's Mississauga Railway Accident Inquiry to committee work with the Federation of Canadian Municipalities for rail safety. As I said, Lac Mégantic in 2013 proved that rail safety continues to be a critical issue today.

Beyond the derailment and Mississauga's recovery, there were still vital issues facing us in the early 1980s as we continued to build our city. The people appreciated the job I was doing, but I had still not won over the powerful developers and their allies.

The reasons were pretty simple. First, they still had not bought into our lot-levies strategy to make development pay its way. This would change, but it remained a sticking point during this period. Second, I was determined to increase industrial and commercial development. We wanted to build a city that was economically viable on its own, and not simply a bedroom community for Toronto. Developers saw home-building as the easiest and quickest way to make money. That was fine from their point of view, but not from the city's point of view.

At first blush, some people thought it odd that I was claiming to put the people first when I insisted on industrial and commercial development. But I most definitely was putting the people first. Without attracting new business like our prosperous life sciences and technology clusters and their high-paying jobs, would I have been creating a real city or merely a giant bunkhouse next to Toronto?

Today, Mississauga has the second-most jobs in the Greater Toronto Area and we have more people coming to our city to work than leaving. But not everyone shared this vision of Mississauga. Not by a long shot.

Don't get me wrong: I was not against home-building by any stretch of the imagination. In fact, I took some bruises for fighting so hard to open up large sections of undeveloped land for thousands of new homes to be built upon. I was definitely pro-development and pro–home-building. I simply wanted a better balance of development. For example, should this or that area be zoned industrial only? Or could it be zoned residential-commercial? And we're talking about huge tracts of land—thousands of acres—not simply a city block here or there.

And it was on this issue that I landed in a bit of hot water with regard to the property Sam and I had bought in 1951 on Britannia Road near Streetsville. Our five acres (2 ha) was located inside the so-called "hole in the doughnut," a huge section near Streetsville that remained designated agricultural land by the Province of Ontario in the early 1980s, and that was surrounded by the growing city. One has to realize that municipalities cannot move to planning and development—whether residential, commercial or industrial—until the province releases farmland from its agricultural inventory.

Throughout the 1970s, a vocal—and well-meaning—group

of citizens wanted to preserve this "hole in the doughnut" agricultural land and stop development. If people from APPEAL (Association of Peel People Evaluating Agricultural Land) showed up at Mississauga council ten times they were there one hundred times. They were diligent.

I liked them, but I disagreed wholeheartedly with their stance. It just made no sense, economic or otherwise, to have this huge tract of agricultural land inside a growing, vibrant, new urban centre. It was good agricultural land, make no mistake, but it didn't add up to keep it as farmland. And it was getting frustrating that the provincial government hemmed and hawed without taking a stand.

I wanted the issue resolved once and for all, so I took this group down to the legislature at Queen's Park to meet the minister of agriculture in 1980. I said to him point blank, in front of everyone: "Is this land in Mississauga known as the 'hole in the doughnut' to remain part of the agriculture inventory for Ontario?"

"No," he said. "That land is going to be urban."

That was the end of that, or so I thought. The good folks from APPEAL took the news graciously and their pressure on council to preserve the land ceased. But other pressure intensified, despite our being able to move on to planning and developing the land. Council decided to release vast amounts of land for development all at once. The land around our property would be designated mostly residential but commercial, too, for stores and restaurants, especially in what is called the Heartland, along Britannia Road today.

But there was no way council, or I, would acquiesce to the developers. After the province released the land's agricultural tag, we'd zone it and release it all for development, but for a price. We were going to make development pay its way in growth with lot levies to cover the cost of infrastructure, libraries, community centres and more. It was only fair new residents and new businesses pay, not existing Mississauga taxpayers. And we wanted all the costs recouped, not just some.

Developers thought we were charging them too much and they didn't like it one bit. Remember, making new development pay was still considered radical; this was about a decade before provincial governments would enact laws based on our formulas to make growth pay. The developers particularly didn't like paying the cost of so-called "soft services" like libraries, hockey arenas, baseball diamonds, soccer fields and community centres. But without these amenities, what sort of a city would we be building for the people, especially new Mississaugans moving into their single-family dream homes?

Regardless, I had poked the bear, the *ancien régime* that was so vehemently opposed to Martin Dobkin not that long before. What came next was a concerted effort to remove me from office. I can't say with certainty how this plan to challenge me came about, or who was involved except Jack Graham and Ron Searle, who emerged as the faces of this group. I believe some were motivated to do this for political revenge; others because they didn't like the "growth must pay its way" lot levies I was pushing forward. Others from the old Town of Mississauga simply viewed me as an interloper from Streetsville.

My understanding is that they believed I had violated the Municipal Conflict of Interest Act because our McCallion five acres was in the "hole in the doughnut" and I had fought to get the area developed. We are talking about the development of 3,800 acres (1,540 ha) and Sam and I owned only

0.13 per cent of this land. We eventually sold our property for $800,000, a nice sum, no doubt. But we have friends who didn't sell and their land is now worth around ten times as much, or $7.5 million for a lot equivalent to what we owned. I just don't understand the conspiracy theorists who think I am out to feather my own nest. I now live in a lovely, but modest, Mississauga home on a cul-de-sac, hardly a palatial residence.

Events unfolded this way: At a private council meeting discussing this development in 1981, I declared my conflict of interest when council first talked about releasing all this land for development and how quickly it would be released. But the next day, during the public debate, I was distracted and didn't declare my conflict until partway through the discussion.

Using Jack Graham as the point man, the group called for an inquiry and took me to court, accusing me of being in violation of the Municipal Conflict of Interest Act. After pre-hearing testimony in December 1981, and a hearing a few months later, Judge Ernest West ruled in my favour in July 1982. The judge noted I had declared a conflict in the first meeting and ruled it a "bona fide error in judgment" that I had not done the same right at the beginning of the public meeting. He said I did not need to step down as mayor.

During this time, many councillors attended the proceedings in full force to support me. Margaret Marland, who represented Ward 2, was always at the head of the pack when it came to supporting me.

It should be noted that all the folks who I was told lined up against me, except perhaps Ron Searle, all became good friends and strong supporters through the years. Still, back in 1982 they were not satisfied with the judge's ruling, and later that fall the *ancien régime* ran Ron against me in the mayoral election. The early '80s were not particularly easy days for me as mayor of this burgeoning new city. But I just had to trust the people. And when they spoke in that election, they spoke loudly, re-electing me with 71 per cent of the vote to 24 per cent for Searle.

With that sort of mandate I knew we could soon move past petty politics and get developers on board to help build this city for the people, with growth paying its way. And once we looked after the basic amenities for each community in Mississauga— like swimming pools, libraries, arenas, community centres and playing fields—we could move on to major projects like a central library, a new city hall, a performing arts centre, a vibrant and accessible waterfront and a whole lot more.

CHAPTER 9

Age Is Just a Number

In November 1985, I was elected to my fourth consecutive term as mayor of Mississauga and I was about to turn sixty-five. The media, being the media, began to ask questions about retirement and whether this would be my final election campaign. There was still so much to be done to build the city, but reporters decided to slot me into old age and possible retirement. Thankfully, the voters weren't so one-dimensional. My age meant little to them. What mattered was the job I was doing.

My response to reporters was simple: so long as my health remained good and I could keep up the hectic pace to serve the citizens of Mississauga, I would have no plans for retirement. This response has stayed the same for nearly thirty years, and the record shows that some of the most productive years of my life occurred after I turned sixty-five. We built a civic centre, a fabulous central library, a centre for performing arts, a state-of-the-art hockey and sports facility and many other civic amenities.

Still, reporters kept asking at every election whether the next would be my last. Age discrimination irks me like few other things. It's as if people think that as soon as you become a senior citizen you must be put out to pasture; that magically you simply can no longer do things, or at least do things as well as you used to be able to do them. It's all so ridiculous.

Your health and your passion and determination should dictate how long you can work, not some age number. There are lots of older people who work harder and smarter than plenty of young people. My friend Don Cherry just turned eighty and he's more popular than he's ever been. He and I are not the only folks who continue working productively well past the so-called expiration date of age sixty-five, but there are countless more forced out before they're ready.

Now, some people tire of work and want to travel, read books, garden and other activities. And that's fine. If they choose to do that, good for them. What I'm talking about is age discrimination that forces seniors to the sidelines when they want to continue working and contributing. I'm ready to slow down now, but I wasn't ready ten years ago at eighty-three. I was fortunate to be in a profession where mandatory retirement comes only from the polling booth, not some bureaucratic edict. Thankfully, the voters of Mississauga viewed me by the job I was doing, not based on my birth certificate.

Which brings me to a question I'm often asked: What's the secret to a long and healthy life?

I've been healthy all my days and I have everything I was born with—tonsils, adenoids, appendix, you name it. (Well, almost everything. I lost two front teeth playing hockey.) I never had any of the childhood diseases like chicken pox, measles or mumps. I've been very healthy and very lucky. The only time

I've been overnight in hospital was when my children were born and when, as I mentioned earlier, I was struck by a pickup truck while crossing the street when I was eighty-two.

Of course, genes and luck play an important role in a long life. I come from a long line of long-lifers. Both my grandfathers lived into their eighties and one almost made it to ninety, which is extremely long for men, particularly a century ago. I had one sister live to ninety-three and another to eighty-two, and both my brothers were very healthy when they died prematurely in separate car accidents.

I was blessed with good genes, but there are other things that I believe have helped me reach the age of ninety-three and counting. For as long as I can remember, I've been interested in health and medical news. I am a voracious reader on the topics and have clippings of articles from nutrition magazines and far-off newspapers, like the *Times of India*. I still have a yellowed ten-year-old clipping entitled "Eating Right at Every Age" from the *Times of India*. If it's useful health information, I keep it.

Since I am "old school" and don't use a computer, my reading material comes in paper form, but I would advocate online reading on health issues. Piles of information are available from credible sources, such as the websites of famous health institutions like the Mayo Clinic, Cleveland Clinic and Health Canada and its affiliated resources.

One specific area that has long intrigued me is blood circulation and its impact on general health. I've never had circulatory problems but I do know poor circulation is often linked to heart disease and strokes. But what people often overlook about blood circulation is how it can prevent many diseases and help your body resist harmful germs.

I am no doctor, but I know that blood carries and circulates oxygen and nutrients all through the body, so it makes perfect sense that good circulation is beneficial to the body's immune system. There are lots of ways to improve circulation and the good news is that most of them are simple everyday things that lead to better overall health like daily exercise, healthy eating and not smoking.

I'm often asked about my exercise routine. It's pretty simple: I stay active and I am constantly on the move. For example, when the family is over, I want to cook and clean up the dishes. When I am visiting, I enjoy getting up and clearing the table after a meal. I simply like to move around, which is good exercise, in my opinion. I live alone and do my own housework and make my bed and clean up the breakfast dishes every morning. I just can't stand coming home at night to a sink full of dishes or an unmade bed.

My son Paul teases me that I am like a bumblebee and that if I'm not moving, I'm sleeping. He says there is only one "inactivity" that doesn't put me to sleep: fishing. I absolutely love to fish. I can sit still for hours on end with a fishing rod in my hand just thinking and waiting for a bite. I don't even really talk much when I'm fishing and I never nod off. But put me in front of the television set in the evening, I will be asleep within minutes.

I began fishing as a little girl on the Gaspé with a piece of wood, string and hook. I even caught the odd fish with that primitive contraption. Since then, I've landed many whoppers over the years, including a thirty-two-pound and a twenty-eight-pound coho salmon in Lake Ontario that hung on my office wall for years, along with a ten-pound brown trout.

In 2012, at age ninety-one, I went on a fishing trip in the Pacific Ocean off Costa Rica with my friend Walter Oster and some other gentlemen, and I actually caught a fish that was bigger than me! It was a sailfish and it took more than an hour to land. Even though all the fish caught on the trip had to be released, my photographer friend Dick Loek did snap a picture of me and the giant fish, and I show it to people if they think I'm telling a fish story.

My friend Jim Murray loves to talk about my energy and stamina. I don't know where my energy comes from. But there's one story Jim tells often about a Caribbean cruise we were on together in 2004, when I was eighty-three years old. I'll let him pick up the story: "She loves to dance and we were in the ship's disco until 2 a.m. My wife and I walked Hazel to her room and said goodnight. The next morning we were feeling pretty proud of ourselves that we were up and having breakfast before 9 a.m. We walked into the dining room; there was Hazel and she tells us she'd already walked two miles on the ship's jogging track and swam twenty-five lengths in the pool. Unbelievable, simply unbelievable!"

I wasn't trying to prove a point or anything that morning. That's just the way I am.

I get a lot of exercise on the job because I go to between ten and fifteen public events each week. A lot of walking—sometimes even dancing—is part of these official functions; I don't just drive up and plant myself in a chair. I want to tour facilities, talk to people, see the things they're proud to show me. Walking is a big part of my life and always has been. When I was a little girl, school was two and a half miles (4 km) away and we walked both ways every day, unless there was just too much snow. I am a huge proponent of walking and its positive health benefits. Maybe that's why I've never met a staircase I didn't like. One of my most memorable walks was along the

Great Wall of China on one of my dozen visits to that country.

And I always walk in parades, never sit in the back of a car. People want to see the mayor up close and the exercise is good for me, too. One parade story involves Peel Region's current chief of police, Jennifer Evans, back when she was a young detective in 1988. She was assigned to walk with me on "protection detail" at the Streetsville Bread and Honey parade. That was kind of silly of her bosses because I don't need protection, but I guess it's protocol when the mayor goes out into crowds. Anyway, I will let Jennifer tell the story.

"It was a rainy day, and I mean *pouring* rain," Jennifer says. "I was hoping they would either cancel the parade or we'd ride in a covered vehicle. But just in case the mayor insisted on walking, I went out and got the biggest golf umbrella I could find. I got to Streetsville and met up with the mayor, who, naturally, said we would be walking the parade in the rain. I showed her my umbrella and told her I was prepared. She turned to me with a stern look on her face, and said: 'If my people get wet, I get wet. You don't need that umbrella.'

"So, we walked for what seemed like miles in the rain and it was like neither the mayor nor the people seemed to care it was pouring. She was waving and people were cheering. I was drenched. The padded shoulders in my jacket were flattened by the rain and my wet boots squeaked with every step just trying to keep up to her. It was quite incredible."

But as for other, more formal exercise, like working out at a gym or lifting dumbbells, I don't do that. I just stay active. You have to stay active. I still even skate a little bit, but not as much as I used to. Well into my eighties, I was regularly skating and even rollerblading the odd time.

It is important to try new things, to challenge yourself as

you age. I've noticed that as people move into midlife, they often stop trying new things. I've read that experts think we stop doing things due to a fear of failing, and if we imagine there is a 50 per cent or greater chance of failure, most people simply don't do whatever the task might be. As we age, we get more frightened of failure. I think this ages us and we should always fight the inclination not to do new things.

That's why at age eighty-nine, I zip-lined a thousand metres above the ground in Italy. Some might think me silly for taking a risk like that, but I saw only risk in missing the opportunity. When would I ever get another chance to glide through the air in Italy at my age? I had no fear of failure because all I was doing was getting harnessed in, helmet on, and soaring over gorges, valleys and hilltops. It was exhilarating. As the saying goes, we should suck the marrow out of life and challenge ourselves more and more the older we get.

I love to travel, especially the older I get. I've been to China and Japan a dozen times and India twice. I've been to the Middle East and Africa and I'm routinely in Europe and the United States. The more you see and experience, the more you break from everyday routines. And that makes you better off as you grow older.

My daily routine during my final year as mayor remained pretty much the same as the previous thirty-five years. My day begins at 5:30 a.m. with a few stretches to get the blood flowing. I then go downstairs to the kitchen and eat a bowl of cereal and read a newspaper or two. Then I take my dog, Missy (short for Mississauga, of course), out in the backyard or for a short walk in the neighbourhood. (When I travel, Missy stays with my daughter, Linda, on her farm.)

After coming back with the dog, I begin work before 7 a.m.

Most evenings, my staff brings over a box of reports and other materials so I always have work to dig into, especially if I was out at an event the previous night. By about 7:30 a.m., I may begin to make phone calls to people I know are up and working by that time in the morning. If I don't have a breakfast meeting scheduled, I usually arrive at the office by 8 a.m. or so. My work day goes well into the evening. The media loves to say "until midnight" whenever they profile me, but that's an exaggeration. I am usually in bed by about 11 p.m.

I absolutely love my job, and that is extremely important to a person's health. The mix of administration, management and dealing with the public is fascinating to me. I just love it. There is always something new each and every day. Now, if you don't enjoy what you're doing, there's a lot of stress and that's no good at all. When you're dreading going to work or doing a particular task, the stress builds and builds and eventually it will be harmful to your health. That's why I tell people to find their passion and do work related to it. Being miserable at work not only affects your performance, it also adversely affects your health.

As for diet, I don't eat a lot and sometimes skip lunch. But I do try to drink lots of water and snack on healthy things like walnuts and fruit. I love broccoli and eat it quite often; sometimes I pop home from the office to get Missy outside and steam up some broccoli before heading out to an event. Fresh broccoli (not frozen) has high levels of sulphoraphane, some sort of thing that not only fights cancer but also reduces joint damage. I figure that it's gotta be good for me and it tastes good, too.

My schedule makes proper eating not one of my strongest suits because I am out so often in the evening. It is not uncommon for me to be out at dinnertime every night for three consecutive weeks, but I also don't eat out of a box as many people do these days.

Healthy eating as a young child on the Gaspé has got to be part of the reason for my longevity. We ate fish at least five times a week and I never knew what a hamburger and French fries were until I was sixteen years old and living near Montreal. Mother had lots of fresh vegetables in her garden that were wholesome and without chemicals of any kind.

This was a tradition I continued while raising my family, growing vegetables in the backyard without pesticides and pulling weeds from the garden by hand. I let that garden lapse, but plan to restart a chemical-free garden again in my backyard in my retirement.

Growing up, I drank "raw milk," which means it was not pasteurized and homogenized. I often wonder whether it was also beneficial to my health. Some in the medical community have a differing opinion and the sale of raw milk is banned in Ontario, where I live. Still, combined with the clean, fresh air on the Gaspé, healthy eating certainly was helpful as I grew from a little girl into adulthood.

Promoting healthy eating and living in a healthy environment is why I got so involved in the World Health Organization and in 1999 joined its advisory board at its Kobe Centre, which studies health programs in cities around the world. Through the University of Toronto at Mississauga we established an ongoing and made-in-Mississauga "Healthy City" model that studies things we can do at a municipal level to help make citizens live in a healthier environment, from by-laws restricting vehicle idling and emissions to creating public spaces that encourage healthy activities. We established the Healthy City Stewardship Centre and won an international award in London, England, in

2006 from the World Leadership Forum for the centre and for Mississauga's commitment to healthy living. It's in all our interests to make cities as environmentally friendly and as healthy as possible for all citizens.

Another key to longevity, in my opinion, is attitude—not just a positive attitude, but a feisty one. Many studies show that, on average, positive people live longer than negative people. Not only that, but if you're social and out meeting people it is also good for you.

I was delighted to hear the story of Olga Kotelko, a ninety-four-year-old track star from Saskatchewan. This is a woman who had been active her entire life—milking cows, stacking hay, playing baseball—who took up track and field at seventy-seven. Today, she still holds dozens of world records. Her advice to people was to try new and challenging things and to stay positive in your attitude. And that's not to say she didn't acknowledge negative things occur. "I choose not to let the dark stuff have a negative effect on me," Olga said in the *Globe and Mail* in 2014 as promotion for a book about her remarkable life entitled *What Makes Olga Run?* (Sadly she passed away in the summer of 2014, shortly after her book was published.) Her feisty spirit is worth emulating. She refused to be typecast as an old person. She was a doer and an achiever. And I believe this sort of attitude can add years to a person's life.

Like me, Olga tries to wash away many of the unimportant things in life and focus on what is really important. Too often we focus on the wrong things. We stress about our fancy cars, our designer clothes and all our "stuff." It has been said that life's winners don't always have the best of everything but they make the best of everything they have. I believe it.

For that reason, try eliminating everything you are not

proud of, won't wear or don't really want. Everything else, take great pride in. If you worked hard for a fancy BMW and simply love the vehicle, then hold on to it. But if you bought a fancy new BMW to impress your friends, then get rid of it. It's the joy and pride of ownership that brings happiness, not the dollar value.

I think this positive attitude also helps in dealing with stress, a far bigger problem when it comes to health than any of us thought until the last decade or two. There are challenges for us all as we go through various stages of life and I think a positive attitude helps us deal with these road bumps along the way, by keeping our minds as clear as possible to help make decisions and by allowing us to move forward after the decision is made. If it doesn't work out perfectly, then we know we did our best and sometimes things just don't work out.

In the role of mayor for thirty-six years, I've had to make lots of tough decisions. Not all of them turned out perfect, but many did. When they went sideways, I didn't lose sleep because I knew I did my homework and made a decision based on the information at hand.

A positive attitude has been one of the most important things that have kept me healthy. I am sure of it. I take no medication, except for a baby Aspirin each morning that most doctors recommend for everyone as a mild blood thinner.

In 2013, the Biotechnology Industry Organization (BIO) annual conference was being held in Chicago and I was asked to say a few words. I try to attend the conference most years because there are some four hundred life sciences firms operating in Mississauga. Walking up to the podium, I thought I'd tell them about how fortunate I was when it came to daily medication. Then it dawned on me, given the audience, it might be better *not* to mention that I don't use any prescription drugs, especially if I wanted to attract a few more life sciences companies to move to Mississauga! At the conference I was asked several times if I had any tips for staying healthy. I passed a few on, but not with as much detail as here.

On my most recent birthday, the *Toronto Star* profiled me, calling me "remarkable" for being so healthy for so long. "The phrase 'one in a million' is usually used figuratively. When applied to McCallion it might be factually correct," the *Star* said. The newspaper quoted McGill University medicine and psychiatry professor Judes Poirier, director of the school's Centre for Studies in Aging, as saying my busy schedule and drive to accomplish tasks and projects work in my favour. "We're starting to see more and more like her. It's a combination of good genetics and living well, being active, passionate and engaged with what you do. The highest-functioning centenarians told me there were not enough hours in the day to do everything. I used to think, 'What the heck, you're supposed to be taking it easy,'" Poirier said.

Hold on, Doc, I am not one hundred years old yet! But I do plan to be one day.

CHAPTER 10

Big Projects

After my first four or five years as mayor, it was time to really start building a downtown core, and it wouldn't be without its challenges—some of which remain today.

Before we went for any big projects we made sure the community had the facilities for everyday life, like community centres, baseball diamonds, arenas, libraries and more. And we cut our cloth according to our needs, not simply to build white elephants or unnecessary shrines.

Most cities grow out from a downtown core. And cities fortunate enough to have a waterfront, like Mississauga, usually have a downtown core close to the water. But Mississauga isn't like that. Our downtown core actually had to "grow into" the new city because Mississauga is an amalgamation of three towns and several villages, not to mention thousands of acres of farmland. And back in 1974 when they were all put together, each had its own distinct downtown area, so there was no natural downtown core to grow out from, especially when you consider the largest municipality of the three, by far, was the Town of Mississauga.

And just to complicate things further, a savvy businessman named Bruce McLaughlin had bought vast tracts of farmland in the Town of Mississauga and was building the country's largest shopping centre, Square One, at the time. So, it was in his economic interest to develop a downtown core near his shopping centre because land prices would rise.

The die was cast and that's how we ended up with a downtown core anchored by a shopping mall with 8,700 above-ground parking spots. At council, we had to play the hand dealt to us, but not before the rest of the city and its neighbourhoods were well on their way.

By the mid-1980s, home-building in Mississauga was going gangbusters with big, beautiful communities like Erin Mills, Meadowvale, Mississauga Valley and others planned or taking shape, with all the amenities: single-family dwellings, two-car garages and spacious lots. These were dream homes for young families leaving tiny postwar homes or apartments in Toronto, or for those coming to Canada for the first time.

At the same time, we also saw tremendous growth in industrial, office and commercial properties that brought with them high-paying jobs in sectors like health sciences, technology, aerospace and financial services. Many of these businesses clustered in the northern part of the city near what I like to call "Mississauga International Airport." For miles south and west from the airport sprang up names like Microsoft, Honeywell, Bell Canada, Ericsson, Royal Bank of Canada, Siemens, Oracle and many more.

This was the beginning of an economic base that today is the envy of most cities. Sixty-two Fortune 500 U.S. companies, 50 Fortune Global 500 companies (i.e., non-American firms) and 96 multinationals from Germany and 71 from Japan have offices in Mississauga.

Too many numbers can make the head spin. But the point is simple: the 1980s and 1990s were a time of explosive growth in Mississauga with six thousand building permits issued annually valued at more than $1 billion.

We were waking from a slumber, getting the sleep from our eyes and no longer simply a "bedroom community" wearily serving our giant neighbour to the east. Mississauga was becoming a lot more than that.

Mississauga is a diverse, progressive and award-winning municipality located on the shores of Lake Ontario, in the heart of the Greater Toronto Area. We became a location of choice for companies wanting to expand globally into the North American market with culturally diverse communities, a strong and growing economy and access to a skilled and talented labour force. Centrally located with easy access to global markets, our city is only a ninety-minute drive to and from the U.S. border and within a day's drive to North America's richest markets with access to 164 million consumers in the northeast and midwest.

But in the 1980s something was still lacking in Mississauga. And that was a downtown known for something more than the giant shopping mall called Square One. We literally—and figuratively—had to go back to square one if we hoped to achieve this.

For downtown cores to flourish they need an exciting city hall, office towers, public places to congregate, places of learning, a great library, fine dining, a venue for arts and culture and more. Some of the things on this wish list were within council's control, some not so much, especially because the land was all privately owned. By this point, we could start moving on to these big projects because we had put in fail-safe plans to ensure all Mississauga neighbourhoods, new and old, had the necessary amenities like arenas, community centres, parks, swimming pools and more. Mississauga really had become a great place to work, live and play.

At the top of the checklist was a new city hall.

The existing city hall was across the street from Square One, near Burnhamthorpe Road and Hurontario Street, Mississauga's main north-south road. It was just an ordinary office building, and not well built, either. I remember one day a heavy wind-storm blew in part of a wall. It was built by developer Bruce McLaughlin after a fire in 1969 damaged the old Mississauga town hall farther south at Confederation Square on Dundas Street in Cooksville.

In typical Bruce McLaughlin style, he and his staff had worked through the night on plans for new municipal offices after fire destroyed the previous one.

Bruce, who studied urban planning in university, began buying up dairy farms between Highway 401 and the Queen Elizabeth Way back in the 1950s until he eventually had about 4,000 acres (1,600 ha) by the early 1970s. He was a crackerjack businessman with great vision. (Where he got into trouble was that he was a micromanager who got himself involved in too much of the day-to-day minutiae.)

"The day after the fire, he presented plans for the new city hall—free of charge—on 10 acres of land at Square One," his long-time associate Ron Duquette told the *Mississauga News* after Bruce's death in 2012. "He 'engineered' the location if you will. It was a shrewd move and he was a shrewd businessman."

The then Town of Mississauga (I was reeve, or deputy mayor, in Streetsville at the time) agreed to give McLaughlin the land where the old municipal offices were in exchange for him building a new town hall on the farmland he owned. It opened in 1971 while Bruce was building the giant shopping centre across the street.

It was all part of Bruce's plan to build Square One, which opened in 1973, and turn the area into a downtown core. He had all these futuristic *Jetsons*-like ideas of moving sidewalks and all the buildings being connected through skywalks above the roads or tunnels below them. His idea was that a downtown core with so many major roads around it would be better for transportation and getting around than one located somewhere along Mississauga's beautiful waterfront. Yes, it was designed with the car top of mind, but Bruce knew pedestrian traffic was essential to a lively downtown, too. The trick would be finding the balance.

One also has to remember that Port Credit, which today has a magnificent waterfront, was its own municipality when the Town of Mississauga's civic headquarters burned down in 1969. The Town of Mississauga didn't have the power to take over the Port Credit waterfront.

It would have taken incredible foresight to build a temporary town hall for the Town of Mississauga based on the mere hope of an amalgamation with Port Credit, so that one day they could build a permanent city core near the water. I don't think Bruce McLaughlin, or anyone else, even thought about a waterfront city core for a future City of Mississauga. "A city centre on the lakefront would have created an unbalanced transportation system," Bruce told the *Toronto Star* in 1998. "We wanted to be at the gravitational centre of Mississauga."

It was obvious that building a new town hall where he did was in Bruce's business interests. But I don't want to place all the blame on Bruce that Mississauga doesn't have a city core on our beautiful waterfront. Business people are in business to make money. Otherwise, they're not in business for long. (Bruce and I sure had our differences and we engaged in some pretty scrappy fights over the years, but in the end I won him over with my businesslike approach to running a city.)

The real decision for the location of Mississauga's city core came down to Town of Mississauga elected officials like Robert Speck and Chic Murray, the old guard I'd battle with so much during the 1970s and well into the 1980s. In 1969 and 1970, they could have resisted moving to lands adjacent to Bruce's holdings and de facto creating a future city core around the Square One shopping mall.

I suppose what I am saying is that the old guard bent to Bruce, a businessman, not an expert urban planner or elected official. And this decision boxed in future councils. As I said many times over the years, the die had been cast and we had to work with what we had.

The first and most important component of the downtown core had to be a spectacular city hall, or civic centre as we call it, that Mississauga residents could be proud of. It had to be unique. We also wanted to demonstrate council's confidence in the city core by building it there, across the street from Square One. The plan was for it to be the first of many spectacular new public buildings that would also encourage commercial towers to be built.

We launched an architectural competition in 1982 with one stipulation: it had to be designed by Canadians. The design for Toronto's new city hall, with its futuristic spaceship look, had been sent out to an international architectural competition in 1958, and we felt we wanted ours to be wholly Canadian.

With 246 competitors, ours was perhaps the most important architectural event for an Ontario public building since the Toronto competition. (The competition for Toronto's SkyDome, now the Rogers Centre, was three years away, in 1985.) Famed British architect James Stirling was on our jury, adding to the lustre of the competition.

In the end, Toronto architects Edward Jones and Michael Kirkland won with a postmodern design that mixes European urban civic design with rural Ontario building types to tie together Mississauga's new urban makeup with its not-too-distant farmland heritage. The concept behind the design was to make it look like a futuristic farm: the clock tower is a windmill, the main building where city staff work is the farmhouse, the council chamber is the silo and the pentagonal office building is the barn. If architecture interests you and you have not seen it, then it's worth a look the next time you're near Mississauga.

Ground was broken in 1984 and it opened in July 1987 with their Royal Highnesses the Duke and Duchess of York at the ceremony. It cost $65 million and it was all paid up by the time it was built. It has been erroneously reported that the Civic Centre was fully paid for by development levies. Much of the money did come from this source, but a significant amount also came from interest on the invested reserves, which were earning 15 to 18 per cent annually in those days. Some taxpayers' money was used, too.

Official opening day in the summer of 1987 was certainly special. My friend Harold Shipp was chairman of the organizing committee and the man in charge of the ceremony. Harold is a developer who less than a decade earlier owned a farm across the street where he stabled his racehorses. (Sadly, my good friend died on September 7, 2014, just weeks before this book was published.) He was the perfect person to be in charge that day because he is so down to earth. He kept the royal formalities as informal as possible. At one point during lunch, he even had the duke and duchess laughing while showing them a trick about getting a linen napkin out of an empty wine bottle.

Harold overlooked no detail. Before the royals arrived, he was in the Civic Centre inspecting things. When he got to the new office of the mayor, he noticed the toilet in the washroom was an ordinary industrial type you'd find in a public washroom, not the sort you'd have in a home—or a castle. Harold immediately ordered workers to replace the toilet with a residential one.

"Madam Mayor, we have to change the toilet in case the duke or duchess ask to use your washroom. They can't use that thing!" he exclaimed, pointing at the industrial model. It still makes me chuckle to think of Harold on toilet patrol.

I've been fortunate to have met so many royals over the years, usually greeting them at the airport along with prime ministers, governors general and premiers. It is protocol for the mayor of the city where an airport is located to welcome royals. I've met Queen Elizabeth many times, including once in Ottawa at the unveiling of the monument of long-time Mississauga resident Oscar Peterson. I find the queen to be very pleasant and friendly. Her husband, however, is a little harder to get to know.

I never met Princess Diana, but I have met Prince Charles and his second wife, Camilla. I also met Princess Margaret, the queen's late sister. My all-time favourite royal was the late Queen Mum. What a delightful person with such a warm and charming personality. I even told her how I was in the sea of people in Quebec City on her first trip to Canada in 1939 with her husband, King George VI. She was Queen Elizabeth back then, not the Queen Mum. She said that she remembered that trip fondly, and it's things like that that show why she was so approachable and engaging to everyone she met.

To say the initial reaction to the new Civic Centre was controversial is an understatement. Some Mississauga residents disliked it immensely; some probably still do. (Don Cherry, who lives nearby, joked shortly after it was built that it reminded him of his hometown of Kingston, a city known for its penitentiaries.)

Even guest of honour Prince Andrew called it "quite remarkable" in the public ceremony to open it, and commented at a private luncheon that it looked like a "gasworks" plant. I had mixed feelings how it turned out, and I guess I still do. I will say it's unique. It just doesn't have that inviting feel that I'd hoped it would have.

Regardless, residents cannot complain they weren't consulted and asked for their opinions. We even had the winning architects, Edward Jones and Michael Kirkland, make up several three-dimensional scale models of the building so we could display them in numerous public libraries and other municipal buildings around Mississauga before it was built. There was two years of public input before the first sod was turned.

Even if there isn't unanimous consent, the building has certainly won many architectural awards and other prizes at home and abroad, including the 1990 Governor General's Award of Merit. I will say this: one of Mississauga's harshest critics likes it and likes it a lot. *Toronto Star* urban affairs columnist Christopher Hume has written: "From the moment it opened in 1987, it has been the most remarkable building in Mississauga, one of the most remarkable in Canada. . . . As a piece of architecture, it ranks among the most respected, and definitely spectacular, examples of post-modernism in the world." This from a writer who routinely uses words like *swampland, sprawl* and *car-choked culture* to describe Mississauga.

Next up on our checklist for the downtown core was a new central library, the jewel of one of the largest public library systems in Canada, with more than 300,000 users and eighteen branches. The architectural firm of Shore, Tilbe, Henschel, Irwin and Peters won the task to create something special and they sure did.

We broke ground for the new Central Library on September 23, 1988, one year after the Civic Centre opened. I was given the honour to turn the first sod at this prime location just south of city hall. In less than three years, in June 1991, the old central library was shut down and staff moved all the collections to the new building, and it officially opened on September 23, 1991, exactly three years to the day after I turned the first sod. At 165,000 square feet (15,400 m²), the library is huge, with five floors and a collection of more than 250,000 items, including one of the largest children's departments in any Canadian library. It's a focal point for learning, attracting young and old to the downtown core. And best of all, like the Civic Centre, it was fully paid for by the time its doors opened, all $43 million of it.

Again, lot levies and high-interest investments on reserves paid for much, but not all. The library is one of my favourite examples of the benefits of our policy to make growth pay its way. Interestingly, it was only two years before the Central Library opened that the Ontario government enacted the Development Charges Act 1989, which that created a formula for all municipalities in the province to make development pay for expansion of services and infrastructure. I would never take credit for the provincial government's policies, but clearly the success of Mississauga had some influence.

It has always been my belief that great communities need strong arts and culture and sports and recreation to flourish. I can't say when or where I developed this belief, but I've held it for as long as I remember. Maybe it came from hearing my mother's beautiful singing voice or seeing all the wondrous culture—theatre, museums and more—on my first trips to New York and Europe in the 1940s. Maybe it goes back to the stories I'd heard about the great sporting traditions in Streetsville long before I moved there—from competitive hockey on the frozen Credit River to first-rate lacrosse being played on the flats to horse races down its main street in the nineteenth century.

We knew Mississauga needed a special venue for the performing and visual arts, but we couldn't put the cart before the horse. First, the Mississauga Arts Council (MAC) was established in 1981 by city resolution and it remains today a non-profit registered charity governed by a volunteer board of directors.

According to its mission statement, the council "engages, connects and champions artists of all disciplines, ages and abilities from diverse communities to develop arts and culture in Mississauga." It supports and promotes the activities of more than 215 arts organizations and several hundred individual members.

So many great people worked tirelessly, most of them volunteers, to develop Mississauga's arts community in the early days; many, many more continue today. It's worth singling out a quartet from the early days: founding member and first MAC chairman Willson McTavish; founding member Joe Macerollo; former treasurer and volunteer Bob Widdup; and MAC's first executive director, Laurie Pallett.

My job as mayor—and one of my dreams for the city—was to build a first-class venue in the city core for Mississauga's arts community while at the same time minding the taxpayers' money. Some wanted us simply to dip into the reserves, some advocated a special temporary levy on the property tax bills, and others thought it best to leave the grand arts venues to downtown Toronto. I didn't like any of those choices and thought there must be a better way to build what became the Living Arts Centre.

Then, out of the blue, an old friend, Avie Bennett, telephoned and wanted to have lunch. I had known Avie since the 1950s, when Canadian Kellogg rented space in one of his family's office buildings. I had always liked Avie and we kept in touch over the years, even as I moved from the private sector into my public sector career.

He is a terrific young man (well, he's not that young but he is seven years younger than me) and he is a truly inspirational Canadian and defender of Canadian culture. In 1985, he bought the iconic Canadian publishing company McClelland & Stewart, rescuing it from the brink of financial ruin. With a commitment to Canadian titles, he published authors like Margaret Atwood, Robertson Davies, Michael Ondaatje, W.O. Mitchell and recent Nobel Prize winner Alice Munro. He donated his 75-per-cent holding in McClelland & Stewart to the University of Toronto in 2000 and established an endowment through it to support Canadian culture.

Back in 1990, at lunch at the Park Plaza Hotel in downtown Toronto, Avie told me his family was selling the Dixie Plaza in Mississauga, one of its commercial real estate holdings, and that he wanted to give $2 million from the proceeds to a worthwhile cause.

Well, you could've knocked me over with a feather. I knew Avie was interested in the arts and Canadian culture, but this was extraordinary. He was willing to give the City of Mississauga four quarterly cheques of $500,000 as the deal to sell Dixie Plaza moved along to fruition. I couldn't believe how generous it was, especially when at that stage the Living Arts Centre was still a dream, nothing more. (We invested his money and by the time we needed to use it to help finance construction it was about $2.5 million, due to interest earned.) Avie had only one stipulation: "I don't want any publicity and I don't want you to tell anyone about this donation," he said.

"Well, the people who cash the cheque in the city's accounts receivable department will have to know," I said.

"Of course, but I don't want it known around city hall where the money came from, so tell them to keep it confidential," he said.

What a lunch. I just couldn't believe it. And that's what really got the ball rolling to build the Living Arts Centre. It wasn't until 2003 that Avie finally allowed us to add his name to the donors' wall at the LAC. Imagine that. There's his name on that wall with all the other donors. It just sits there among all the rest, but the story about how it got there is quite remarkable.

Willson McTavish and his volunteers with the Mississauga Arts Council were diligently working on plans for a city-wide fundraising campaign, but after Avie's generosity I saw there could be a faster way to raise the money. We needed another "whale," as they call the extremely wealthy patrons in Las Vegas.

City Manager Doug Lychak and I went to meet Bruce Heyland, chief executive of Hammerson Canada, the giant British retailing landowner that had bought Square One from Bruce McLaughlin a few years before. Heyland, who was also chair of the Ballet Opera House Corporation in Toronto, liked the idea of an arts centre in Mississauga but told us we'd have to go to London, England, and pitch for a donation directly to his parent company's board of directors. Off the three of us flew to London, but not before Heyland told us: "They'll want to see your plans as part of the pitch for the donation."

Plans? What plans? I thought. I'm sure Doug was thinking the same thing. All we had was a big idea and Avie's $2 million in the bank and a consultant's report saying it was a good idea. But we hadn't spent money to develop any formal plans at that point. Doug and his staff cobbled together pictures and descriptions of beautiful arts facilities around the world and cut and pasted them into a presentation. That was about all the "formal plans" we had boarding the plane to London in the spring of 1991.

Bruce Heyland took us to Hammerson's head office and up to the boardroom. You can just imagine how stuffy and proper everything was. "Hi, I'm Hazel McCallion, mayor of Mississauga," I said to one director while extending my arm to shake hands. He stiffened right up, his shoulders thrust back like a soldier coming to attention at reveille. After introductions and pleasantries, we made our presentation to the eight or ten directors present.

Each sat in their big boardroom chairs, some with their arms crossed, and they asked very few questions, listening intently. When we were done, the chairman thanked us and invited us to a formal dinner the next evening at his club. That was it.

I thought we either didn't make much of an impression or, possibly, bombed, judging by the reactions. Doug thought the same. But Bruce told us later that it wasn't bad. "It's just the way they are, very formal," he said. I asked Bruce when we would likely hear whether they'd be interested in making a donation. "Oh, probably in two or three months," he said.

The next morning, Bruce, Doug and I flew over to Amsterdam for a few hours because there was an arts facility someone told Bruce we should tour. It was so funny; as we walked down the street in Amsterdam, strange women kept coming up to the two men asking if they'd be interested in any of their services. The men were getting quite embarrassed, especially with me standing there listening. But I was getting a kick out of watching their reactions.

Since I enjoy walking so much, I started having some fun with them, telling them I'd like to walk down this street or that street. Each time they'd say, "No, no, Hazel. It's time for us to get back to London for the dinner." Then I would prod them a little more until we really did run out of time. I don't remember much of the tour of the arts facility in Amsterdam, but I sure remember the conversations with the ladies in the street.

Back in London, we arrived for cocktails and dinner at a really posh club with leather chairs, crystal glasses and the aroma of expensive cigars. After cocktails we were called to the dining room, and on our way in, the Hammerson chairman, a lovely elderly gentleman, took me by the arm and said: "I will be making an announcement tonight."

I looked over and both Bruce and Doug had surprised looks on their faces.

At the dinner, the chairman stood up and announced that Hammerson would donate $3 million towards a new facility for performing and visual arts across the street from their Square One shopping centre in Mississauga, Canada. Then he turned to Bruce, his CEO of Canadian operations: "And I want you to commit as much of your time as necessary to make sure this gets built for the mayor."

And that he did. Bruce volunteered to chair the Mississauga Arts Council and push the project forward. He even stepped down from the Hammerson board in London in 1993 to devote more time to operations in North America, including the Living Arts Centre, which was designed by the renowned Toronto architectural firm of Zeidler Partnership Architects.

After returning from London with the Hammerson donation, I started lobbying for money elsewhere and we ended up getting $13 million from the federal government, $13 million from the Ontario government and $5 million from the Region of Peel. The City of Mississauga kicked in $20 million. It's worth noting that Rogers Cablesystems gave us $1 million, which was extraordinary for the mid-1990s when Ted Rogers's company was struggling to stay afloat. It was not the powerhouse then that it is today. There were many other corporations like RBC and individual donors, and you can see them all on the donors' wall where Avie Bennett reluctantly allowed his name to be added in 2003.

As everyone knows, the devil is in the details and so much credit must also go to Willson McTavish and his volunteers for really pulling everything together so the Living Arts Centre could open its doors in the fall of 1997. I was honoured that the official grand opening night on November 15, 1997, was for the annual Mayor's Gala fundraiser, and Canadian superstars Anne Murray and Ashley MacIsaac were the entertainment. What a night!

Bruce Heyland, then the LAC's chairman, gave me too much credit, even telling the *Mississauga News* that it would never have been built if not for my relentless drive. "She has been so focused on this project for the past five years, and for five years before that," he said in 1996. "It's tough, I think, politically, to maintain that kind of vision for a long period of time."

That is nice of him to say, but the reality is I had a great team around me and we built all the necessities for everyday life in Mississauga before we undertook the Living Arts Centre, so it was not that difficult to stay focused.

In 1998, a year after it opened, we lost a great corporate partner. Hammerson sold Square One to Ontario Municipal Employees Retirement System (OMERS) and began consolidating its business in Britain and France. Still, they came through with the biggest corporate donation and their name still adorns the largest performing theatre in the building, even though most people would not know the significance of Hammerson to the creation of the LAC.

And, like the Civic Centre and Central Library, when the Living Arts Centre opened, it was paid for.

More than 5 million people have visited the LAC since that first night. It's an important resource for the arts, education and business. It is 225,000 square feet (21,000 m²) of multiple performance venues, studio spaces and exhibition display areas. The two main performing arts venues—Hammerson Hall with 1,300 seats and the RBC Theatre recital hall with 400 seats— are the sites for a range of arts, cultural and entertainment events presented by both the Living Arts Centre and community partners.

And it's not just for the performing arts. Seven studios are the home of professional resident artists. The studios are also used for dozens of recreational classes for all ages, including school trips. Laidlaw Hall features constantly changing art exhibitions from local artists. The LAC is also used by others not involved in the arts. The meeting and conference rooms are utilized by community organizations and businesses for a variety of events, from church services to luncheon meetings to international videoconference business meetings.

I am very proud of the Living Arts Centre, but I would be lying if I said things have always been rosy. In the beginning, it was difficult finding and holding qualified senior staff and it lost money for the city. In the early days, it was not being run like a business. At one point, shortly before opening, we even had to send in the very capable Dave O'Brien, Mississauga's city manager who succeeded Doug Lychak, to be acting CEO.

But those days are long behind us now. In 2003, businessman and accountant Gerry Townsend, who ran for mayor in 1976, took over as CEO. He righted the ship and stopped the operational losses. After almost ten years at the helm, Gerry handed the reins to Ron Lenyk, former publisher of the *Mississauga News*, and the LAC continues to help nourish and grow the arts and culture of Mississauga.

For a great city, arts and culture and sports and recreation go together like salt and pepper. It's worth talking about the Hershey Centre, a premier sports and entertainment facility in the Greater Toronto Area. One reason to mention it is because I sometimes get accused of being autocratic and forcing my will upon people to get things done in Mississauga: the Hershey Centre refutes the notion I can get everything I want. If that were true, the Hershey Centre wouldn't be located east of the city core and nowhere near current or future main public transit routes.

The city wanted the Hershey Centre in the city core and we even offered to build Hammerson a multi-tier parking lot if they would sell us city core land near Square One for the Hershey Centre. I don't know if it was because Hammerson was preoccupied in negotiations to sell Square One and surrounding properties to OMERS in 1997, but they refused to budge. I still remember city manager Dave O'Brien coming into my office absolutely dumbfounded that his parking lot deal was turned down.

Next, we tried to get the Hershey Centre built on the school board's lands north of the city core because long-range plans called for a rapid transit line running up Hurontario, right past the school board's lands. We couldn't get land there, either. (Indeed, construction for the rapid transit line on Hurontario began in 2014, and it probably would have begun earlier if the hockey arena had been built there.)

That left us with our current location, well east of the city core and north of Matheson Boulevard, on Rose Cherry Place, named for the late first wife of Mississauga resident Don Cherry. Don, who was an owner of the first junior hockey team to occupy the Hershey Centre, the Mississauga IceDogs, is like me: he doesn't suffer fools and he wants things done right. We broke ground in the middle of winter in January 1998 and the Hershey Centre was opened in October 1998 for the Mississauga IceDogs' first home game. Naturally, before the doors opened, the cost of $22 million to build the facility was paid from our reserves and investment income.

The Hershey Centre is a tremendous facility, not only for watching fast-paced junior hockey with 5,500 up-close seats, but the complex also supports other sports. There is an indoor soccer field and two outdoor lit soccer pitches, a gymnastics centre, three NHL-sized community ice surfaces and a basketball court. No sense crying over spilled milk, but the Hershey Centre could have added to the city core's night life and pedestrian traffic had it been located centrally, or even up the street on Hurontario.

Still, all these are excellent examples of how ensuring growth pays its way is not only fair, but beneficial to all residents. The strategy has been essential in supporting Mississauga's phenomenal growth. All municipalities should remember this as they grow, because developers want to make a buck, but they're often willing to do more if asked. At least the ones I've known.

For example, the *Mississauga News* reported a story about a ribbon-cutting ceremony I attended during the 1990s with "the handsome young scion of a noted development family." While we were posing for photographers, the *News* reported me turning to the executive and saying: "Mississauga has been good to you. Now, I think you should consider being good to Mississauga by making a donation of $100,000 to the Erindale College Building Fund."

This was when Erindale was a satellite campus of the University of Toronto and looking to expand into its current stand-alone University of Toronto at Mississauga campus with its own medical school and other first-rate facilities. I've always believed great cities need great post-secondary schools.

After my request, the reporters and photographers apparently overheard the young man stammer out: "Ah, ah, we have someone at our firm who looks after that." To which I replied: "No, I don't want to talk about that. I want you to phone my office on Friday and let me know it's been done."

I don't recall that specific incident because I did things like that all the time. I still do in my final days as mayor. And I have to say, business usually responds, and usually in a big way. The developers would pay their lot levies and then they'd donate to the community in other ways. So many businesses have been partners in building this city, and also in helping with our post-secondary institutions like University of Toronto at Mississauga and Sheridan College's fabulous new campus in the downtown core, not to mention our two world-class hospitals. Developers understand that it's a two-way street. And I like to think I helped them realize this.

For example, Orlando Corp., one of Canada's premier industrial and commercial property landlords, credits the city with helping to fill their Mississauga business parks with multinational companies like Bridgestone-Firestone and PepsiCo.

"What we appreciate about Hazel is she understands business and how it operates," Orlando executive Doug Kilner told the *News*. "And because she understands business, she has assembled a top-notch team who . . . make it so much easier for us to work with."

There's been grumbling about lot levies over the years but developers and business in general understand they're worth the price when used to create a positive business environment. We do that by creating amenities where a large and talented pool of workers want to live and where a solid economic base creates more and more business opportunities.

I don't know if Mississauga was the first to develop the lot-levies growth strategy, but we were certainly one of the leaders in Canada. Indeed, Streetsville could have been the first, because when I was mayor of Streetsville, we charged fifty dollars per new housing unit to pay for upgrades for the town's hydro utility. I honestly can't recall where the idea came from, but I've always thought it only fair that existing residents shouldn't have to pay the capital costs for so-called "hard services" like sewers and roads and "soft services" like recreation facilities, community centres and libraries.

We introduced lot levies before provincial laws were enacted. Some developers called them illegal. We simply said,

"Then go develop elsewhere. Our levies are the price of admission to Mississauga." And the policy worked fine, even if we didn't have a statute or law behind it until several years later.

As for Mississauga's city core, it's coming along and we have a plan called "Downtown 21" to make it even more livable and pedestrian-friendly in the twenty-first century. We're reworking streets to make them more walkable. We're enhancing public transit and building a BRT (bus rapid transit) system so a station is within a five-minute walk anywhere downtown. Also, we're refurbishing and redeveloping waterfront areas in the Port Credit and Lakeview communities.

With condominiums rising, the population of Mississauga's downtown core is expected to double to between 70,000 and 80,000 residents by 2031. It's "smart growth" too, showcasing Mississauga's commitment to sustainability and green initiatives. Downtown 21 sets a new course for the future of our downtown and hopefully will help show the world Mississauga is not simply urban sprawl and built for the car, as so many of our critics like to say.

And I have lots to say to those folks, but first I want to return to some non-political aspects of my life.

CHAPTER 11

Hockey

M y big brother Lockhart bought me my first pair of hockey skates for Christmas in 1926 when I was five years old. The skates were one of the most memorable gifts of my life because they sparked my passion for the game, a passion that has never dwindled.

Lockhart, who was scouted for the NHL, was a terrific hockey player, and he took me outside to the pond and had me skating in no time. The cold air on my face, the numbness in my toes, the crackle of the ice each time the blades moved—these are the memories so familiar to millions of Canadian hockey players over the years.

To get an idea how long ago that was, my all-time favourite hockey team, the Toronto Maple Leafs, were still called the Toronto St. Patricks; legendary goalie Georges Vézina collapsed on the ice in the first game of that season and would die of tuberculosis within weeks; Howie Morenz, the legendary Stratford Streak, was in just his second NHL season; and the now-long-forgotten Montreal Maroons were about to win their first Stanley Cup.

My first few winters of hockey are ingrained in my memory. It seemed as if I played hockey from the time I got home from school until bedtime, with only a break for supper. I'd play with Lockhart when he was around, or more likely he'd give me lessons as he was just too good a player for me to actually play against him.

Before I was ten years old, I remember organizing games in Port Daniel. I would always play on my sisters' team. Gwen and Linda played defence and I was a forward. I was a pretty strong skater and not too bad at carrying the puck and passing. Our equipment consisted of skates, stick and mittens, and occasionally we'd strap on old Eaton's catalogues as shin pads. Those hockey games were quintessentially Canadian.

Before long, my older sisters were on to other things. Linda, a teacher, was almost ten years older than I was, and Gwen was six years older. I'd still play hockey as much as possible with any kids who wanted to lace 'em up. Though we'd be chilled to the bone, the memories still warm the heart.

Years later, while running the office for Louis Rolland in Montreal, I heard about a women's professional hockey league. I went down for a tryout and made the team. We were sponsored by Kik Cola, a soft drink company, and I played the 1940–41 and 1941–42 seasons for five bucks per game, a princely sum in those days when most people weren't making that much for an entire day's work.

Here's what Canadian Olympic gold sprinter Myrtle A. Cook said about me in her *Montreal Star* column called "In the Women's Sportlight" on January 12, 1940:

> *There's a bit of chuckling going on around the Kickees hockey camp. The club just persuaded Hazel Journeaux, ex-Port*

*Daniel star, to sign on the dotted line. She makes her bow
tonight against the Sevens at St. Laurent Arena. This player,
who hails from the Gaspé Coast League, is reported to be a fast
skater and a hard shot. We need a few really good shots in our
fraternity. . . . Hazel Journeaux plays left wing, weighs 122
pounds and is 5 feet 3 inches tall. Welcome Gaspé!*

The season was short and there were only three teams in
the league. I think we played six or eight games per season
so it wasn't like I didn't need my other job with Mr. Rolland.
Besides, I still had to pay the sixty-dollar debt to my landlady,
Mrs. Lucy Wilson, who picked up my dental bill after I took a
stick to the mouth in one game and lost two teeth.

Considering the dental cost, I guess I broke even on my
professional hockey career. When Canadian Kellogg transferred me to Toronto in 1942 that was the end of my professional involvement with hockey. There was no women's league
in Toronto that I could find, and at the time we were working
until nine or ten o'clock every night building the first synthetic
rubber plant so I wouldn't have had time anyway.

It didn't take long for me to develop my fondness for the
Toronto Maple Leafs, my favorite team ever since. I've cheered
for them for more than seventy years and have gone through
all the highs and numerous lows. I must be one of the few Leafs
fans who have been alive for all eleven of their Stanley Cups.
I guess today, most Leafs fans haven't been alive for any of
their Cup wins since it's been almost fifty years since their last.
Believe me, I intend to be around for their twelfth Stanley Cup!

Women's hockey has always been important to me because
I loved playing and I've always encouraged other girls and
women to play. In the late 1970s, I was asked to join the board

of regents of the Ontario Women's Hockey Association. I am still on the board. Along with my good friends at the OWHA, Fran Rider, who is president and CEO, and Pat Nicholls, director of operations, we've fought to ensure girls get the coaching and the ice time to develop their hockey skills.

We also spent two decades lobbying for women's world championships and to get women's hockey included in the Olympics. One thing I learned over that period is that there is more politics in sports than there is in politics. I remember Fran and me being told by some high-placed international hockey officials that there would not be a women's world championship in our lifetimes and there would never be women's hockey in the Olympics. Can you guess that these officials were all men?

But not all men were against the women's game. I remember inviting Don Cherry to the Meadowvale arena near Streetsville in 1980 to watch women's hockey. It was the first time he'd seen women play at that level and he commented on the skill and pace. He was hooked right from the start and has been a huge supporter of women's hockey ever since.

In 1987, the OWHA staged the inaugural Women's World Hockey Tournament in North York (which is now part of Toronto) and Mississauga. We ran this first tournament, not the International Ice Hockey Federation (IIHF).

Brian McFarlane in his book *Proud Past, Bright Future: One Hundred Years of Canadian Women's Hockey* called the event "an overwhelming success," with reporters from *Sports Illustrated* and the *New York Times* covering the tournament. Teams representing Canada, Ontario, the United States, Sweden, Switzerland, Holland and Japan all competed. "It was because of this event that the International Ice Hockey Federation decided that female hockey must become more prominent in the world of hockey," McFarlane wrote.

I was the honorary chairperson of the event, just as I was in 1997 and 2000 when it changed into the Women's World Championships run by the IIHF. At the first world tournament in 1987, I dropped the ceremonial first puck and, being a sprightly sixty-six years of age, I then skated around the ice in my CCM Tacks! The trophy was named the McCallion World Cup, which was quite an honour. The IIHF Women's World Championships has its own trophy and the McCallion World Cup now resides in the Hockey Hall of Fame in Toronto.

Though it could be frustrating trying to knock down the prejudices of the male-dominated hockey establishment to grow the women's game at the grassroots and international levels, it was also so satisfying. Here were literally hundreds and hundreds of women all fighting for a common goal: to create leagues and tournaments for their daughters and granddaughters to excel in and enjoy the great game we all loved.

In *Picks and Sticks*, author Michele Muzzi kindly says that I was "the first person, it seemed, in any kind of political position in Canada to acknowledge women's hockey." That may be so, but it was the tireless work of Fran Rider and so many volunteers that put women's hockey in the position it has today in Canada and the United States, and growing around the world.

Both Fran and I were on hand in Nagano, Japan, in 1998 for the first gold medal game in women's hockey at the Olympics. It was such a thrill to see so many dreams come true for so many talented hockey players. It would have been better had Canada beaten the U.S., but we got our revenge by winning gold in 2002, 2006, 2010 and 2014. The gold medal game in Sochi in 2014 was one of the great hockey games of all time, regardless of gender. The U.S. was ahead 2–0 with three minutes to play and Canada roared back and won in overtime.

Fran Rider gives me far too many accolades when she speaks about the recent success of the women's game. "Hazel gave women's hockey credibility. Without her, we wouldn't have gotten here," Fran told the *Mississauga News* in 2008. "She not only put her name to [women's hockey], she believed in it and would attend any women's hockey event and ask, 'What else can I do to help?'" She once told the *National Post* that if not for me, women's hockey might not be in the Olympics today. "The women's hockey community calls her our mayor," Fran said. "Mississauga has to share her with the world of women's hockey."

Women's hockey has grown far beyond tournaments for the elite players of each country. While fewer young boys are taking up the game in Canada, the girls' game is growing at the grassroots level. In October 2013, the International Ice Hockey Federation held a World Girls Hockey Weekend for atom, pee-wee, bantam and midget players in Brampton, Ontario. In the official program, the IIHF said, "Hazel is an icon in the world of women's hockey."

I don't know about that. But I do agree with this: "Girls' hockey struggled against tremendous hostility. It was almost impossible to get ice time, sponsorship support or any credibility," the IIHF writes. "Hazel became an active lobbyist. If girls and women could not get ice time, she made phone calls and secured support. Hazel encouraged the corporate sector to get involved and they did, making it possible for more girls to enjoy hockey and gain valuable skills."

It pains me greatly when I see so much violence in the sport I love so much. It's even creeping into women's hockey. In a pre-Olympic exhibition game between Canadian and American women late in 2013, an NHL-style donnybrook broke out. There is no love lost between these two squads, but there is no place for that sort of behaviour. And the worst part was that the media loved it and played up the fighting. Women's hockey got far more attention for this violence than it ever gets for its talented players and exciting games. That saddens me.

Few cities, if any, have built more hockey arenas than Mississauga over the last twenty-five years. Don Cherry even says that this hockey arena construction is helping the development of players and leading to so many young men from Mississauga reaching the NHL. "You know why?" Don asked on *Hockey Night in Canada*'s "Coach's Corner" in April 2013. "There's fourteen arenas so you can walk to them in Mississauga. You know why? Hurricane Hazel. She loves hockey. . . . She built them all for the kids, she loves hockey. The best mayor that ever was." The number is even higher because some of our arenas have multiple rinks, so there are twenty-five artificial ice pads in Mississauga. I love Don and his passion for the game I love so much. Hockey has been in my blood since Lockhart bought me those skates.

Heck, Canadian comedian Rick Mercer even featured me playing hockey on his popular television program *Rick Mercer Report* in 2009. That six-minute clip had been viewed 3.4 million times on YouTube the last time I checked in 2014. Can you believe it? It's been viewed in 212 countries and the vast majority of viewers—some 2.4 million—were Americans, according to Rick Mercer's production team.

I love the game and I need to say this: fighting and violence, at all levels, but especially in the NHL, are absolutely ruining our game today.

Like any red-blooded Canadian, I have an opinion about all things hockey and my views are quite different from those of Don Cherry. (Don is no longer involved with the Mississauga IceDogs but its current owner, Elliott Kerr, tells me he is having trouble attracting fans, especially families, in part because of all the violence in the game.) My friendship with Don aside, I feel I have an obligation to express my opinion. Don and I have agreed to disagree on whether fighting should be banned from hockey.

The fact is, if people carried on and did the same things on the street that they do on the ice they'd be arrested and thrown in jail. It just makes no sense to me that in football, another tough and demanding sport, you don't have fighting, but in hockey it's allowed. Sure, in football you'll have the pushing and shoving but in hockey you've got bare-knuckle boxing where players pound opponents and throw them down on the ice to pummel some more.

I will acknowledge that the NHL is starting to take the issue of on-ice violence more seriously lately, with tougher penalties and longer suspensions. But these changes are incremental and I believe more radical changes are needed right now. My goodness, the NHL should ban fighting like they do in the National Football League and the National Basketball Association. There is no fighting during the NHL playoffs and during the Olympics, so let's get rid of it once and for all.

Is it going to take an on-ice fight where one of the combatants ends up dead before they come to their senses?

I know Don Cherry and others say that you need fighters to keep the dirty players honest. Without fighting and the fear of getting beaten up, chippy players would take liberties on the star players, so the argument goes. But I'm not buying it.

In the NFL, with its ban on fighting, defensive players are not allowed to take liberties on star quarterbacks, for example. If a star quarterback like Peyton Manning or Tom Brady is running down the field and he slides feet first, defenders are not allowed to hit him. Even if the star quarterback is standing "in the pocket" behind his offensive line, defenders are not allowed to go overboard and put the quarterback at undue risk. When a defender goes overboard, he's assessed a costly personal foul penalty. The deterrent works.

I am not saying football rules are 100-per-cent applicable to hockey, but surely the smart young fellows running the NHL can figure out ways to stop the fighting and the violence that are driving so many young, talented players away from the game. Nine out of ten Canadian kids no longer play organized hockey. The sport is expensive, but this culture of violence is also a big part of the reason why parents aren't putting them into hockey.

I'm opposed to hockey violence and fighting for several reasons: first, as a fan for almost ninety years I prefer to watch skillful hockey plays, not bare-knuckle boxing; second, as a mayor it concerns me that we have all these arenas with rising operating expenses and dropping revenues as more young people drop the sport; third, it's an absolute waste of our police resources to be sending officers into hockey arenas to break up fights, either on ice or in the stands. Police chiefs tell me their officers are being called to arenas surprisingly often.

For more than a decade, I have been crusading to get violence and fighting out of hockey. Just as when Fran Rider and I were told women's hockey would never make it to the

Olympics, I refuse to give up when it comes to trying to get the game cleaned up, especially at the NHL level where so many kids watch their heroes on TV and then mimic them on the ice.

In 2002, I instituted the Mayor's Sportsmanlike Award for boys' and girls' hockey teams in Mississauga. The eight different hockey organizations in Mississauga nominate teams with the fewest penalty minutes and each player on the team gets a medallion acknowledging their sportsmanship. Punishing dirty play is one thing, but you also have to give an incentive for good and fair play.

I recognize this is only one city, but the program has been wildly successful. The kids love getting their medallions from the mayor and we've had to move to bigger locations three times as more teams get nominated and proud family members come to see the kids honoured for their sportsmanship. The fact is, if we don't clean up hockey we're soon going to have empty arenas in cities and towns across Canada.

But don't take my word for it. The world's leading manufacturer of hockey equipment, Bauer Hockey Inc., started a program called "Grow the Game" in 2012 in part because "hockey in Canada has experienced historically low participation rates over the last few years, and today approximately 90 per cent of Canadian families and their children choose not to play hockey," according to a Bauer news release.

And it gets worse. Bauer's research looked at the barriers to participation and found that beyond the cost of hockey "many parents do not perceive the sport as safe for their children to play, including risk of concussion and a belief that the game promotes violent behavior." Well, hello, NHL executives. It's time to acknowledge that what kids see on the ice in the NHL is what far too many emulate.

Don Cherry and I don't even talk about this anymore. He knows where I stand and I, obviously, know where he stands. His intentions are good: he detests the cheap shots and unsportsmanlike behaviour, just as I do. It's just he advocates the "enforcer" role and fighting. We believe in the same thing but disagree on how to get there. To me, banning fighting will cut down on the violence. To him, banning fighting will increase the dirty stuff. Neither of us can convince the other.

On September 30, 2013, after yet another NHL melee, this time in a pre-season game between Toronto and Buffalo, I wrote to NHL Commissioner Gary Bettman. I know a lot of Canadian hockey fans don't like Mr. Bettman, but I think he's smart and has the best interests of the game at heart.

"As Mayor of a city that has built many arenas to encourage the game, we are now facing a decrease in the registration for male hockey," I wrote. "There are a number of reasons for this such as the cost, changing demographics and the violence."

I went on to say that the Greater Toronto Area is "Maple Leaf Nation," but not really a hockey hotbed beyond the Leafs and that many junior and minor league teams struggle for fans. Worse, parents are keeping their young sons away from the game.

"I have spoken to many parents and one of the issues they raise is that they do not want their son to play hockey due to the violence that is present in hockey today, both at the local level and at the national level. It is disappointing that the NHL seems to glamorize violence on television and encourages the belief that in order to play hockey you should know how to fight. . . . If what happens on the ice at NHL games happened on the street those involved would be arrested and charged."

I think Mr. Bettman is doing a pretty good job; he just

happens to be stuck between a rock and a hard place. I don't believe he wants hockey to be viewed as "mixed martial arts on ice," but he is employed by pugnacious old-boys owners who think violence and not the artistry of Sidney Crosby, the speed of Alexander Ovechkin, the laser-like snap shot of Phil Kessel or the goaltending prowess of Carey Price is the best way to sell tickets. Gary Bettman is too smart to fall into that trap. He wants a beautiful game, just like most of us.

Mr. Bettman wrote back on January 7, 2014, and pointed out that the league is implementing tough new rules to protect players, like suspending those who hit others in the head. He said fighting is on the decrease with the number of "fight-free" games at their highest level since 2007. "Cultural changes of this magnitude evolve over time, and we are seeing on a nightly basis concrete examples of this culture change taking effect," he said.

Is he snowing me or is he sincere? Being a person who always looks at the glass as half full, I like to think Mr. Bettman and the NHL head office want to cut down the violence in the game. The question is: Will the culture change quickly enough so that parents feel the game is safe for their children, particularly their sons?

That is why I advocate an immediate ban on fighting and tougher penalties for dirty play. For example, you slash Sidney Crosby, you get a two-minute penalty; you slash him a second time in the game, you get a five-minute major penalty; a third time and you're out of the game and suspended. Or, if you injure a player with intent, you're suspended until that player returns. It makes no sense that Todd Bertuzzi can pummel a player into the ice and end his career and still collect multi-million-dollar paycheques for years and years.

After playing and watching this great game of hockey for almost nine decades, I look forward to one day seeing the game return to its roots where skill, artistry and sportsmanship dominate instead of bullying, brutality and violence. You know what real hockey is? Real hockey is beating the player at the game, not beating up and knocking players out of the game. It's a wonderful sport when played that way.

CHAPTER 12

Sam

Imet Samuel Robert McCallion through the Anglican Young People's Association in 1945. Living in Toronto's west end, I was attending St. Michael and All Angels Church and Sam was at nearby Church of the Good Shepherd in Mount Dennis, a neighbourhood in the Borough of York, just on the western outskirts of Toronto at the time.

Our paths first crossed at the AYPA's West Toronto council and then later, and often, with the national council. We started out as colleagues and friends, both of us working on various committees of the organization.

To describe our early relationship as a "whirlwind romance" would be untrue. We were good friends with similar interests, not only our faith but also our work ethic. My mother taught me that hard work never killed anyone, and Sam's parents instilled the same thing in him. He and his two brothers and sister were raised in a working-class neighbourhood of Toronto during the Great Depression. The value of hard work and money was not lost on anyone in the McCallion family.

When I met Sam, I had a demanding job with long hours

at Canadian Kellogg so there wasn't much time for courting in the traditional sense. The AYPA and Kellogg consumed all my time. After about two years, I began to think of Sam as more than simply a friend and colleague at the AYPA. I was attracted to his quiet confidence, dignity and roll-up-your-sleeves attitude in getting things accomplished.

Sam claimed he was a little slower to acknowledge there was something more to our relationship than simple friendship. In fact, it took Sam almost four years from our first meeting to acknowledge there was a spark between us. By this time, I had risen to national president of the AYPA. This is what Sam said years later about our romance, in an article in *Today's Seniors*: "I was program director of the Canadian AYPA when Hazel was president and we spent two weeks at camp on Lake Couchiching. That's when I fell in love."

It was the summer of 1949 and I remember long talks in front of the crackling campfire. We talked about our future together. We talked about the AYPA. We talked about our jobs. We talked about all the things young people in love talk about. Of course, for the times, we weren't really that young. That summer, I was twenty-eight and Sam was twenty-five, and we wouldn't marry for another two years.

After serving my two-year term as AYPA national president, I married Sam on September 29, 1951.

Sam was a remarkable man, especially when you think of the times—when the male-dominated culture in North America predominantly thought a woman's place was in the home. He did not have a chauvinistic bone in his body. He knew I wanted a working career and he supported me every minute of every day. I loved that about him. He was a wonderful husband.

When I became mayor of Mississauga and more well known,

not only in the city but across the country and beyond, Sam never fretted about being overshadowed. He came to most events and was there to support me, not to share any limelight. "I married Hazel Journeaux," Sam would say. "I didn't marry the mayor of Mississauga. I have my own identity in the community."

And that he did. He once told the *Toronto Star* he never minded being teased as "Mr. Mayor" or "Prince Consort." "We got married because we were in love and wanted to spend life together," he said in a January 1979 article. "She is an individual and I am an individual. We melded two individuals together into a partnership. If I'd been chauvinistic and said a woman's place was in the home, we probably would have broken up years back."

Sam was a lot of things—a devoted husband, loving father, businessman, neighbour and friend—but one of the things he was most proud of was his community involvement, especially when it came to his beloved Streetsville. As our daughter, Linda, says, he had an undying love for his community.

For more than forty years, Sam was a lay reader and preacher at our church and he would travel to small country churches to preach when the congregations were without a minister. Often one or two of our young children would be in tow, trying to sit quietly in a pew, but often unsuccessfully. Sam would muddle through despite the distraction.

Sam was a founder and president of the Streetsville Chamber of Commerce and served as its volunteer president for five years. He was the founder of the Streetsville Bread and Honey Festival in 1973 and charter president for ten years. He gave thousands of hours to that festival over the years. Though he started it as a one-time wake or send-off party for Streetsville before its impending amalgamation with Mississauga in 1974, it has endured and grown. In the early years, Sam would take three weeks off work each year just to organize the Bread and Honey Festival.

His community work didn't stop there. Sam was a member of the Streetsville Rotary Club and the Probus Club of Streetsville. In 1988, Sam received the Rotarians' highest honour by being presented with the Paul Harris Fellowship Award. The year he died, Sam was named Mississauga's Volunteer of the Year.

And it wasn't just the big events and organizations in the community that appealed to Sam. He did so many little things, most of which went unnoticed by most people, sometimes even me until I heard about them later.

For example, Streetsville's long-time clothier, the late Eric Ladner, told a story about how in 1959 when he was twenty-six and a new father, he took a gamble and started his own business. Knowing the risks involved, Sam wanted to show his immediate support for the young entrepreneur. On the very first day the clothing store opened, Sam was the first customer in the door and the first to buy something.

"Sam gave of himself 100 per cent," Eric Ladner told the *Mississauga Booster* in its edition commemorating the publication's fortieth anniversary in 2004. "He was always ready to help and truly cared about people's welfare."

After the fact, I would also hear stories about how Sam did not charge customers for printing if money was really tight for them. Most would make good later, but that was Sam, always giving others a helping hand.

Sam died on May 14, 1997, and my dear friend Margaret Marland gave a beautiful eulogy at the funeral a few days later at Trinity Anglican Church in Streetsville. The church was packed with people from so many different parts of our lives, including Catholic Bishop Pease Lacey, whom Sam liked so much. Two words from that eulogy summed up Sam: *gentle man*.

He most certainly was a gentle man, as well as a gentleman. And that makes this part of Sam's story harder to tell: his battle with that insidious disease called Alzheimer's, which changed my beloved gentle man.

In the early 1990s, I started to notice little things like Sam getting forgetful, being a tad disoriented at times and not sleeping as well. When his signature changed, that got me really thinking. Still, I chalked it up to the aging process. Then one day in 1993, Sam was taking some newspaper advertisements up to local car dealer Laurie Williamson for the client's approval. He pulled his car up to the front of the dealership to park. Disoriented, Sam hit the gas instead of the brake and drove his car through the showroom window. No one was hurt, including Sam, thank God, but I knew this was more serious than simply aging. Medical professionals told us the news that he had the debilitating neurological disorder Alzheimer's disease, for which there is no known cause or cure. This was a body blow to everyone in the family.

After the car accident, they took Sam's driver's licence away and that was when we really began to see the Alzheimer's symptoms of irritability and anger. For a couple years, Sam continued working and our son Paul, who was working most closely with him at that time, kept a close eye on his father. (All the kids worked with Sam in the printing business and at the *Booster* at one time or another.)

By 1995, Sam's condition got so bad that he had to give up work. Nurses had been coming to the house for some time but

Sam's care was getting harder and harder for everyone. By this point, his personality was significantly different.

It's not worth going into details; suffice it to say that my "gentle man" was no more. He wasn't violent, as some Alzheimer's patients become, but he was belligerent and horribly stubborn—something he never was in all his life. He began to use foul language, which he had never done before. Indeed, when our son Peter was younger and using foul language in the house, Sam would sit him down and calmly give a lecture about how people with limited vocabularies used swear words, not members of his family. Now, sadly, I routinely heard Sam cuss like a sailor.

It is not easy for me to write these things about my dear husband. It feels like I am besmirching his memory, his legacy. But I feel a need to talk about Alzheimer's because so many families have to deal with it, just like we did. I hope families reading this will learn something or at least feel some comfort knowing they are not alone.

By the fall of 1996, some three and a half years after he drove through the showroom window, Sam simply could not remain at home. The doctors and medical people told us so. In November 1996, the family decided we had to put him in a nursing home built specifically to look after patients like Sam. Talk about a tough decision. Sam did not want to go and he told me so.

His last Christmas was very difficult. We brought Sam home for the day and he did not want to return to the nursing home after dinner. It was so hard taking him back and saying goodbye that Christmas night.

I'm not one who is overly emotional, but these were emotional days laced with feelings of guilt. Sam and I had been partners in everything for forty-five years and now I was going against his wishes. It felt like I was going against him at every turn. It was for his own safety and health, but knowing that didn't make it any easier.

In the nursing home, Sam brooded. I'd visit and try to be cheerful, but he'd say hurtful things and our visits would end badly. I know he didn't mean to be hurtful. But, as I said, his personality had changed, which is so often the case with Alzheimer's. After six months in the nursing home, Sam developed pneumonia and died at age seventy-three. He had suffered enough. And the Sam I had fallen in love with, the Sam who would give so much to his community and others, the Sam who was my most trusted advisor—that Sam had gone long before he took his last breath.

In Canada today, an estimated 750,000 Canadians are afflicted with Alzheimer's and related dementias, according to the Alzheimer Society of Canada. That number is astounding. It is equivalent to the entire population of Mississauga—every man, woman and child. Think about how many families and how many lives are affected by this menacing disease! And the number is expected to almost double to 1.4 million Canadians by 2031.

Until it happened to Sam, I never really gave Alzheimer's much thought. I sure do now and it is one of my favourite charities to help. The disease affects so many lives and we've got to find a cure or figure out ways to mitigate its devastation. I am delighted that right here in Mississauga there's a life sciences company called Amorfix Life Sciences Ltd. doing exceptional work on Alzheimer's research. And I am proud that the Alzheimer Society in Peel has a daycare centre in Port Credit named for Sam, where loved ones can go in safety while allowing caregivers needed breaks. (After Sam's death, dear friends donated more than $45,000 and this money all went to the Sam McCallion Day Centre.)

The Alzheimer Society says that family caregivers spend 444 million unpaid hours a year looking after loved ones with dementia, representing $11 billion in lost income. And the combined direct (medical) and indirect (lost earnings) cost of the disease is $33 billion a year in Canada.

If you or someone you love is showing signs of dementia, see the proper medical professionals, read about the disease and visit the Alzheimer Society website, which is an incredible resource for learning and coping. There are so many useful tips on the website for family members. Things like:

- *Talk and share the pain. Go beyond your family and talk to a person such as a counsellor or trusted friend or join an Alzheimer Society support group.*
- *Keep a journal and use it to express your personal feelings of guilt, anger and anything else.*
- *Don't forget about yourself. If you spend a lot of time with the person with dementia, take planned and regular breaks and stay in touch with the outside world.*
- *Tread carefully before making decisions. Thoroughly explore all options before making major steps.*
- *And, finally, know that tears can be therapeutic. Let them cleanse and relieve the pain inside.*

I'm no expert, but I did live through it and I feel for every family that is living through it. As for tears, I do not show my emotions openly, but I will admit to tears helping me.

After Sam's death, I was so busy and consumed with work. Maybe I intentionally tried to be more busy than usual. I really think being busy after losing a loved one helps with the grieving process. It's not that you don't have time to grieve and think about your loss, but your mind is occupied with other things, too, and I think that it is healthy to know that life must continue.

CHAPTER 13

Sprawl

During a wicked storm in June 1796, Upper Canada's first lieutenant-governor, John Graves Simcoe, and his wife, Elizabeth, were forced to take shelter at the mouth of the Credit River, in what is now the Port Credit community of Mississauga.

Incredibly, they were returning on their own by canoe from Niagara for government business in York, now known as Toronto. He must have been my kind of politician, travelling on his own without all the government trappings of the day. I have long been offered a taxpayer-funded chauffeur to drive me around, but I prefer driving my hybrid-electric car on my own.

Anyway, after the storm subsided late in the afternoon, the lieutenant-governor looked around and thought this would be a perfect place to build an inn for weary travellers on their way to and from government business in York. And so was built Government House Inn, just east of the river near what is now Lakeshore Road. The Upper Canada government leased it to innkeepers who ran it for almost forty years before the wood structure was demolished. It was also the site of the historic meeting in 1805 where chiefs of the Mississaugas agreed to sell the southern portions of their territory.

Soon after the land purchase by the British, United Empire Loyalist Mrs. Sara Grant became the township's first official landowner when she was granted 200 acres (81 ha) in the area of what would become Dixie and Dundas streets. She immediately sold the land for five hundred dollars, according to Roger Riendeau and Marian Gibson in the book *Mississauga: The First 10,000 Years*.

And so began the great urban sprawl of Mississauga. I am being a little facetious to make a point: buying, selling, investing and developing land is not a new phenomenon. (Interestingly, had Mrs. Grant held that land for her ancestors, today it would be worth about $300 million. Quite a nice nest egg.)

For thirty years, I've taken a lot of heat over the issue of urban sprawl. First, I was dubbed the "Queen of Sprawl" by the media, who also called Mississauga things like "the poster child for unbridled urban growth." Then I was called an evangelical convert to smart urban growth—but not until most of the farmland in Mississauga had been developed.

After decades in the political arena going back to my planning board days in Streetsville, I can take the heat. And I'm not going to deny things that we can plainly see: there are thousands upon thousands of single-family homes today sitting in lovely neighbourhoods that were farmland not long ago; indeed, only back as far as the last time my Toronto Maple Leafs won the Stanley Cup. Okay, I can see snickering fans of other NHL teams thinking that's a long, long time ago. In some respects it is. In terms of building a city from what was basically a collection of towns, villages and farmland, it's not that long ago.

Take Erin Mills, Canada's biggest planned community and home to more than one hundred thousand people. When Maple Leaf captain George Armstrong hoisted the Stanley Cup on May 2, 1967, Erin Mills consisted of engineering and architectural plans hanging on the drawing boards of E.P. Taylor's Cadillac Fairview Corporation. Back then, the future Erin Mills was just farmers' fields with no infrastructure like sewers, water pipes or roads.

Over the next twenty-five years or so, Cadillac Fairview and its Erin Mills Development Corporation, which developer Marco Muzzo bought in the early 1980s, turned this giant piece of land into the community it is today. Others did the same all around Mississauga.

Call it sprawl, if you like. Or call it planned communities based on what families wanted: affordable housing close to Toronto with two-car garages, all the amenities and terrific schools and nearby recreational facilities. Either way, there's more to the urban sprawl story than meets the eye.

Plenty of things aren't talked about often enough when the subject of urban sprawl comes up. First, every municipality starts out as urban sprawl, even Toronto. Especially Toronto. Don Mills, Rosedale and Forest Hill are all neighbourhoods of single-family homes, with few apartments, and they are all examples of urban sprawl. In fact, Don Mills was Canada's first planned community and, like Erin Mills, it was developed by E.P. Taylor.

It's just that things boomed and happened so quickly in Mississauga, whereas it took twice as long for all the land to be developed in Toronto after the urban sprawl movement began. If you want to get a sense of what Toronto looked like before urban sprawl, watch an episode of CBC's *Murdoch*

Mysteries television series, which is set in the late nineteenth and early twentieth centuries.

Second, sprawl was created by market demand, not municipal politicians, or any politicians for that matter. People wanted comfortable single-family homes with all the latest amenities like central air conditioning, walk-in closets and en suite bathrooms. We call this low-density housing, as opposed to high-density apartments and condominiums. Developers are not going to build things that people don't want to buy. During the 1980s and '90s in particular, people wanted to leave apartments and small bungalows in Toronto and move out to Mississauga and get value for their housing dollars. Today, more and more people want to buy and live in condominiums so we're seeing many built in Mississauga's downtown core and around our waterfront. But it wasn't that way in the 1980s, 1990s and early 2000s when the urban sprawl movement rolled through Mississauga.

Lastly, there is a public misconception that municipalities have the power to stop development. We don't. We're simply part of the process. It's the provinces through their various planning acts that control development.

Municipal leaders can throw up roadblocks, and we have at times, but ultimately it's up to the province and, where I live, its appointed members of the Ontario Municipal Board. That's because when local councils rule against something, developers often appeal to the OMB. Every time an appeal happens, it costs local ratepayers money for their municipality to defend its actions.

I've even seen many examples where developers actually use the threat of the OMB as a negotiating tactic when they come before the city if they think they can get more concessions from the board than from us. Ontario is the only province in Canada that has an appointed body that can so easily over-rule locally elected municipal officials. It's ridiculous.

Now, I'm not saying we turned down developers over and over in a bid to stop urban sprawl, because we didn't. If we had, all the appeals to the OMB would've bankrupted the city, and, as I said, people wanted beautiful single-family homes and we wanted to build a great city. The point is that suburban cities (I dislike *suburban* as it implies we're less than Toronto) and politicians take the heat for urban sprawl when there were all sorts of other variables involved, too.

Quite frankly, the unelected OMB simply has too much power and yet it seems to get off scot-free in the court of public opinion when it comes to urban sprawl. Councillor Pat Mullin said it best after drafting a motion that council passed urging the government to disband the OMB after yet another example of the panel going against the wishes of the locally elected representatives of the people. (This particular case was from 2011, after the agency overruled council's decision to stop a 280-megawatt gas power plant from being built near the lake in south Mississauga. But there have been so many other examples of the OMB sticking its nose into local business, especially when related to urban sprawl.)

Members of the OMB "are not elected, they're not account-able, and as far as I'm concerned, we are; the buck stops here," Pat Mullin said while introducing the council motion. "We are in our community, we know our community, and while we may not always support the community in terms of an application, they have the opportunity to get rid of us in the next election. In my view, it's time to take back the planning."

Ironically, the power plant never did get built because there was such an uproar that the provincial government was worried about losing seats over it; so it cancelled the plant for political reasons before an election and during construction, costing tax-payers more than a billion dollars.

It's the same thing that happened with urban sprawl. The provincial government and its unelected OMB members pushed for development and played a large role in urban sprawl. But it's the local politicians like me who wear the issue as the "Queen of Sprawl."

In the late 1990s, a notion came to me as I looked around at our gridlocked roads and highways in the Greater Toronto Area: we've got to grow differently. It wasn't just that Mississauga's land was getting close to being filled, it was also that our housing density was too low to support an efficient public transit system. I set up an eighteen-member volunteer Citizens' Task Force on the Future of Mississauga to look for solutions to urban sprawl, traffic gridlock, waste management and other pressing issues not just for our city, but for the entire GTA in which we reside.

One of the recommendations in its final report in May 2002, called *Securing Our Future*, was to dispense with regional government, something I've advocated since before I was mayor as a way of saving millions of dollars a year by eliminating the duplication of services between regional and city governments.

That extra tier of regional government is an expensive luxury that big cities like Mississauga and Brampton don't need. Way back in 2004, an accountant's study for the city and region found Mississauga would save $31.8 million a year by becoming a single-tier government. How much would we save today—$50 million, maybe $60 million every year? That money could be used to buy new buses, fix roads and a whole lot more.

In its report, the Citizens' Task Force also called for a "GTA-wide Coordinating Body and ensure that it is given the tools and resources necessary to perform meaningful, effective, and assertive planning and coordination."

This task force was effectively ignored by the provincial government, but some of its early progressive ideas found their way into the public debates, from linking public transit systems across the GTA to stable funding paths from upper-tier governments to support infrastructure upgrades and maintenance at the local level.

Also in 2002, the provincial government called on me to chair a new Central Ontario Smart Growth Panel to look at urban sprawl in the Golden Horseshoe area of Ontario from Peterborough to Kitchener-Waterloo, and Niagara to Barrie. This panel was made up of quite a disparate group of folks: politicians, bureaucrats, academics, environmentalists and developers. At some meetings it was like herding cats, as it seemed we'd travel on tangents of individual interests and agendas.

Critics thought, at best, it was a waste of time or, at worst, a smokescreen set up by a tired Conservative government on its last legs with a looming election. A *Toronto Star* columnist said I was looking like a "stooge" for then-premier Mike Harris. I've been called a lot of things over the years, but that was a first for me being accused of acting like a lapdog. (The *Star* had a very different take on me on the gridlock issue a little later, as you'll read.)

Within a year, in April 2003, we presented the government with a final report. Nobody on the panel got everything he or she wanted, but I was proud of the work we did. We concluded smart growth for Ontario must centre on four priorities: balanced growth; public transit priority, especially when it comes

to integrating all the public systems around the GTA; environ-
mental protection; and a more collaborative and innovative
approach to waste management.

There was a provincial election later that year and, as
expected, a new government was elected. I was delighted
when the new government used our report as the bedrock for
its plan to develop a green belt in the Golden Horseshoe area
and a new planning policy called "Places to Grow" that has
tried to slow down urban sprawl and improve public transit in
the entire region.

"The focus of the Places to Grow plan is the creation of
complete communities, with a greater mix of businesses, services, housing and parks that will make them more livable," the
provincial government said in announcing the new plan. As
I read that, I couldn't help but think: That's how we've been
building Mississauga since day one; moving from a bedroom
community into a strong economic base of its own where more
people come to work and live.

The government also set up what would be called Metrolinx,
the first step in integrating the area's various public transit
systems, and I served on its board for several years. Full inte-
gration of GTA transit systems is still in the future but we are
seeing links in fares and other moves in the right direction.

My biggest *mea culpa* has to be public transit. One of the
things Mississauga did not do well was transportation. And no
fast-growing municipality that I know of did do it well. We simply didn't think about it enough and plan for it from the earli-
est stages of building Mississauga. The city and the citizens have
resisted high density for years and that was one of the toughest
impediments. It doesn't make sense for empty buses to be driving
through meandering neighbourhoods of single-family homes.

High density remains contentious. If you ever want to fill the seats in the council chambers, just have a discussion about a proposed high-rise building. But things are slowly changing as we build up, instead of out, in Mississauga. A little-known fact is that after Toronto, Mississauga has the highest density in the GTA. We're building density in the right locations, like the city core and along the corridors, or hubs, as we call them. About forty thousand people reside in Mississauga's city core in 2014 and that is expected to double within fifteen years.

We're starting to get the density needed to support public transit in a big way, which encourages more people out of their cars. As it stands, Mississauga has the third-largest municipal transit system in Ontario with more than 50 million riders per year. MiWay (the Mississauga transit system's brand name) connects to transit systems in Toronto, Brampton and Oakville and all GO Transit (short for Government of Ontario transit) stations in Mississauga. Our fleet of buses is one of the most energy-efficient, too.

In the late 1990s, we also started to set aside land for dedicated bus lanes along the Highway 403 corridor. We finally began construction of a bus rapid transit line (BRT) in 2010 that stretches eleven miles (18 km) with twelve station stops east-west through Mississauga from Oakville to Toronto's subway system. It was just so difficult getting all the necessary government people to fund the $259-million project. As the *Mississauga News* quoted me saying at the groundbreaking ceremony in November 2010: "I ought to tell you it's been 12 years in the making. It's hard to believe it took us up to 2008 to get the federal and provincial governments on board to help finance it. And this is just the beginning of our effort to put public transit on the road in a big, big way in Mississauga."

The other big transit project is an LRT (light rail transit) line up our main north-south road (Hurontario Street) from Lake Ontario to Brampton. It will be connected at the city core to dedicated bus lanes encircling the area, and every rapid transit station will be within a five-minute walk from anywhere in the downtown. Construction has been pushed back as we await funding guarantees from upper governments, but we're hopeful it can begin in 2015.

So, we're making strides. We're doing our darndest to make Mississauga a transit-oriented city. But we're playing catch-up. If we'd planned our neighbourhoods a little differently, if the upper governments would commit ongoing funds to transit instead of on a project-by-project basis, if we'd thought more about public transit, we would be in better shape now.

Still, our BRT system is an example of what can be achieved when we put our funding together to move our transit plans forward for the people of Mississauga. It's the key to our city's future and that of the GTA.

We're also building bicycle lanes around the city. I even rode the four and a half miles (7 km) from home to my office one day when I was eighty-seven as a gesture to show our support for living "greener" and becoming a more sustainable city.

One lesson that other fast-growing municipalities across North America can learn from Mississauga is that transportation, both public transit and roads and highways, should be a real and basic condition of any development, whether it's fifty homes, five thousand homes or ten thousand square metres of industrial space. You have to be able to move people and goods to keep the economy moving and competitive. It's not that we didn't think about roads, but we didn't think enough about future traffic patterns and loads on the roads. We certainly didn't think enough about public transit and moving the maximum number of people in the most efficient and environmentally friendly way possible.

I look around our province and elsewhere, and I see where public transit and roads still aren't a basic condition of development. This has got to change, and if our smart growth panel taught us anything, it's that local, provincial and federal governments have to work together. We've got to stop the squabbling and the turf wars. We must strive jointly to meet the genuine needs of the people if we want to ease the gridlock, the stress of sitting in traffic and the inability to move people and goods efficiently around the GTA.

And it's going to cost money, *lots* of money. I've been saying this for more than a decade and I was delighted that the *Toronto Star* came around to my way of thinking in a June 2012 editorial after I said we've got to raise taxes to ease the gridlock that is choking our roads and our local economy in Southern Ontario. "Mississauga Mayor Hazel McCallion didn't become one of Canada's longest-serving and most popular municipal leaders by being a tax-and-spend squanderer of public funds," the editorial begins. "So when she says a crisis looms and we'll have to reach into our wallets to deal with it, people should pay attention."

The *Star* goes on to say that with 1 million more cars expected on GTA roads by 2030, we need to find $50 billion through taxes, tolls or parking levies to enhance public transit systems and improve the network of roads.

"McCallion deserves praise for boldly saying what the public needs to hear—we'll all have to pay more, and soon, to avoid intolerable gridlock. It would help if politicians at every level of government quit wallowing in denial and admitted the fundamental truth," said Canada's largest newspaper.

CHAPTER 14

City Power

Taxes are a topic on which everyone holds an opinion. Nobody likes to pay more taxes. I know I sure don't like to, but taxes are essential and rising taxes are inevitable if we're going to solve today's greatest urban issues such as traffic gridlock, aging infrastructure and affordable housing.

In none of my twelve election victories did I ever promise to cut taxes, but I always promised to deliver value for the taxes my constituents pay.

In fact, I did cut taxes in 1993 by a small amount, and it made news headlines across Canada and the United States, and even got me on American TV networks again. (My first appearances on U.S. networks were during the train derailment crisis and I have been featured many times over the years for watching out for taxpayers' money and stories about how senior citizens can still make a big contribution to society.)

But, looking back, it was a mistake to reduce taxes that one year. Instead of cutting taxes, we should have put the extra money into reserves and saved it for future use. It wasn't a lot of money, either way, but it was the wrong signal to send that we were tax-cutters. Sure, tax-cutting platforms would soon become vogue for federal and provincial politicians and propel some to election victories, but my job has always been to deliver value to taxpayers, not cut taxes.

And my record speaks for itself. In 1991, Mississauga was the first municipal government to publish an annual report on its revenue and spending so residents could examine, scrutinize and offer input on where their hard-earned money was being spent and why. We still do this, as do many other municipalities. We've won numerous awards for our transparency in financial reporting and we welcome public comment at council on each annual report.

Mississauga maintains an "AAA credit rating" from Standard & Poor's and has been debt-free almost as long as I have been mayor. In 2013, we borrowed $30 million to replace all the fluorescent street lamps with high-efficiency LED lights that not only save us on energy but illuminate streets much better. The generated energy savings will pay for the 49,000 new lights' capital cost within ten years.

For a decade, from 1992 to 2002, Mississauga residents faced zero tax increases year after year, including that 1 per cent tax cut in 1993. Later on, during years of tax increases in the 3 to 5 per cent range, I was criticized for not raising taxes during that earlier period. But we were accumulating surpluses of $15 to $20 million a year, thanks to the booming construction in the city. We were ploughing those surpluses into reserves and saving the money for rainy days. It just wouldn't have made sense to increase taxes in those days. (Indeed, some residents asked us to cut taxes, but I wasn't about to let that happen.)

Hindsight is 20/20, and critics who look through a lens of revisionist history are probably correct: from a long-term point of view, we probably should not have frozen taxes for a decade but should have increased them incrementally. But from a practical, political point of view, it didn't make sense raising taxes while we enjoyed annual budget surpluses.

How could I advocate raising taxes when citizens could freely see our surplus budgets? I treat taxpayers' money like my own. The voters knew that and they would have had trouble paying higher taxes when we were racking up such big surpluses and watching our spending.

Our sound financial performance and our development levies were sometimes a double-edged sword, especially when dealing with upper-tier governments at the province and in Ottawa. The new provincial legislation empowering us to charge the lot levies in 1991 made it more difficult for developers to challenge us in the courts, but it also created a formula that was complicated. It actually reduced the amount of money we could charge in Mississauga. And then when Mike Harris and his "Common Sense Revolution" rolled into power in 1995, his government yielded to developers and amended the Development Charges Act, reducing further what municipalities could get in lot levies. Harris's minister of municipal affairs, Al Leach, argued at one point that since Mississauga had $250 million in development fees in reserves, it proved we were charging too much and we were creating gold-plated edifices on the backs of developers and first-time home buyers. One of their mouthpieces even accused Mississauga of paying for the entire Civic Centre with development fees, which was not true.

No, we shot back, the unspent fees were in reserves because we wanted to spend wisely, unlike upper-tier governments, and save the money for rainy days or public transit and other public projects like community centres and recreational facilities.

Besides, I argued, in the days of the late 1980s and '90s, we were earning 15 to 18 per cent interest so the reserves grew rather quickly through investment returns, not simply from charges to developers.

These proposed changes from Harris and Leach in Bill 98 really got under my skin. Mississauga Council immediately put a temporary freeze on development to show our displeasure after Leach introduced the proposals in late 1996. As chair of the Greater Toronto Area Mayors' Committee, I headed down to the legislature with Oakville Mayor Ann Mulvale to testify at a committee hearing about the proposed changes. Here's what I said on March 24, 1997, to that committee: "What this legislation does is remove one of our existing sources of revenue. We cannot work with reduced revenues from the province and at the same time be expected to pass the cost of new development on to our existing taxpayers. We need every cent we can get our hands on just to pay the cost of keeping the existing infrastructure in place. Siphoning off these much-needed dollars to pay for the new development just doesn't make common sense."

In the end, Mike Harris and Al Leach made some changes and today municipalities can't charge as much for the capital costs of "soft services" like community centres and libraries as for "hard services" like roads and sewers. I hesitate to say "minor changes" because any changes to reduce development fees, in my opinion, were not warranted. We fought hard and had to take some water in our wine, but it could have been worse.

It was one of many examples of the "Common Sense Revolution" being little more than a cunning strategy to download responsibilities onto municipalities while pretending to get the provincial government's spending under control. It was a trend started in Ottawa and refined by Mike Harris's crew. Other provincial governments have also found it a useful political strategy to download onto municipalities.

But long term, this shirking of responsibility by federal and provincial governments is dangerous to the entire country. The property tax was brought into being to service property, not humans. It was intended for community centres, fire halls, parks, libraries and such. But the property tax bill today includes many provincial responsibilities such as education, public health and social service costs that municipalities should not be paying.

Upper-tier governments pretend to be getting their financial houses in order, but it is really a house of cards. For example, the Common Sense Revolution didn't rein in spending. After they were defeated, former provincial auditor-general Erik Peters found the Tories left office with a deficit of $5.6 billion. I am not playing political games here and picking sides. Lord knows, from 2003 to 2013 Dalton McGuinty's Liberals didn't run a tight financial ship either, and they wasted millions, if not billions, of taxpayers' dollars.

My point is that too many provincial and federal governments have been playing fast and loose with the public's money the past several decades and something has to be done. And this culture of "government downloading" has got to stop. It is ridiculous and unfair.

I have been banging this drum for years. Here's something else I told that committee on March 24, 1997, at the Ontario Legislature: "I want to say that local government in this province and in the country has a much better record financially than either the provincial or the federal governments, and I think we should say that. Sometimes people don't really appreciate that our record is much better than the provinces, and I'm speaking of all provinces, and the federal government. We think a lot already before we do things. I think we're noted for it."

Again, I am not picking on anyone or any party in particular. People used to urge me to run in provincial or federal elections, but I never did. Party politics would be very difficult for me to play. If I believe in something, I would never vote against it just because the party whip said so. If I had run provincially or federally, I would either have quit party politics really quickly or worn out the carpet crossing the floor of the House. My independence and integrity are too important to me to compromise.

Downloading costs onto municipalities—including child care, transit, housing and public health—has led to higher property taxes and an infrastructure deficit across the province. So many municipalities simply couldn't cope initially and were forced to make drastic cuts. In the short term during the Harris years, we were okay in Mississauga because of the reserves we'd built up. We kept property taxes in check during the first decade of downloading, but we knew it was unsustainable.

In Mississauga alone, we have an "infrastructure funding gap" of almost $100 million a year. What this means is that as infrastructure ages and deteriorates, money has to be spent to repair and replace. It's like your home. If you need a new roof but wait year after year before putting on a new roof, eventually it will leak and cause damage. So, not only does the roof cost more to replace, but you could have higher repair costs for damaged walls or windows.

It's the same principle with the infrastructure funding gap. Upper governments aren't giving municipalities enough of the tax dollars for infrastructure and are also asking us to pay for services that those governments should be footing the bill on. So, like you deferring on fixing your roof, municipalities are deferring infrastructure improvements as long as possible.

Numbers don't lie, but too many tossed around can bore so I have to be careful. Still, some numbers just have to be mentioned. Today, municipalities simply do not get their fair share of the tax pool, according to Statistics Canada and the Fraser Institute.

For example, Ontario municipalities receive only eleven cents of every tax dollar raised in Ontario, yet we own 65 per cent of the capital infrastructure. The provincial and federal governments receive thirty-four cents and fifty-five cents and own 32 per cent and 3.2 per cent of the capital infrastructure, respectively. This is a recipe for disaster.

I recognize the provincial and federal governments have other responsibilities such as health care, education, defence and equalization payments. But all the various parties talk about spending wisely, and none do. The waste is staggering, from billions of dollars on used helicopters and submarines to the Ontario government cancelling construction of power plants in Mississauga and Oakville that never should have been started. Don't even get me started on the Senate, the "House of Entitlement" in Ottawa for defeated politicians and their friends.

The wanton disregard for taxpayers' money drives me crazy. And yet election after election, taxpayers allow Conservatives, Liberals and New Democrat politicians in Ottawa and all the provinces to buy their votes with *their* money.

And then voters look around in their own town or city and see roads, playgrounds, swimming pools and other infrastructure all decaying. These same taxpayers turn a blind eye when their provincial and federal governments squeeze finances and download responsibilities onto their municipality. Why? I don't understand why there hasn't been an uprising from coast to coast by ordinary Canadians.

Sure, federal and provincial governments toss municipalities a bone from time to time—like Paul Martin's Liberals sharing the gasoline tax or Stephen Harper's Conservatives channelling temporary money during the recession of 2009–10 for municipal infrastructure—but municipalities need more control and sustainable funding beyond the property tax base. We're now asked to provide services well beyond what the property tax was set up to achieve. The federal government needs to provide permanent infrastructure funding to assist cities, not simply piecemeal plans.

Cities are the economic engine of this country and our concerns are critical to the nation's success. How can we compete against other countries where large capital infrastructure projects to help move people and goods efficiently are funded by their national governments and ours aren't?

Equally important is the issue of housing. Affordable housing is quickly moving out of reach for a large number of Canadians. Where I live has one of the longest wait lists for subsidized housing in the country. For years, we've been asking the federal government to adopt and implement a national housing strategy to alleviate the problem.

Early in 2014, I was at an opening of an affordable housing building in Mississauga and the federal and provincial ministers in attendance went on and on about the great co-operation between the three levels of government. They were taken aback when I got to the microphone and talked about downloading and how property tax was never intended to be paying for such things as social housing. These are important issues and they won't get solved without some bold and creative thinking from the upper governments.

For example, in my province of Ontario, municipalities do not have the power to charge a hotel room tax. Sure, we can ask for it, but we don't have the legislative authority from the province to enforce it. Hotels just opt out of any municipal tax for their customer. Have you ever looked at your final bill and the taxes on it when you've stayed at an American hotel? I have and I simply can't believe how much each municipality gets from every visitor. Why aren't we doing the same here in Canada to help municipalities?

Municipalities also require more of the tax money collected at gas pumps. It's our cities and towns that are choked with gridlock and ever-higher levels of pollution. Between 2005 and 2013, Ontario municipalities received $3.2 billion from the Gas Tax Fund, according to the Association of Municipalities of Ontario. That may seem like a lot of money but it is divided between 443 Ontario municipalities over eight years.

Transit and road transportation are the largest infrastructure needs across Ontario. It is imperative that we move people and goods. Over the last decade, there have been some important strides in concert with the federal and provincial governments. But municipalities need long-term and predictable funding for these infrastructure programs. The property tax bill, along with one-time grants from upper-tier governments, cannot support the building and operating of public transit.

I was delighted in April 2014 to see Ontario Premier Kathleen Wynne announce bold new transit initiatives. But the proof of the pudding will be in the eating. We'll have to see if she follows through with these plans after winning a majority government in June 2014.

There's an old saying, "Fool me once, shame on you, fool me twice, shame on me." Municipalities have seen what happens when federal or provincial policies change and the impact on our municipalities—in the areas of water quality and quantity, public transportation infrastructure, housing options for vulnerable people or potential loss of housing funds.

The other thing that drives me crazy about the upper-tier governments is that they don't reward well-managed municipalities. We've run a very tight ship in Mississauga for years, but never did we get a bonus from the province or the federal government. Bonuses work well in the private sector as an incentive to increase productivity and eliminate waste, but God forbid such a notion be embraced in Ottawa or at Queen's Park.

We've heard things like "There's only so much money to go around and we have to spread it evenly" or "Hazel, you don't need any more because Mississauga is in great shape but such-and-such a place needs the money more." Usually other municipal governments need it more because they haven't been watching expenditures closely enough and they run into financial troubles. In other words, if you do a poor job, the federal and provincial governments will reward you with a bailout, but if you do a good job you're rewarded with a pat on the head but no financial incentive.

I got into quite a row with Toronto Mayor Mel Lastman on this issue back in 2003. Toronto, besides being a suburb to Mississauga and supplying our businesses with so many talented employees, as I like to tease, is incredibly important to the overall economic health of every municipality around it.

Toronto must exert fiscal responsibility and when it doesn't, it creates negative news. This makes upper-tier governments question whether to give municipalities more autonomy and makes businesses question whether to locate or expand anywhere in the region. Such was the case in 2003 when millions of Toronto taxpayers' dollars were wasted on a computer-leasing scandal and questions were swirling about monkey business involved in the redevelopment plans for Union Station, the public transportation hub for Toronto and the entire region. It was embarrassing picking up the morning newspapers and reading something new about mismanagement in Toronto.

About a week after getting out of hospital after that pickup truck hit me, I had a breakfast speech scheduled at the Toronto Board of Trade. Since Toronto is so important to the region (and when it sneezes the other municipalities catch a cold), I felt a need to say something, and right in Mel's backyard. I urged my neighbour to get its fiscal ship in better order. "We've got to build confidence that we can run our municipalities efficiently," I said. "It's time municipalities like Toronto started to run like a business."

Mel was none too pleased. He said all the fiscal problems in Toronto were related to downloading. "Maybe the truck hit her harder than I thought," Mel quipped when reporters asked what he thought of my speech. Mel's quite a jokester (and I even made headlines for calling him that) but it was wrong to try to use downloading as the excuse here. Yes, downloading was and is a real problem, but it clearly wasn't the reason for all of Toronto's financial ills at the time.

I'll give this to Mel for his downloading cries: the province did cough up $64 million to Toronto to help with that year's budget. The money came under the guise of transit help, but if Toronto had been watching its nickels and dimes more closely, it would not have needed so many dollars from Queen's Park.

And Mel's boy-who-cried-wolf howls set us back in our arguments for more municipal autonomy by giving the province
a perfect example of a city not running a tight fiscal ship and
needing a bailout.

What do you think would happen if well-managed cities
like Mississauga were given a little extra money from Ottawa
or the province because they did a good job? Yes, a bonus for
doing a good job. And maybe that extra money would go to
things like high-efficiency street lighting or retrofitting municipal buildings with the highest-efficiency energy-saving tools to
save even more money.

Guess what? The less efficient municipalities would take
notice and they would keep an eye on their budgets more
closely because they'd want some of that extra money, too.
And if they didn't, the taxpayers in their community would
take notice and vote in politicians who could save them money.

It's a culture thing. Things wouldn't change overnight, but
I guarantee things would change if councils were rewarded for
watching taxpayers' money more closely, instead of the feds
and provinces doling out money based on simply getting votes
and signalling that inefficiency is okay. I have always believed
there should be rewards for cities, towns and all governments
that don't blow taxpayers' money.

And it's simply high time for municipalities, especially large
municipalities in Canada like Mississauga, to be given more
autonomy. We need a better deal. Our annual city budget in
Mississauga hovers around $750 million and our infrastructure
is valued at $8 billion. This city is home to many cultures and
faiths, with more than seventy languages spoken among our
750,000 residents, and we deliver far more services affecting
their daily lives than any other level of government.

It's time for upper-level governments—and for voters—to acknowledge that for too long provinces have treated municipalities like their children, not their partners in delivering necessary services to Canadians. The status quo is not sustainable. Getting a better deal for all municipalities is an area I plan to work on after retiring as mayor of Mississauga because it is something that is long overdue.

It is my dream to see municipal powers and responsibilities added to the Canadian Constitution, which unfortunately is a document confined to federal and provincial powers. Local government is simply not a "full level" of government without such a bold move. Is it likely to happen anytime soon? No, probably not. But I would sure like Canadians to start talking about the idea.

CHAPTER 15

Eye of the Hurricane

The year 2005 was one of the best I could remember in a long, long time, so how could I know a hurricane was forming that would batter me politically in the not-too-distant future?

I desperately missed Sam, and always will, but my health was terrific, council was working well together to ensure the city continued growing comfortably, our trade missions to Asia and Europe were reaping investment and jobs for Mississauga, and the public was ready to talk seriously about smart-growth issues and the impending gridlock crisis on Greater Toronto Area roads.

There were still challenges, of course. We had to continue raising property taxes each year, especially with the added strain on the city's budget from downloading by the provincial and federal governments. Our reserves remained around $600 million, below our peak of $800 million, but we continued to be debt-free, as we had been since shortly after my first election as mayor in 1978.

On a personal note, I would receive honours around this time that I never could've dreamt of while growing up in the Gaspé, not least of which was the Order of Canada.

I'll never forget that day in the summer of 2005 when between meetings I dashed home to pick up a few things and let out Hurricane, the gorgeous German shepherd I owned back then. By pure chance, the mailwoman happened to arrive with a letter while I was there. I signed for the letter and opened it. To my complete surprise, it told me I had been awarded the Order of Canada. I had no idea my name had been put forward and, quite frankly, I didn't think anybody in an elected position could receive the Order of Canada. I figured you had to be retired from public life before you could get it.

What an honour! Of course, the tough part was keeping quiet about it for a couple weeks until the official announcement of all the recipients that year was made public by Governor General Michaëlle Jean. How I wished Sam were there when the letter arrived. I would've shared the news with him with no fear of it getting out before the official notice. Hurricane may have been my favourite dog of all time, but it just wasn't the same sharing this news with her!

And the funny thing was that my friend Dorothy Jamieson, ninety-six, is the one who nominated me, but I didn't know it at the time. Had I known that day, I would have immediately picked up the phone and given her a call. It's just like her to do something marvellous for someone else and not say anything or look for accolades.

Dorothy is a fascinating person. She was born in Britain and served as a sergeant and systems operator in Fighter Command for the Royal Air Force during World War II. She was a war bride who married Canadian pilot Ronald Jamieson, and they settled in Mississauga in 1945 after the Allied victory. Her nephew is CBC's Peter Mansbridge.

One of my favorite Dorothy stories is about when Prime Minister Winston Churchill came to the Fighter Command bunker in Lincolnshire, where she was in charge of the facility's day-to-day operations. An officious pilot introduced her to Churchill and then dismissed her, saying he would take over the tour for the prime minister. Churchill immediately responded: "Excuse me, Squadron Leader, you are dismissed. The sergeant will give me the tour."

Dorothy has done so many wonderful things for our community and she is an inspiration. She was the first female commodore of the Mississauga Canoe Club and the first female Olympic judge in the sport of canoeing at the 1976 Olympic Games in Montreal. She's left a legacy and she's a role model with her determined can-do attitude in everything she has undertaken in life.

I travelled to Ottawa in November for the formal Order of Canada ceremony and, I have to admit, I was a little nervous. I'd been in the public eye for years and met numerous prime ministers, premiers and governors general, not to mention the Queen and the Pope, but for some reason hearing my name and listening to the description of my career gave me butterflies. It's difficult to explain why, but it's kind of like an accomplished golfer standing on the first tee at the Old Course in St. Andrews for the very first time. Every single golfer who has told me about that experience has said they were nervous and couldn't really explain why. Same with me at Rideau Hall.

The official program called me "a visionary leader" and went on to say, "Hazel McCallion, whose tireless optimism has earned her the nickname 'Hurricane Hazel,' has cultivated a reputation for her skill at governing, shown by Mississauga's dynamic evolution into one of Canada's most successful cities. . . . Encompassing qualities quintessential to a true role model, it has been said that no politician in Canada is so closely associated with his or her community; Hazel *is* Mississauga."

Of all the honours bestowed upon me—from libraries, schools and hospitals taking my name (not to mention a wine and a rose variety) to the governments of Germany and Japan awarding me their highest civilian honours for strengthening ties between our countries, to Hazel McCallion bobblehead dolls and my picture on the front of the box of a Monopoly game using Mississauga streets—none is more important or prestigious than the Order of Canada.

There was also another surprise in that calm-before-the-storm year of 2005. Out of thousands of mayors, I was runner-up in the World Mayor competition. In a contest run by the City Mayors Foundation, an international think tank on urban affairs, people from around the world voted online for their favourite mayors. The winner was declared based on votes and the quality and conviction of supporting statements.

Dora Bakoyannis, mayor of Athens, beat me out, but I was thrilled nonetheless, especially when I read some of the online comments from supporters: "Mayor Hazel cares deeply about Mississauga. . . . Madam Mayor doesn't have wrinkles, they are pockets of knowledge!"; "She is tough, yet resilient, hard-nosed, yet compassionate, and old, yet young"; "She gets the job done without delay in the simplest, cost effective way without political fanfare"; "This grandmother can definitely teach the young mayors of the world a lesson or two in City Management 101"; and "Too bad we can't clone Hazel McCallion."

It was around this time that I was chosen as one of the "American Women of the Year" in *Who's Who of American Women* (which refers to North American women), *Reader's Digest* picked me as Best Mayor in Canada and Hockey Canada presented me with its Female Hockey Breakthrough Award for my work in promoting women's hockey. Things were really on an upswing.

And a book came out called *The Ten Greatest Canadian Political Leaders* and I was ranked ninth on the list. Imagine that—Hazel McCallion included with the likes of René Lévesque, Agnes Macphail, Lester Pearson, Louis Riel, Nellie McClung, Tommy Douglas, Sir Wilfrid Laurier, Pierre Trudeau and Sir John A. Macdonald, who was ranked first, of course. "We ranked these leaders," the book stated, "based on the following criteria: the impact the leader had on the nation, province, or local community that he or she led; the influence the leader had while in office; how long he or she held the position; the significance of the changes made; and whether the person's accomplishments have endured."

There have been so many influential political leaders in Canada not on this list (William Lyon Mackenzie King, Joey Smallwood, Brian Mulroney, Jean Chrétien, Bill Davis, Jean Drapeau, Peter Lougheed, John Diefenbaker, Robert Borden, Charlotte Whitton, to name a few). I was not only on that list, but I was the only mayor, and the City of Mississauga was barely thirty years old at the time. Quite remarkable.

Back in the mid-2000s, there was even time for me to do a little police work with the SWAT team. A distraught man climbed up on his roof with a rope around his neck and threatened to jump and hang himself. Police were called to his home in Port Credit at 11 one morning. I was in Toronto at a meeting and when I was leaving around 3 p.m., I called my office and was told the man was still on his roof.

So, on my way home, I stopped in Port Credit, where a crowd was watching as police tried to get him down. I told him police had a lot of other important things to do and he was wasting their time. He waved at me and even blew me a kiss as I shouted to him to come down immediately. Much to my surprise, he did. He was fine. It was all a misunderstanding over the piles of junk he'd collected in his yard. But it's a story I like to tell the chief of police, Jennifer Evans, and I remind her I am still owed my off-duty police pay for helping them out.

Around this time, Mississauga was also stretching its legs, literally. The annual Mississauga Marathon, which started in 2004 and is a qualifying race for the famed Boston Marathon, now attracts more than ten thousand runners. And what I really like about it is that it has a charitable component that raises more than $100,000 for local charities every year, and it stages races for all levels, not just the gruelling 26-mile (42.2 km) marathon.

"When I approached Hazel about the idea for a marathon she immediately 'got it' and got behind it," said race founder Elliott Kerr. "Great cities have great marathons because they're good for tourism, good for promoting healthy lifestyles and good for civic pride. Hazel understood this right from the start. As part of the festivities, we've even named a five-kilometre fun run 'The Hazel,' in her honour."

During this time, I was travelling a lot, too. I still do, but I travelled even more then. I love to travel and see new things. I was in India for the first time in 2005, and China, Japan, Germany and Tanzania. As mayor, it's my job to drum up

The Fire Fighters, The Police,
The Volunteer workers.
All those who helped
Bless and thank you everyone.

Hazel McCallion

Mayor of Mississauga

The derailment on November 10, 1979, became the "Mississauga Miracle" without the loss of even one life. Managing that harrowing week was the single biggest achievement of my political career. Note that I was still on crutches in this picture from a fall during the derailment week.

I often get teased for being autocratic, but people want strong leaders. Take the Mississauga train derailment. People needed clear and concise information. They didn't need "best-case scenarios." That's sugar-coating. Instead I said things like, "If you think you'll be out of your home for two days, then plan on being out four days."

I've had the pleasure to meet so many famous people as mayor of Mississauga. Actor Tony Curtis was charming.

Ron Duquette

Canadian impressionist Rich Little had the audience laughing at the 1992 Mayor's Gala, even if he admitted he had trouble finding my unique voice.

Ron Duquette

Ottawa's Paul Anka was fantastic at the 2000 Mayor's Gala; he even sang his legendary "My Way" with lyrics personalized for me.

Ron Duquette

This is my long-time friend Dorothy Jamieson, ninety-six, who surprised me by nominating me for the Order of Canada. Dorothy was born in Britain and served as a sergeant and systems operator in Fighter Command for the Royal Air Force during World War II, and she knew one of my political heroes, Winston Churchill.

I have met the Queen on numerous occasions, usually to greet her and other royals at Pearson International Airport, which is located in Mississauga. Of all the royals, I got to know her mother—the Queen Mum—best.

For a hockey lover like me, it was a thrill to meet the Great One, Wayne Gretzky. We both look a lot younger in this photo!

Wry comedian Bob Newhart (wearing black tie), who was the headliner at the 2003 Mayor's Gala, along with my friends Ron and Kathy Duquette.

Jean Chrétien was one of my favourite prime ministers, even if he didn't help municipalities as much as I'd hoped. But his word was his bond, and he was so down to earth.

Stephen Harper is the eighth prime minister in office since I was elected mayor of Mississauga in 1978. And a funny thing: I was born before seven of them; only Pierre Trudeau was born before me.

Bill Davis was the Ontario premier who created the City of Mississauga and forced the amalgamation with my town of Streetsville, which I fought tooth and nail. Despite that political fight we became lifelong friends, and he has been there for me in the best and worst of times.

With Hillary Clinton in 2013, months after she stepped down as U.S. secretary of state. Could she become the first woman president of the United States?

Walter Oster

Relaxing on Lake Ontario and taking in some sun while salmon fishing.

Ron Duquette

Drumming in a traditional Chinese dragon boat race to help keep the strokes rhythmic.

Mississauga resident Oscar Peterson was one of the great pianists, and I am proud to say he was a close friend. He often invited me to his home for dinner, and I was in Ottawa, along with Queen Elizabeth, for the unveiling of his beautiful statue on Parliament Hill.

Regis Philbin headlined the 2008 Mayor's Gala, and I made the mistake of telling him I didn't know who he was. He used that as one of the biggest jokes in his act. He and I have stayed in contact, and he even had me to New York to appear on television with him one time.

CBC star Rick Mercer featured me playing hockey on his popular television program *Rick Mercer Report* in 2009, when I was eighty-eight years old. That six-minute clip has been viewed 3.4 million times in 212 countries on YouTube the last time I checked in 2014.

Maple Leaf legend and Mississauga resident Johnny Bower with me in 2006. Johnny, who was a goalie on the last Leaf team to win the Stanley Cup in 1967, and I are getting restless to see the Leafs win another Cup.

That's me with two of Mississauga's leading builders and citizens, Bruce McLaughlin (on the left) and Harold Shipp.

In 2003, I visited Tanzania for the first time to see the ravages of the HIV/AIDS epidemic on the children of the country; 800,000 had lost one or both parents. From my visit came a charity called Hazel's Hope, to which Mississauga residents gave more than $1 million through World Vision. It provides safer water, education, HIV/AIDS awareness and prevention training, health care and more in Tanzania.

I do not generally show my emotions openly, but the trip to Tanzania really was heart-wrenching. Here my friend Maggie Bras gives me a hug while we are touring a local community.

Just before my eighty-ninth birthday, it was a thrill to carry the Olympic Torch as it made its way through Mississauga on its way to Vancouver for the 2010 Winter Games.

In June 2010, when I was eighty-nine, the University of Toronto at Mississauga presented me with an honorary doctorate of laws for my lifetime of work in public service. It was quite a thrill for someone with only a grade 11 education.

investment, primarily for Mississauga, but also for the entire Greater Toronto Area. A rising tide lifts all boats, as they say.

One of the reasons I love to travel and meet new people is to tell them the story of Mississauga. There are incredulous looks on the faces of executives when they hear Mississauga has some of the lowest business taxes and the city has not borrowed money since 1978. They just can't believe that. They're intrigued. They want to find out more about Mississauga. (The city went into debt for the first time with me as mayor in 2013 when we borrowed $30 million to change all the street lights to high-efficiency LED lamps.)

I was delighted to be part of the Greater Toronto Marketing Alliance's 2005 mission to South Asia. Mississauga's Indian community was growing steadily and strengthening business ties with the country made sense. I was eager to see India for myself, and it was an eye-opening trip. India was just really taking off then and I didn't know much about it, not like China or Japan, both of which I've visited about a dozen times over the years. My good friend Jake Dheer, who produces my *Mayor's Hour* television show and runs Rogers Community Channel 10 in Mississauga, still has a lot of family in India, and he told me I would love it. He was right about that.

When I came home from that trip, I was scheduled to visit north Mississauga's Lincoln M. Alexander Secondary School's first annual Holi festival, a Hindu celebration in the spring. All I did was mention that I'd just returned from India and the place erupted. I don't know what it is, but young people just get a kick out of me. Before I knew it, there was a lineup of girls in saris wanting to get their picture taken with me. It made me wonder if they paid that much attention to their own grandmothers. Even the boys began lining up for pictures.

I've always tried to visit as many schools as possible, especially schools with high populations of new Canadians. I want these children to feel welcome. I also try to instill confidence in all young people because sometimes in today's world, children can lack confidence for whatever reasons. I want them all to know how important they are, not only to their families, but to everyone in their community. I tell them to do their homework and be prepared for whatever is thrown at them—whether it's from family, teachers, employers or the general public.

And you know what? So often these kids teach the mayor a thing or two with stories they tell me or poems they write. I was so moved by a book of poems and life stories written by grade 5 students for my visit to St. Veronica Catholic Elementary School. One story, in particular, really struck me. It was from a boy born in the Philippines. He thanked me for Mississauga, a safe home that keeps him dry at night, unlike the home of sheet metal he once lived in, and he thanked me for the clean water to drink. *He thanked me.* I want to thank him because with an attitude like that I'm sure he will grow into a fine young man and be an asset to our country.

It's easy for Canadians to take things for granted, to get wrapped up in everyday problems that we think are so important. But when a grade 5 boy thanks me because he can drink clean water, that puts everything into perspective.

Mississauga is one of the most multicultural cities in the country, with half of our population born outside Canada. To celebrate this, we have an annual Carassauga Festival of Cultures, the largest multicultural festival in Ontario and the second-biggest in Canada. Its success depends on hard-working volunteers, more than six thousand of them. Active volunteerism, as you'll soon read, is part of the DNA in Mississauga.

Carassauga started in 1986 as a way to promote under-standing, respect and co-operation among Canadians of different heritages. Over three days each May, visitors experience the cuisine, culture and entertainment from seventy-two cultures at thirty pavilions in thirteen locations across Mississauga. Opening the 2014 Carassauga for the last time as mayor was bittersweet, indeed.

In Canada, it's absolutely amazing how we receive people from all over the world and integrate them into our communities in so many ways. That's such a wonderful part about Canada and being Canadian: we welcome people from whatever country, whether refugees or landed immigrants, and make them feel at home and part of our society. We do a great job of that in Mississauga, as do places all across Canada, and new Canadians make such an outstanding contribution to our country.

Most of those trade mission trips I made were low-profile from the Canadian media's standpoint, but not all. I remember one trade mission to the Far East in 1997 that I briefly considered boycotting because Quebec Premier Lucien Bouchard was going. I was born and raised in Quebec. I love Quebec and I return to the Gaspé most summers. But I don't like the separatist movement and I even called Bouchard a traitor for his efforts to take Quebec out of Canada. In 1995, I was one of the hundreds of thousands of Canadians who travelled to Montreal just days before the referendum on separation to rally support for people to vote to stay in Confederation.

And then, less than two years later, I was to go on a trade mission to the Far East to drum up business with a guy who wanted no part of Canada. In the end, I decided to go and you know what? I enjoyed Lucien's company. We had several conversations and I was delighted and surprised by his enthusiasm, but I'd never agree with his politics. I was delighted to see Pauline Marois's Parti Québécois government get trampled at the polls in April 2014. Hopefully, this defeat will put to rest the separatist movement for many years, if not forever.

As a Quebec-born politician who has considerable experience, I had written Madame Marois some months before the election, offering political advice that she should put aside talk of separation and concentrate on the economy, including the plight of unemployed youth in the Gaspé region.

"It is most difficult to understand your priorities of insisting on a strong control of the language bill and sovereignty when so many people in Quebec and other parts of the country are unemployed and would give their right arm for a job," I wrote. "Politicians should be working together to build our economy and provide opportunities for people to work, especially young people. I can't believe that the issues of language and sovereignty seem to be your priority."

The letter went unanswered, but election results indicate that she and the PQ would have been better served had she taken my advice and concentrated on the economy.

Returning to the mid-2000s in Mississauga, it really was the calm before the storm. In 2005, the city opened Riverwood Park, 150 acres (61 ha) of pristine land on the scenic east bank of the Credit River, from Burnhamthorpe Road to Highway 403. Over the years we've added trails, renovated the historic Chappell and MacEwan houses on the property and built a stunning $1.5-million MacEwan Garden Terrace for the public to enjoy. More than two-thirds of the site is preserved in its natural state, for more than 350 species of native plants and forty-six species of birds and animals, including herons, owls, red-tailed hawks, turkey vultures, white-tailed deer, hare and breeding frogs. For all those people who call Mississauga sprawl with everything paved over, I urge them to spend an afternoon at Riverwood, especially in June when the flowers are in full bloom.

Riverwood is a gem but it's tucked away so that many residents don't even know it exists. To attract more attention from motorists along Burnhamthorpe, the city plans to build a majestic new entranceway and name it in my honour as a retirement gift. I can't think of a nicer gesture as I have always supported parkland and the need for natural environments where people can walk, exercise and simply enjoy the beauty of nature.

Shortly after opening Riverwood, and as my eighty-fifth birthday approached on February 14, 2006, I started to give some thought to stepping down and not running in the election that November. I thought about what had been built in Mississauga and what was left to do. The downtown city core still needed more attention and more "growing up, not out," with office towers and high-density residential buildings.

The biggest need was for a major convention centre and luxury hotel in the downtown core. Smaller cities like London and Windsor had them, but we did not. Such a convention centre had been part of the official city plan for a decade or more. It was my dream to link it up via tunnels or skywalks with the Living Arts Centre, to maximize that facility's use during non-business hours. And I wished I had a dollar for the number of times visiting executives with operations in Mississauga had told me that we needed a four- or five-star hotel so they didn't have to travel into Toronto.

Immersed as I was in smart-growth issues and trying to untangle the Greater Toronto Area's gridlock, I wanted to get the bus rapid transit line built along the Highway 403 corridor and a light rail transit line built through the centre of Mississauga from the lake to our neighbour in the north, Brampton.

But despite having a lot of things on my plate, I still wondered if it was time to step aside. I talked to a few of my closest friends and advisors and to my three children. Everyone asked: "How's your health?" I told each one of them that it was fine and I could still handle the hundred-hour work weeks. I was reminded that for years I had said I would stay so long as my health allowed me to do the job.

Everyone urged me to run again and move forward with the plans for the city. My son Paul was concerned I wouldn't know what to do with myself without the job because I love it so much. I decided to run again. To say I was "seriously" thinking about retiring would be an overstatement. But I did entertain the idea briefly in 2006.

Whether it was my age or someone mentioning a rumour indiscreetly, whispers began that I was contemplating retirement after all these years. This, unfortunately, caused some problems on council with personal ambition and jockeying and politics coming to the fore in the minds of some councillors, instead of working hard and keeping the best interests of the people of Mississauga top of mind.

When I publicly declared my candidacy in the 2006 election, some members of council who were eyeing the mayor's office were probably disappointed, though none were prepared to seriously challenge me head-to-head in a mayoral campaign. And the election drew some candidates for council whose intentions, I believed, were to further their political careers ahead of the interests of the city and its residents. As I told the *Toronto Star* not long after the 2006 election: "There's a lot of things going on and it's not healthy for the City of Mississauga. I would feel better if I didn't know deals were being made" by councillors competing for positions.

I can live with losing battles on council, if for the right reasons. For example, I wanted to ban drive-thrus because I think keeping people sitting in their cars with engines idling is counter to promoting Mississauga as a healthy city. But other councillors sincerely believed such a ban would be detrimental to Mississauga businesses, as people would make a point of going to drive-thrus in nearby Etobicoke, Brampton or Oakville. I lost the vote but respected councillors for sticking to their sincere beliefs, even if I disagreed. But when council sessions turned into grandstanding, showboating and voting based on political ambition, I knew things were not working.

Even an old nemesis agreed with me. Former councillor Larry Taylor often battled me and called me "autocratic." But in the same *Star* article he said this about the tomfoolery at council sessions: "There's an expectation and anticipation, based on her age, that this indeed may be her last term. When Hazel leaves there will be a battle for the mayor's position and those mayoral candidates will be forced to present a view, a vision of Mississauga, that's going to set the scene for the next election. I see this as council's way to try to create some personal political identity."

I continued working hard and doing my best for the people of Mississauga, but the next several years were difficult. They would culminate with a political storm hitting landfall in Mississauga in 2009.

To say I had battened down all the hatches and was ready

for what was to befall me would not be accurate. To say I would survive it thanks to all my supporters—like that grade 5 boy who was thankful for all the work I'd done over the years for the people of Mississauga—would be correct.

CHAPTER 16

The Inquiry

It has come time to address the issue of the Mississauga Judicial Inquiry that lasted for two years from October 2009 to October 2011, the lowest and most demeaning point of my entire political career.

It's with no great pleasure that I rehash something that cost Mississauga taxpayers $7.5 million so that my political opponents could try to extract their pound of flesh from me. But I must and will say some things here either that I have never said before publicly or that I said publicly, but my words were ignored by the media hyenas covering the inquiry.

Before I do, I'd like to make a few things perfectly clear: First, I've always put the best interests of the people of Mississauga ahead of everything else, including at times my family; second, I did make some errors and would handle some things differently if I could do them over again; third, it was me—mayor of Mississauga—who insisted on the clause in the contract to build a downtown convention centre that ultimately killed the deal that triggered the witch hunt. If I were trying to feather the nest of my son, why would I be the one person to insist on something that in the end destroyed the deal?

In today's society, the public has become so cynical of political leaders. And this cynicism is not without good reason. Too many political leaders have exhibited reprehensible behaviour. My opponents, for whatever reasons, played to this public cynicism and taxpayers paid for it.

I knew all along that I did the things I did to benefit the City of Mississauga and for no other reason. Thankfully, citizens recognized that, too, and elected me for the twelfth and final time in 2010, during the frenzy of this vindictive political inquiry.

Ahead of moving into the details of this part of my life, I should point out that there is a 386-page report on the public record and available online at www.mississaugainquiry.ca. It was written by the Honourable J. Douglas Cunningham, the judge who presided over the Mississauga Judicial Inquiry.

I encourage Mississauga residents to read it. After all, their tax dollars paid $19,400 for each page of this report. "Commission counsel and our investigators interviewed nearly 100 people and collected about 35,000 documents. In the end, 35 witnesses testified over 38 days of evidence," the report states. Without question, it is thorough.

What you will read below is a synopsis of some of the things Commissioner Cunningham wrote in his report, along with my personal reflections since the report was published on October 3, 2011. The judge found that I did not contravene the Municipal Conflict of Interest Act (MCIA), although he did not like that I used my influence to try to get a deal when my son was involved.

My intention is to state the facts plainly. I will not gloss over important facts, but I will not rehash ad nauseam when interested parties can read Commissioner Cunningham's report in full.

I want to address the central issue of the inquiry: that by working my darndest to get a four- or five-star hotel and convention centre built in Mississauga's downtown area I was in a conflict of interest because my elder son, Peter, was involved with a company that wanted to build it.

Let's go back to the beginning. In 1997, Mississauga's Living Arts Centre (LAC) opened across the street from the Civic Centre, our city hall. The LAC, with a main auditorium of 1,200 seats, two smaller theatres and numerous meeting rooms, was always thought to be a terrific annex for a nearby convention centre, should one ever be built. Indeed, the official city plan envisioned a convention centre in the city core. And I am on record that this would be a dream for me to see it connected, via either tunnel or skywalks, with the LAC.

I am a great supporter of the arts. Performances and artistry will always be the prime purpose of the LAC, but I believe that combining the building with a convention centre could create a positive economic impact for Mississauga. As the third-largest city in Ontario, Mississauga's lack of a downtown convention centre and hotel with 200 rooms or more is striking. I still hope such a complex will be built one day. We aren't trying to reinvent the wheel and compete with the giant Metro Toronto Convention Centre, but we could see many mid-range conventions attracted to Mississauga with our downtown being so close to Pearson International Airport and so many health sciences and technology firms clustered in Mississauga. In a nutshell, a downtown convention centre and luxury hotel would create jobs in the short term and long term, attract tourists and pay upwards of $1 million in property taxes every year to the City of Mississauga.

For a decade, we tried—the council and staff—to get such a convention centre built but, for whatever reasons, developers and hotel operators were not stepping up. No one ever told me it wasn't economically viable and yet no project was in the works.

"In June, 2005, the city's Economic Development Office solicited more than 30 developers and hoteliers to build an upscale hotel and convention centre adjacent to the Living Arts Centre, to no avail," Commissioner Cunningham wrote in his final report.

Around this time, my son Peter, who was selling real estate, came up with an idea to broker a deal to get the convention centre and hotel built, along with condominiums. He approached his friend Leo Couprie, a successful businessman in the import/ export world, and suggested they set up a company called World Class Developments (WCD) to acquire the land and to find a developer to take over the project. Leo was the prime investor but Peter borrowed money from him for a financial stake in the company. I didn't find out about Peter borrowing money and acquiring a 16-per-cent equity stake in WCD until long after the deal fell through. My impression was that Peter was acting as a real estate agent looking for a commission on the sale of the land and on sales of condominiums one day.

Regardless, the wheels were set in motion to finally fulfill a goal that had been in the city plan for more than ten years. Or so I thought. In hindsight, I wish someone else's son had come up with the idea to broker a deal and attract an investor interested in building the convention centre and hotel.

Two giant pension funds, Ontario Municipal Employees Retirement System (OMERS) and the Alberta Investment Management Corporation (AIM), jointly own significant parcels of land in the Mississauga city centre core. "OMERS and

AIM were equal partners and co-tenants of the city centre land," Commissioner Cunningham wrote in his inquiry report. "Oxford Properties, the real estate investment division of OMERS, was responsible for day-to-day property and development management of this land for both OMERS and AIM."

Peter approached Oxford about selling land across the street from the Living Arts Centre. As large landowners in the city centre, the pension funds knew I wanted a convention centre and luxury hotel built. Initially, they were not keen on selling. I convinced them it was in the public interest to sell at fair market value and I insisted that a clause go into the contract stipulating that the convention centre and hotel be built before the condominiums. This was the clause that eventually killed the deal. In the end, the developer wanted the condominiums built first and Oxford used the clause to scuttle the agreement.

So, again I ask: if I was more interested in helping my son ahead of the City of Mississauga, why would I insist on the clause that killed the deal? But that side of the story didn't get out for whatever reasons, even though I tried and tried.

In testimony at the inquiry, it was plainly stated by me and Oxford that I told Oxford to include the clause to get the convention centre and hotel built before any condominiums. Later at the inquiry, my lawyers also underlined this point in final submissions. Liz McIntyre and Freya Krisjanson are terrific lawyers, but the media conveniently ignored this important information.

Even Commissioner Cunningham, in his final report, referred to the co-landowners (OMERS and AIM) as putting the clause in but he neglected to mention it was me who insisted on such a clause. "Given that the hotel was the reason for the transaction from *their* perspective, *they* [emphasis added] needed assurances that it would be built," he wrote.

(Without confusing matters, after the inquiry there was a lawsuit brought forward, again instigated by a political opponent, and this judge plainly pointed out the significance of this evidence about the clause to build the convention centre and hotel first. In tossing out the lawsuit, Ontario Superior Court Justice John Sproat wrote: "Mayor McCallion intervened and pressured OMERS to sell the land to WCD. Mayor McCallion's evidence, which was not challenged, was that she recommended to OMERS that it stipulate that hotel construction must precede any condominium development.")

Yes, I took part in discussions to help get a deal done to sell land where a convention centre and hotel could be built. Yes, I have taken part in numerous discussions to get development deals done to further the economic growth of Mississauga, especially when it comes to the city centre core. That is the job of the mayor. For example, I rolled up my sleeves and helped the YMCA acquire land in the core to build a facility that has added so much to the downtown area. No one seemed to have a problem with me doing that.

Yes, my son was part of the company that wanted to develop the land. Yes, I would have done the same thing for any other company trying to build a convention centre, whether my son was involved or not.

Most importantly, I declared my conflict of interest and did not vote on any council decisions involving my son or World Class Developments to build a convention centre. (So charged was the atmosphere that a red herring arose at one council session where I forgot to formally declare my conflict, but I had done so previously and everyone knew about it. The "gotcha" journalists seized on this for a day or two.)

Even before the inquiry was launched, the city—not me, but

the council, including my opponents—hired two independent legal firms to research whether I had overstepped the rules. Both law firms came back with confirmation that I had not violated the Municipal Conflict of Interest Act.

Senior city staff all supported me and testified I did not pressure them to do anything untoward. It's all there in the report, what Marilyn Ball, director of development and design, Mary Ellen Bench, city solicitor, Janice Baker, city manager, and Ed Sajecki, commissioner planning and building, all told the inquiry.

Those are the clear facts.

The deal between World Class Developments and Oxford ultimately fell apart because the purchaser could not abide by the clause that the hotel and convention centre would be built first, before the condominiums. I insisted it be added for that very reason: my interest was all about the benefits to Mississauga, not my son.

After the deal fell through, the city and council moved on and we got a deal to buy the land and put a campus of Sheridan College where the convention centre could have been built. As the Sheridan plans moved forward, lawsuits and sworn affidavits flew around over the failed convention centre deal. Now my political opponents saw a chance to pounce. They voted in October 2009 for a judicial inquiry that lasted until Commissioner Cunningham's final report in October 2011.

Council and I are delighted with Sheridan's campus and the thousands of young vibrant people it brings to the city core, but the city had to buy the land for $15.1 million and there are no property taxes generated because it is a learning institution. Instead, the city receives $75 a year for each student, and at 5,200 projected students that works out to about half the revenue a convention centre and hotel would have paid annually in property taxes. On a strictly financial basis, the taxpayers of Mississauga would have been better off with a convention centre in that location.

Was I wrong to push for a convention centre, something that could have attracted more tourists to the city centre, created jobs and added up to $1 million a year in property taxes for the City of Mississauga? I don't think so. As mayor, it is my job to do such things.

Commissioner Cunningham said I did not contravene the Municipal Conflict of Interest Act, but he did not think I should have been involved as mayor in the deal to purchase the land. And yet he also wrote this: "The business community has had the benefit of many years of stable leadership and a mayor who understands business. Mayor Hazel McCallion enjoys a considerable measure of public trust, as demonstrated by her history of electoral success."

Do I have regrets? Yes, I wish other developers, without connections to my son, had come forward with convention centre plans. But none did. They cited several reasons, from poor economic conditions at various times to Mississauga being so close to Toronto with its major convention centre and luxury hotels. No company ever told me it was a losing proposition and made no sense. But none stepped up to the plate, either.

Should I have known more about my son's business dealings? Perhaps. But at the time he was almost sixty years old. Let me ask parents: Do you know what your grown children are doing at all times? Do you know if they pay their taxes on time or their parking tickets? Do you know who all their business partners are? My son Peter is a person who doesn't communicate well, and there were lots of things I didn't know about him and this deal.

It's not as black and white as the media laid it out. The *Toronto Star*, for example, said "optics really do matter" even if what I was doing was good for the city. Really? Here are writers with little business experience—and certainly no experience in building a city—sanctimoniously preaching that they know best. Today an integrity commissioner works for the City of Mississauga. If we have any questions of possible conflicts, we go to him beforehand for clarification.

Even though in the end I was found not to have breached the Municipal Conflict of Interest Act, it's my strongest belief that it needs major surgery. As of 2014, the Act has not been updated. It's just too vague and leaves elected officials in precarious situations that political opponents can use for partisan reasons.

For example, the Act does not clearly define what things are covered in possible conflicts, leaving so much open to interpretation. Suppose a city needs to expropriate land and part of that land is owned by someone the mayor or a councillor knows from high school or a relative or a friend of a relative. As a councillor or mayor, are you in a conflict? It's open to interpretation with the Act as it stands today.

Such situations happen often. One city's mayor called me recently to ask advice over a light rail transit plan that will include the expropriation of land. The reason is that members of his council have relatives who own homes along the corridor where the transit system is being built, and the value of the land is sure to increase. This mayor went to court beforehand to get a ruling on whether his council was within its rights. Can you believe it has come to that? The Act doesn't specify dollar amounts, either, so an elected official could be in conflict over something involving five dollars or $5 million.

In the end, what was achieved by this public inquiry that cost Mississauga residents $7.5 million? That is up to others to decide. John Snobelen, a former Ontario cabinet minister, wrote in a *Toronto Sun* column that the inquiry "revealed the square root of nothing."

As a taxpayer, it makes me wonder why these inquiries cost so much and seem to take so long. It doesn't help when lawyers can sometimes strut like peacocks or shuffle papers endlessly. I realize there are plenty of professional fees to be earned, but couldn't that $7.5 million have been better used for social housing, renovating kids' playgrounds or other things? Even if the cost of the inquiry were restricted to $3 million, that would have left $4.5 million for kids' playgrounds instead of legal fees.

Regardless, the media had a field day—day after day—during the testimony phase of the proceeding. As a politician, I long ago developed thick skin, but the relentless pounding on me and my reputation was vicious. I remember waking in the night on several occasions and wondering what would happen the next day. For someone who never in my life had trouble sleeping, this was unusual and uncomfortable. I don't take any daily medication but I could sometimes feel my blood pressure rising.

Then there was the stress of legal bills piling up. My lawyers were terrific and they didn't waste court time or demand payment immediately. Fortunately, almost all my legal fees were reimbursed by the City of Mississauga and the Region of Peel, but at the time I had no idea how much I would receive and I am not a wealthy person. I have received a fair salary and worked hard, but I certainly do not have tens of millions of dollars tucked away. In the end, I still had to pay about

$35,000 out of my own pocket, which is not an insignificant amount of money.

On that note about money, I even had to hand over my bank accounts and financial information to the inquiry investigators at one point. Of course, there was nothing to find, and there was never any issue raised at the hearing. Still, it was enough to make me feel like a common criminal.

Looking back, I am so thankful to four Mississauga councillors—Maja Prentice, Pat Saito, Katie Mahoney and Pat Mullin—who time and again stuck their necks out and supported me. If they and their voices of reason hadn't been there I am not sure I would have made it through.

By the end of the inquiry, my old nemesis, the *Mississauga News*, compared me to Jimmy Stewart in the Frank Capra classic movie *Mr. Smith Goes to Washington*. "You think I'm licked. You all think I'm licked. Well I'm not licked, and I'm gonna stay right here and fight," roars Jimmy in the film, and these lines were quoted by the *News* in one of its many jabs, taunting me to step down.

The *News* was comparing me to perhaps the best-ever, most positive depiction of a politician in film history. Jimmy Stewart played a decent, honest, hard-working U.S. senator who always put his constituents first, even if powerful forces were out to get him. I was honoured by this comparison, however unintended it may have been.

But I must admit, during the deepest, darkest days of the inquiry, I was reminded of Jimmy Stewart in another famous Frank Capra movie: *It's a Wonderful Life*, where he played the civic-minded but despairing businessman George Bailey.

I cannot lie. There were times when I was so beaten down that I thought about packing it in and resigning. I didn't tell my family or any of my closest confidants, but I was thinking seriously about ending my long run as mayor then and there. I remember longing for Sam so we could sit down and talk things through. He was always my best advisor. But he wasn't around and I was alone.

After all these years serving the great citizens of Mississauga, I thought maybe I should give up the fight. (In June 2011, the *Globe and Mail* reported a rumour that I was thinking about stepping down. For the life of me, I don't know where that came from because I have no recollection of telling anyone about my true feelings at the time.)

Throughout these long months, I received phone calls and notes of support from friends like Don Cherry, former premier William Davis, former Mississauga councillor and provincial cabinet minister Margaret Marland and so many others. Even former Peel Region chairman Lou Parsons, an old political foe, called me from Florida shortly before he died in December 2010, urging me to hang in there.

Friends like Harry Ziad Malawi, Diane Kalenchuk, Betty Merkley, Silvano Belmonte, Haroon Khan, Pat Anderson, and Wally and Tina Matskofski were always there for me to lean on no matter what. Betty organized rallies and websites in my support. Haroon hosted parties in his home to cheer me up. They were all there, always. Harry kept writing positive things in the *Canadian Arab Network*, a publication he founded, despite what other media were saying. "Madam Mayor's work and love for the people of Mississauga speaks for itself," Harry wrote. "Her good deeds to humanity are enormous, and her integrity and reputation are unquestionable. She is whiter than white and cleaner than clean."

Ted Woloshyn was another person in the media who resisted piling on and gave me a fair shake in his newspaper columns and radio broadcasts. There may have been others, but I can't think of any.

All these heartfelt gestures helped, but the public pounding I was taking day after day in the major media was taking its toll. I was really being laid out in lavender. I was being called a liar, a dictator, greedy, petulant, self-serving and more. You name it. They were dishing it out at me, ladle upon ladle. I knew the accusations were not true, but part of me simply wanted the whole mess to go away.

Then I remembered *It's a Wonderful Life*, and how George Bailey is at his deepest despair and ready to give up when his angel, Clarence, shows him what his town would be like if he chose to end his life. Clarence shows him a vision of mean-spiritedness and nastiness in his beloved, idyllic Bedford Falls. Without George, the town's curmudgeon manipulator, Henry Potter, would seize control of Bedford Falls, remaking it in his own image.

Such thoughts gave me the strength to realize that I simply could not resign. Sure, I knew I couldn't last forever. But I wanted to leave when I wanted or when the people wanted, not be forced out by my political opponents.

I was ninety at that point, but there was still a heck of a lot of fight left in this so-called "Queen Lear." The people of Mississauga had placed their trust in me twelve times and there was no way I would simply give up. I would finish my term and get the wheels in motion for projects like light rail transit and waterfront redevelopment, and battle other emergencies like an ice storm that crippled Mississauga and Southern Ontario for days. I came in with a train derailment and it looked like I was going out with an ice storm, not some trumped-up accusations attacking my integrity and reputation.

As Commissioner Cunningham wrote in his report: "There is no doubt that the mayor's interest in the WCD project was driven principally by her desire for a four- or five-star hotel in Mississauga, and not simply by a desire to assist her son."

Political opponents with much to gain and the media could question my character as much as they'd like. It never felt good, and still burns. But the most important thing is that the people of Mississauga know I'm honest and I've always had their best interests at heart.

As Bob Rae, a former Ontario premier I'd battle with at times, once said: "She's a remarkable kind of force. I can understand her political appeal because she has a very good and a keen sense about what matters—what is essential. She's a tremendous fighter for what she is and for what she does. Hazel's first and last interest is Mississauga."

That's why the people of Mississauga elected me for a twelfth term in 2010—at the height of the political feeding frenzy upon my reputation—and why days after Commissioner Cunningham released his report in October 2011, I was named Canada's Most Popular Mayor from the country's fifteen biggest cities in a Forum Research poll, with a 78 per cent approval rating.

"With Hazel McCallion at the top, we're reminded that love is blind," Myer Siemiatycki, a municipal politics expert at Ryerson University, told the *National Post*. "It tells us that the branding of a mayor—the persona—can go a long way. The mayors who inspire are the ones who win confidence."

Like I said throughout my career, the next election campaign starts the day after the last election by working hard every single day for the people of Mississauga. I was bruised, but not battered, and there remained much unfinished work ahead.

CHAPTER 17

Hazel's Hope

City hall, or a mayor for that matter, cannot make a community. For a municipality, elected officials can set guidelines and plans to build neighbourhoods, roads, public transit, hockey arenas, libraries and more. But it's the people who truly make the community.

I've always believed a big part of making a community is volunteering and giving your time. Getting involved, meeting new friends, working together and having a stake in your neighbourhood, your children's schools, your city or town. Some call it "having skin in the game." I call it pride of ownership.

Mississauga residents have always been community-minded; from the 280,000 who lived here in 1978 when I was first elected mayor to the 750,000 today. It's no coincidence that year after year the experts who analyze crime statistics across Canada name Mississauga the safest big city in the country.

Yes, we have crime, I won't deny that. But things are much better than they would be without such a strong volunteer culture. Mississauga even has an incredibly active volunteer organization dedicated to helping young people turn away from a path towards crime and move towards becoming productive citizens. Founded in 1992, Safe City Mississauga is a registered charity that works closely with the police, the city and other partnering agencies to deliver youth and neighbourhood programs, events and awareness campaigns to the community. It does great work.

When it comes to a culture of volunteerism, it's big things and little things; they all add up. From volunteering at music festivals like the renowned Southside Shuffle in Port Credit and the Mississauga Waterfront Festival to the annual Bread and Honey Festival in Streetsville and the Carassauga Festival of Cultures, the province's largest multicultural celebration.

This culture of giving and activism in Mississauga is about parents raising thousands of dollars every year for their children's schools through fall fairs and public barbecues. (If any parent organizations want to learn first-hand how to run these things, they need only visit two schools in south Mississauga, Kenollie Public School and Mineola Public School, any September or June. For more than thirty years, one generation of parents after another has taken up the baton with clockwork precision and raised hundreds of thousands of dollars for their schools.)

This culture in Mississauga is about even smaller, less formal things that volunteers do to build a community. I once had a caller on my cable-TV phone-in show tell me how he loved Mississauga, but he had one complaint. "Madam Mayor," he said, "we have so many great parks and recreational facilities in Mississauga. But the one behind our home where my kids play soccer and baseball doesn't get its grass cut often enough. After two weeks, the little kids can barely move the soccer ball because the grass is so high."

"Sir," I said, "thank you for calling and enjoying our facilities. I have an idea. Why don't you organize a group of parents— those with children who use the park—to cut the grass between the times that city workers can get back to cut it? That way the people using the park will make sure it's in the best shape for their children, and other residents in Mississauga won't have to pay for hiring more crews of workers." I'm not sure if he did, but I hope so.

Mississauga has 480 parks spread over 6,700 acres (2,711 ha) and twenty-three major trail systems, including one along the waterfront that connects to Toronto in the east and Oakville in the west. Every little bit of help from people enjoying the parks helps us all.

It's worth mentioning the community collaborative called the Peel Newcomer Strategy Group. Immigrants are the jewels in Mississauga's crown because they bring valuable knowledge and experience. But coming to a new country creates many unique challenges. This newcomer group works to make the transition easier for immigrants and helps to ensure that our rich social fabric continues to be adorned with diverse threads.

We've seen so many waves of immigrants from Italy, Portugal, Poland, Croatia, China, Southeast Asia, Ukraine, the Caribbean islands and elsewhere come to Mississauga and add to our mosaic without changing our city's culture of working and living together in harmony. And volunteers who've welcomed newcomers and helped them transition have been invaluable.

Sometimes the best ideas create the simplest solutions and that's the case when it comes to volunteerism. Take the example of a Streetsville school teacher who saw the correlation between a healthy breakfast and better learning for children. Audrey Pritchard set up a breakfast club at Forest Ridge Public School in

1991, the first of its kind in Peel Region. Today, more than one thousand healthy breakfasts are served each month to children by volunteers. The program was renamed the Audrey Pritchard Breakfast Clubs after she died of cancer in 2005.

I'm singling out Audrey simply because like so many great volunteers, she had an idea and did something about it to improve her community. She was thinking of others. That's what makes great communities.

Speaking of Streetsville, it is worth mentioning the culture of volunteerism in that specific community. It is remarkable, all the volunteer efforts in Streetsville. And it's been like that for decades, long before Sam and I arrived in 1951. Why is volunteerism so embedded in Streetsville residents? Maybe it's the rural roots or the history of being an underdog against larger neighbouring municipalities. I don't know, but I wonder if that is the reason the community has maintained its distinct identity even though it became part of the much bigger Mississauga.

People have sometimes talked about Streetsville's distinctiveness, even written about it. But it might be worth the time and effort for some bright sociology or urban affairs students at the University of Toronto at Mississauga or at Sheridan College's Hazel McCallion Campus to really study Streetsville and come up with hard data on what makes this community tick and what other communities across Canada can learn from it. I would be happy to help in any way I could.

Enough about Streetsville. There are so many other wonderful examples of great volunteer work in Mississauga, and across Canada. Rotary, Kinsmen and Lions Clubs, church, synagogue, mosque and temple groups, choirs, minor league sports organizations of every stripe—hockey, soccer, baseball, basketball, cricket—and so much more. Go to any hospital and you'll see the volunteers and what they mean. There are also an impressive three hundred volunteers at the Living Arts Centre. I always make a point of talking to and meeting volunteers. They don't give so much of their time for recognition, but they deserve to be told how important they are every once in a while. I cannot say enough about volunteers.

I've always believed in volunteering. Now, being mayor and working eighty to one hundred hours a week, I just don't have the time to volunteer beyond the committee work in Mississauga and at the Region of Peel, or when the provincial or federal governments ask me to serve on panels such as those for the safe transportation of dangerous goods or smart-growth urban planning in Ontario.

By the time I was elected mayor, I had sat on virtually every committee at the Region of Peel and the City of Mississauga. I have also served on the executive of many national and provincial committees and associations, including president of the Association of Municipalities of Ontario (AMO) in 1978–79 and chair of the Large Urban Mayors' Caucus of Ontario (LUMCO) for more than twenty years.

Over the years, I've received many volunteer awards, including the Paul Harris Fellowship from Rotary International in 1985 and 1992, the Lions International President's Award, the Helen Keller Fellowship from the Mississauga Lions Clubs and the Melvin Jones Fellow for dedicated humanitarian services from Lions Clubs International.

They've all meant a lot, but what means even more is setting an example for others. As Albert Einstein so eloquently put it: "Setting an example is not the main means of influencing others; it is the only means." I do not believe in the philosophy "Do as I say, not as I do." I've volunteered my time and I know how important it was to others, but also to myself.

That's why we've created so many important citizens' committees in Mississauga for individuals to collectively come together and make a difference. Governments and political leaders should set a tone, but residents are the ones who truly make communities.

We set up the Mayor's Youth Advisory Committee to get young people more involved. We set up the Mississauga Sports Council and Arts Council to get parents and patrons more involved in deciding how we should spend tax dollars on these important community activities, especially with demographics changing. We set up ecoSource Mississauga to get everyone more aware of the changing environment they live in and better utilizing resources, whether they be energy, garbage collection or our natural lands like the Rattray Marsh and our parks across the city. For the most part, all these committees and others have sparked community involvement and helped make Mississauga a better place to live.

Charity goes hand in hand with volunteerism. Some say charity starts at home. That may be so, but charity extends well beyond that. Some time ago, I asked supporters to stop donating money to my political campaigns and instead give the money to charity. The 1991 election was the last time we accepted political donations. "When I was Hazel's campaign manager my sole job was to return cheques to donors and ask them to give it to a charity of their choice. I never had an easier job," my friend Ralph Hunter used to joke.

Now, I am not a wealthy person, so my personal giving to charity is not about opening my chequebook and writing donations with lots and lots of zeroes. I give what I can to help raise funds for hospitals and other charities, but I leave it to others to cut the really big cheques.

Sometimes I am amazed when my name shares the spotlight with others who have given millions of dollars. Such is the case at Trillium Health Centre in south Mississauga, where the Hazel McCallion Heart Centre gets the same billing as the Harold and June Shipp Stroke Centre on the outside of the building.

Harold is a successful developer and he and his late first wife, June, were very generous in their gifts of time and money to the hospital. He followed in his father's footsteps. Gordon Shipp was always giving back to the community, especially the hospital, known as South Peel Hospital and then Mississauga Hospital before being called Trillium.

Harold was on the board for years and June was a volunteer for thirty-five years before a stroke took her. Harold, whom I can call a good friend, knows I've given my time and name at fundraisers to help out, but financially I haven't given near what he has. I know of one cheque he wrote the hospital for $6 million and no doubt he's given even more privately.

Which, I guess, just goes to show there are so many different ways to give to charity. You don't have to be wealthy to give. Every little bit helps. It's worth noting the Trillium hospital came into being after a sixteen-year-old boy in 1952 died en route to a Toronto hospital. Immediately, the Port Credit Rotary Club and the Credit Valley Lions Club joined forces to lay the groundwork for a $500,000, fifty-five-bed hospital. This was volunteerism at its best. It has expanded over the years to 750 beds, in large part through government money, but the community has always played an active role in the hospital, too.

And also in Mississauga's second hospital, Credit Valley, which opened in 1985 in what was then a farmer's field we bought from Cadillac Fairview Corp. I was on the founding committee that searched for the perfect site at Erin Mills Parkway and Eglinton Avenue.

Way back in 1979, the Credit Valley Hospital Volunteer Association, chaired by Carol Townsend, had a vision to provide "healing and hope" for the growing community of Mississauga when the city was one-third its current size. By 1982, Dr. Keith MacDonald was appointed chief of medical staff to begin acquiring equipment and key personnel three years before the doors would open. There was vision and volunteerism hard at work.

One of my largest charity endeavours over the years was the annual Mayor's Gala in Mississauga, which raised more than $4 million. It started in 1987 when city employee Olga Carmen in the public affairs department came to me with the idea of a Mayor's Gala as a way to dispel negative views by some residents over the city's newly opened Civic Centre. She wanted to stage the dining and speaking portions of the event in a large tent in the public square, followed by dancing in the Great Hall of the award-winning Civic Centre. My friend Ron Lenyk was the first chair of the gala.

It sounded like a fun idea, but I insisted the gala must not cost taxpayers a single dime. It didn't, but who would have thought what a huge charity event it would become over the years? After two years, the event was moved to the convention centre near Pearson Airport. And then the gala moved to the Delta Meadowvale Hotel ballroom, farther west in Mississauga. It moved permanently to the Living Arts Centre in 1997 after that venue was built in the downtown core. In fact, the Mayor's Gala was the official opening event of the LAC on November 15, 1997. (It remained there until the last annual Mayor's Gala in 2011.)

Because it was a smashing success right from the beginning, a group of people came to see me about what to do with the surplus money being raised. These folks had all heard me go on about how important the arts are in building vibrant, livable cities so it was decided to use the money for arts, culture and heritage.

Over the years, the Mayor's Gala grew and grew with headliners like Wayne Newton, Paul Anka, Bill Cosby, Regis Philbin and so many other stars all coming to Mississauga to perform.

I have so many fond memories of the galas. Regis Philbin and I danced together and became fond friends. Until that gala, I had never heard of Regis and I told him so. He was a bit taken aback at first, but even made a joke about that during his performance. We got along so well he even had me to New York to appear on his show and he still refers to me as "his favourite mayor" whenever we talk or write.

Another year, Paul Anka personalized his song "My Way" for me and sang it with much applause and laughter from the audience. And I have to tell a story about Wayne Newton. He was the entertainer for the 1998 gala and he flew in from Las Vegas to a strange city and an event he knew little about. "What's this about a charity auction being a part of the gala?" he asked.

"Yes, we've got some great things up for grabs tonight," said Jim Murray, handing him a program listing the items. Jim, the son of an old political nemesis, Chic Murray, who was the reeve of the Town of Mississauga, has been a close friend for more than thirty years and he was the master of ceremonies at almost all of the galas.

Without hesitation, Wayne Newton said to Jim: "If you can use it, I will donate four days in Vegas, use of my jet to and from Vegas, tickets to my show, a private dinner at my ranch and a suite at the MGM Grand."

You should have seen the look on Jim's face. I thought he was going to pop all the buttons off his tuxedo shirt. I have been a big Wayne Newton fan ever since. That trip alone raised more than $25,000 and it was purchased by the chairman of A & P grocery stores, John Dunn, who gave it to the company's manager of the year.

Of the more than $4 million raised over the years, all has gone to arts and culture. The first $700,000 was dispersed to various groups, such as the Mississauga Symphony. Then the Hazel McCallion Foundation for the Arts, Culture and Heritage was set up, and in 2006 we donated $2.34 million to the Community Foundation of Mississauga, which administers a new arts, culture and heritage endowment fund with that money.

Today, the Hazel McCallion Foundation for the Arts, Culture and Heritage retains more than $1 million and it is invested and generating interest income. With this income and without touching the principal, the foundation awards grants of up to $5,000 to "innovative initiatives or projects that will contribute to the arts, culture and heritage in the City of Mississauga, or ones that showcase the art and ingenuity of Mississauga citizens to the rest of the world."

It should be noted that I do not have a say in who gets any of this money. It is up to the Community Foundation of Mississauga or the granting committee of the Hazel McCallion Foundation for the Arts, Culture and Heritage. I simply lend my name and hard-working volunteers do the rest.

The colour, life and excitement of a city are defined through its arts, culture and heritage projects. Through the Mayor's Gala we've provided sustained funding for these projects to make our city an even more vibrant place to live, work and visit. And it will remain so long after I am gone.

Beyond arts and culture, my name is used to help raise money for many other worthwhile initiatives, too. More than thirty years ago two City of Mississauga employees, John Rogers and the late Rick Mortensen, approached me about a charity golf tournament in my name. I said okay so long as they guaranteed all the money raised went to local charities. They created the Hazel McCallion Charitable Fund, a federally registered charity that disburses proceeds from the golf tournament and is run by volunteers.

Well, lo and behold, after thirty-two annual tournaments they've given more than $2.5 million to some three hundred different charities, including Mississauga Children's Choir, Alzheimer's Society of Peel, Credit River Anglers Association, Mississauga Hockey League (boys and girls), Safe City Mississauga and Hazel's Hope, one that is particularly dear to my heart.

Back in 2003, I met with the World Health Organization (WHO) and learned of the terrible plight of Tanzania, where an HIV/AIDS epidemic was affecting millions of people. Back then about 800,000 children had lost one or both their parents in Tanzania alone. I visited Tanzania with the World Health Centre based in Kobe, Japan, and I witnessed many dying and starving children left orphaned as a result of HIV/AIDS. When you see that kind of human suffering, it awakens something inside you and you feel compelled to help, to make some kind of difference. I decided I needed to do something, but what? After church one Sunday I met with Reverend Harold Percy, the minister at my church, and David Toycen, president of

World Vision Canada, which is headquartered in Mississauga. We came up with a plan to launch a charity called Hazel's Hope and administered by World Vision. I went back to Tanzania for a second visit, this time with World Vision.

I am an optimist by nature but, my God, my heart was broken on those trips to Tanzania. I met so many children without both parents. I saw grandparents becoming parents again because sons and daughters were dead from AIDS. I talked to teenagers who were raising their brothers and sisters.

On this trip I was accompanied by my friend Maggie Bras, herself a wonderful philanthropist who runs the Robert & Maggie Bras and Family New Drug Development Program at Toronto's internationally acclaimed cancer facility, Princess Margaret Hospital. Their program will be spending millions and millions of dollars on research to find personalized drugs to treat cancer. I am the honorary chair of the program and a director of the Bras family's foundation.

Maggie and I shared some tears on that trip to Tanzania— never in front of the children, but later in private. Upon my return to Mississauga I was determined to raise money for Tanzania in a number of ways: I asked Mississauga residents to give a toonie to Hazel's Hope and, if they could, sponsor a child through World Vision.

Then I asked friends like Oscar Peterson to help. The great jazz pianist did a concert at Roy Thomson Hall in 2005, just two years before his passing, with all proceeds going to Hazel's Hope. (After his death, Oscar's youngest daughter, Celine, continued to partner with World Vision Canada to help youngsters in other parts of Africa.)

Others organized a five-kilometre Hazel's Hope Fun Run. Mississauga schools helped, too, with raffles, bake sales and "dress-down days." The Mississauga Chinese Centre on Dundas Street, a wonderful tourist attraction with shops, restaurants and replicas of famous Chinese architecture, throws me a birthday party and raises thousands of dollars for Hazel's Hope every year.

In all, Mississauga raised more than $1 million for Hazel's Hope, with World Vision taking the money to Tanzania to provide safer water, education, HIV/AIDS awareness and prevention training, health care and more. We're still raising money for Hazel's Hope and if you'd like to donate, visit the World Vision Canada website.

When we all do a little, our combined efforts make a big difference. A great city like Mississauga proved the greatness of its residents in helping to turn the tide against HIV/AIDS in Tanzania.

We also proved the old adage, sometimes attributed to Winston Churchill: "We make a living by what we get. We make a life by what we give."

CHAPTER 18

Leadership

I'm often asked what the secret to my success has been over a long career in politics and if leadership qualities are something you either naturally have or you don't.

To begin with, leadership skills—whether in politics, business, sports, ministry or whatever—most definitely can be learned and refined over time.

There are some innate qualities good leaders possess, such as integrity, sound moral and ethical principles and compassion. A good leader, especially a political one, should have compassion, to be able to recognize needs and adopt policies and courses of actions that result in the greatest benefit for the most people.

Some leaders are more naturally gifted than others but some hone their skills with practice and determination. Some of Canada's longest-serving prime ministers are sparkling examples of this. They were decisive leaders on policy decisions, but their leadership styles in dealing with the public were very different.

Pierre Trudeau had a natural charismatic presence that electrified audiences. I remember one time he showed up at the

Streetsville Bread and Honey Festival and the women were swooning as if he were Mick Jagger, Marlon Brando and Albert Einstein all wrapped up into one. Brian Mulroney, on the other hand, never had the star power of Trudeau but he exhibited different leadership qualities with the public. He'd write notes or pick up the phone and call people to wish them luck with an important endeavour or offer condolences if someone lost a loved one. When he'd talk to a person one-on-one, whether a captain of industry or captain of a softball team, he had this knack of making that person feel he or she was the most important thing on the prime minister's mind at that particular moment.

Jean Chrétien was a populist who played up his small-town roots, the street-fighter-from-Shawinigan image. I always liked Jean, even if I disagreed vehemently with some of his government's downloading manoeuvres that hurt cities. He was honest and his word was his bond. That's a quality I admire in politics. He was also so comfortable in his own skin. There were no airs about him. I remember one time when Jean was visiting, I presented him with a City of Mississauga necktie. In front of the crowd and the TV cameras, he pulled off the tie he was wearing and put the gift around his neck. The crowd just loved it because it was a gesture not too many prime ministers would do, but it was natural for him.

I don't know exactly where I fall on the leadership spectrum. I am definitely decisive and I don't beat around the bush. And I love getting in the middle of a crowd and meeting new people, talking and exchanging ideas. I'd like to think, at age ninety-three with thirty-six years' experience wearing the mayoral chain of office, that I can, in some way, inspire people to set and achieve important goals in their lives, whether it's senior citizens who still have lots to give to their community, or young people who are filled with energy and zeal to make a difference. Or women in politics or business who want to be mayors, premiers, prime ministers and CEOs, or someone who's come to live in a new place and wants to be an active part of the fabric of his or her community. Or simply a person raised modestly without family connections who wants to give his or her life to public service to make Canada an even better place.

Most importantly, I hope my record shows that having a purpose in life—whatever that purpose, be it grand or modest—is a pretty darn good way to spend your time. So much better than drifting, rudderless and without goals.

Life is an opportunity for each of us to do a lot of great things. And by great, I don't necessarily mean building a city like Mississauga. I mean everyday important things like coaching kids, building a business, helping at hospitals and nursing homes, and making your community a better place.

I have trouble understanding people saying they have a lot of time on their hands. You know what they say about idle hands being the devil's workshop. Personally, I feel like there is not enough time available to do all the things that I would like to do and I wish there were more days in the week.

A few years back, I stumbled on something called "Everything I need to know I learned from Noah's Ark." The advice from the unknown author is simple, but so true that I decided to use it often in my public speeches, whether to students, service clubs or at ceremonies to open new businesses across Mississauga. Here's what we can learn from Noah and his ark:

- *First, don't miss the boat—and remember we're all in the same boat. Always plan ahead: it wasn't raining when Noah started building the ark.*

- *Next, stay fit and active because when you're six hundred years old like Noah—or ninety-three like me—you never know if someone will ask you to do something really big.*
- *Don't listen to naysayers and critics—just get on with the job that needs to be done. And in a similar vein, build your future on high ground. Let others take the low road, if they must.*
- *It's best to travel in pairs like I did with Sam. Remember, speed isn't always an advantage. The snails were on board along with the cheetahs. And when you're stressed, float a while.*
- *Most important, listen to and take advice, but trust your instincts above all else. The ark was built by an amateur, the* Titanic *by professionals.*

By nature, I am not a person who sits back and reflects. I'm always looking forward for the next project or for the solution to the current problem. But over the last few months as mayor, I have reflected on many things. I guess it's natural to become more reflective as we age and move into new phases of our lives.

I've thought a lot about the question I am asked so often: what are the keys to my success and my longevity? I've come up with seven core things that have related to my life in politics. But I think they are applicable to success in general, whether it be politics, business, sports or anything else.

They are: Be honest; work hard and always do your home-work; be organized; know your motivation; work together; don't be afraid to fail; and be tenacious.

It sounds so easy to be honest and truthful. And it is, but it can also get complicated. If a friend or colleague brings an idea to you, do you tell them what you really think or do you some-times sugar-coat so as not to hurt their feelings? Sometimes, it's tough to be truthful, but I've found honesty really is the best policy. I have a reputation for being blunt. I've earned it and I've put plenty of noses out of joint being blunt. But deep down, people prefer the truth, even if it stings at first.

Over all my years, I never once promised to cut taxes but I did promise to deliver value for taxpayers' money. People appreciated that. They don't like politicians, or any type of leader, telling them one thing and doing something else. They also don't like politicians telling them they'll look into a matter when there is no intention at all that they will. Bosses can fall into this trap, too, and it ultimately will catch up to them. Directness and truthfulness inspire people into action, not meaningless niceties. It's worth remembering that.

My motto of running the city like a business is truthful and we were consistent. Of course, I know government must provide services that businesses would not or could not do because it would go against the rights of shareholders. So, yes, governments can't run exactly like businesses, but they can and must be more fiscally accountable to their shareholders—the taxpayers.

I speak frankly to everyone. I don't change who I am for a resident coming before council or a premier meeting me at Queen's Park. "You never forget a meeting with Hazel," Premier Mike Harris told the *Toronto Star* on my eightieth birthday. "You always know where she stands. There's no beating around the bush. She won't tolerate that from either side. I really and truly have to say there are very, very few leaders who ever come to personify their communities the way Hazel does."

Maybe it's because I am a child of the Depression and we didn't have a lot but I sure know the value of hard work. Sometimes I wonder whether there is too much entitlement in today's culture. My mother always said, "Work never killed anyone but lots of idle people die young." There's something to be said for rolling up your sleeves, setting an example and working hard.

As the late former Peel chairman Lou Parsons told the *Toronto Star*: "Hazel came up the hard way. Everything she did, she worked hard for. She didn't wear figure skates."

With only a high school diploma, I am often not the smartest person in the room. But I sure as heck want to be the best prepared person in the room. And I can tell you this, too: when city staff or councillors have done more homework than me on a certain topic, nothing gains my respect faster. I bet all bosses feel the same way about their underlings, certainly all successful bosses.

My entire career as mayor, I worked seven days a week. Some weeks, I would attend fifteen or twenty events outside of the office, meeting people, getting to know their concerns, and cutting ribbons and celebrating new businesses. I prided myself on being a mayor who cut ribbons *and* red tape.

The last two decades as mayor, I often wouldn't get out on the political hustings during the official campaign period in the fall. That's because my campaign never stopped. As soon as one election was over, I was back working hard the next day. My people knew I was on the job all the time.

I don't like politicians who show up six months before an election. What have they been doing the rest of the time? Voters often think this, too, and I can't say I blame them one bit. There's nothing worse than feeling like you only hear or meet politicians when your vote is needed.

Not me. I used to drop by barber shops or grocery stores to meet people, hear what was on their minds and let them know their mayor was on the job and working hard for their vote and for their city. I worked hard every day, not just during election campaigns. In fact, I found election campaigns were often a good time to get away for a short vacation because councillors were all out on the campaign trail and city hall business slowed down. That sounds crazy, for a politician to take a vacation during an election campaign, but it was made possible by working hard, day in and day out.

Being organized is so important to success. All my life, I have organized my next day with to-do lists before going to bed. If I was out in the evening and didn't have the time to do it before bed, I would get up a half hour earlier and set up my plans for the day that morning. It's a very small thing to do, but it is so effective in saving time and effort.

Another key to success is to know what motivates you. If you're driven by money and making a lot of it, stay away from politics. You'll do so much better in the private sector. I was never motivated by money. If I had been, I would have retired long ago and taken a much-higher-paying job in the private sector. What motivates me is building, solving problems and making sure Mississauga is the best place to live for all residents.

Some dedicated and hard-working politicians retire from politics and cash in with big corporate jobs or appointments to boards. That's okay after you've made the sacrifices in public service for ten years or so and you want to retire. But one should never be motivated to get into public life thinking there is a big pot of gold at the end of the rainbow. Such motivation does not make for good public service.

Another path to success is to build alliances and listen to trusted advisors. I enjoy working with city staff. I love the administrative part of the job, and the talent on our team in Mississauga has always made things even more gratifying. The talented and hard-working staff at the city, whose first priority has always been the taxpayers of Mississauga, have helped me greatly over the years.

I've been fortunate to have a core group of people in the mayor's office who share this vision and passion for public service, especially my executive assistant, Carol Horvat, who's been with me for twenty-four years and provided unwavering loyalty and support.

It's worth noting that the mayor's staff in Mississauga, which also includes Christina Diggle and Michelle Bown, is made up of city employees, not political appointees. This gives them the independence to speak up without fear of losing their jobs. Not that they have had to do that often, but I appreciate and respect their views. Problem solving is one of the real treats of the job for me and it helps having diverse opinions and perspectives.

When situations arise, I just try to find the best solution in the timeliest manner. The city staff, for the most part, have the exact same attitude: "That's a problem," I'll say. "Now, how do we solve it?" And, by and large, solutions will be found in no time.

Really good leaders also delegate and inspire others to work hard and do the right thing. Micromanaging people is fruitless. If a leader's team isn't performing, find new players.

Generally, during my years as mayor, council has operated as a team. Sometimes we've had agitators who were more interested in their personal political careers than finding solutions for Mississauga. Eventually the people decide they want a council that can work together. And, as the old political saying goes, the voters are always right.

I've also found working with other municipal leaders drives results better than squabbling. In the early 1990s, I organized a mayors' and regional chairs' committee across the Greater

Toronto Area to speak in a unified voice. It helped somewhat when the upper-tier governments started downloading on us. I can't imagine how bad things could have gotten had we not stood together.

An even more successful situation followed the massive ice storm in December 2013, when I invited mayors and regional chairs from across the Greater Toronto Area to meet in Mississauga to speak in one voice to ask the federal and provincial governments to help with the $275-million cleanup. Ontario later announced it would pay $190 million, but we were still awaiting word from the federal government months after the fact.

We also formed the Greater Toronto Marketing Alliance (GTMA) in 1997 to help grow the economy of the entire area by raising the profile of the region internationally to attract new investment and employment. The GTMA's mandate is to provide all-encompassing services to investors interested in the Greater Toronto Area and to ensure that the GTA is positioned internationally as a preferred business location.

My next secret to success may sound counterintuitive, but it may be one of the most important towards gaining ultimate success in anything in life: never fear failure. Don't go out looking for failure, but never let the fear of failure paralyze you in making decisions, finding solutions to problems or taking chances to fulfill dreams. In failure, so much can be learned.

When I lost that first election for a seat on Streetsville town council in the 1960s, I could have walked away and returned to the corporate world or worked side by side with Sam, building his business. But I'd been bitten by the bug of public service and I felt I had something to give. So I worked harder, delved deeper into the issues and built up my profile so everyone in

Streetsville knew they could count on me. I never lost another election in my life.

Every time I've failed, I've learned. Now, I have this reputation that I always get what I want, that I can be like a dog with a bone. Yes, I am tenacious and I believe that is a worthwhile quality in striving for success. But to suggest I have never failed is just plain wrong. One need only see that we have no convention centre in downtown Mississauga to realize this. But I've also been thwarted on other fronts and each time I acknowledged defeat, took my lumps, learned some things and moved on.

I failed in keeping Streetsville its own independent municipality. I've tried for years to separate Mississauga from the Region of Peel, but my arguments that such a move would save taxpayers' money have fallen on deaf ears.

From both of these, I learned that some political decisions are made for reasons other than relying on simple facts. But, and this is important, once a decision has been made—even if it's a bad decision—you have to move forward and find ways to make it work as best you can. There's no sense being negative.

This lesson is applicable in politics, business and life. If your boss or a relative makes a decision you don't like, you've got to move past being negative. Make the best out of it. Your career or your family life will be better off. How many times do we see family members let something small grow into something big that creates deep divides?

I recognize it sounds simple, but oftentimes we still must move on and make the best of a bad decision. I guarantee that simply being negative only makes things worse.

I still think the Region of Peel creates a duplication of services that costs taxpayers money, but we've had successes at the region, too. I have a loud voice at the region and everybody knows where I stand, but you'll not find me sitting back being negative and sabotaging things while the situation is what it is.

One other high-profile loss for me was the seemingly never-ending fights with the federal government and Pearson Airport. There were smaller battles about runways and noise, but the biggest battles involved lot levies and Ottawa's refusal to pay them like others did in Mississauga when they built things.

Now, don't get me wrong, I knew how important the airport was to Mississauga's ultimate success, primarily for attracting businesses and good jobs for the city. But what always irritated me was the highfalutin attitude from the folks at the Greater Toronto Airports Authority who thought they could operate their own city inside of my city. Who did they think they were: the Vatican, and I was the mayor of Rome? We were persistent, but ultimately lost in the Supreme Court of Canada in 2001, which ruled in favour of the federal government that the airport's $4.4-billion expansion was exempt from municipal lot levies. The Federation of Canadian Municipalities stood solidly behind us at the Supreme Court, but to no avail.

I had only one small victory during the two decades of battles with the airport authority, but it was sweet. It was when they were building Terminal 3 in the late 1980s. As always, they steadfastly refused to pay development fees so I simply told them that they had better build the world's biggest septic tank because I would not allow the new terminal to be hooked up to Mississauga's sewage system. They immediately sent over a cheque for $2 million and that was the only money we ever got from the airport. It just goes to show the power of leverage when you're up against a bigger foe.

Like most people, I don't like to lose. But these high-profile losses for me (and many other smaller battles) taught me so many things that helped me immensely for many successes.

Speaking of success, I am often asked to rank my achievements and I always answer this way: one, the management of the derailment crisis that became the "Mississauga Miracle" with not one single loss of life; two, establishing a strong and lasting economic base in the city; three, building a city for the people with great everyday services like arenas, libraries and 6,920 acres (2,800 ha) of parkland before doing anything else; and four, retaining our waterfront for the people by buying the Rattray Marsh in the 1970s and redeveloping the Lakeview area today, all with the needs of people being the priority.

CHAPTER 19

Moving On

W hen I was in my mid-fifties, just before I become mayor of Mississauga, my vision began to improve. Literally. It was at this point that I could set aside the eyeglasses I had worn for many, many years.

It was also at this point that I could envision how we could turn Mississauga from a bedroom community into a city with its own strong economic base. We did this successfully, in part by giving preference to industrial/commercial development over residential, but always keeping the needs of people first. Today the trend of people going out in the morning and coming back to Mississauga in the evening has been reversed. They're now coming into Mississauga in the morning and leaving after work. I am proud of this and that in all the Greater Toronto Area the most jobs are in Mississauga, after the giant City of Toronto. I ran a three-pronged program: that development must pay its way, that we must plan for people and that we must run the city like a business.

The city is run like a business and city staff long ago adopted that philosophy. When business wants to come and locate in our city offering good jobs, our building department turns cart-wheels to make it happen.

Reflecting back over a long career in public life—and a long life, period, that isn't over yet—I can think of only one personal regret: I never went to university. I would have loved university life and exchanging ideas and challenging the norms of the day.

But I never got the chance because my parents just didn't have the money during the Depression. In 2010, the University of Toronto at Mississauga presented me with an honorary doctorate of laws for my lifetime of work in public service. I received the degree from the then-chancellor, no less than David Peterson, the former Ontario premier whom I'd had a few battles with over the years. He'd once made headlines by saying I was "a terror to every premier in Ontario. Don't mess with her." (Over the years, as we've become friends, we've laughed about that one.) So, technically, with that degree, I am Dr. Hazel McCallion, university graduate.

As nice as that is, it can't replicate attending university. Education really is our best hope, in Canada and around the world, to finding solutions to so many challenges today and tomorrow.

Not attending university as a young person is probably why I have done my darndest to help build the UTM and Sheridan College in Mississauga into the terrific schools they are today. The UTM even named its biggest building the Hazel McCallion Academic Learning Centre, which the students simply call "The Hazel." It's actually the third-biggest library of the U of T's forty libraries across all campuses. "The Hazel" houses 350,000 volumes and thousands of the most advanced e-resources such as journal indexes, abstracts and past exams.

Sheridan College named its Mississauga campus in our

downtown city core the Hazel McCallion Campus, where about five thousand students and new Canadians are getting the post-secondary experience I never did.

It's all rather overwhelming. Over the years, council did commit about $20 million of taxpayers' money to the two institutions (which has already paid dividends in many ways) and I did all I could to help fundraising campaigns for both, including twisting more than a few arms of developers, business people and friends. Avie Bennett, for instance, gave a big cheque to the Hazel library at UTM. Avie, being Avie, declined to tell me exactly how much but I know it was big. (UTM wouldn't even tell me how big!) Great cities need great learning institutions. And Mississauga has two great higher-learning institutions.

Leaving a legacy is far more important than leaving an inheritance, in my view. I hope I've left behind my love of learning and the pursuit of education as worthy endeavours. It is my dream that the students who will be filling the halls and classrooms of these institutions in the years to come will share that love and be inspired to become all they were destined to be and more.

As I write this, the farewell and retirement parties for me have already begun. By the time you read it, I will likely be packed up and out of the mayor's office and someone else will be leading Mississauga.

So, what will I be doing? It's hard to say, but time will tell.

I know one thing I will *not* be doing: I will not be involved in Mississauga politics and acting like some back-seat driver. No way. I'll be around if the new mayor wants any advice, but I will not be making public pronouncements or comments about how things should be done. I had a great run, but it's time for a change.

It was in 2010 that I announced I would retire from office in 2014. I did this as a way to provide an orderly transition so that potential successors and residents would have time to prepare for a new mayor. City manager Dave O'Brien told *Toronto Life* in May 2000: "When you think about Hazel and Mississauga, you think about them as one. You don't think about them as a city and a mayor, but as one occurrence in history. She has developed the city in her own likeness."

That may be so, but it's time for others to take what I helped build and enhance the city further: improve public transit and help ease the gridlock; "grow up, not out," with higher-density buildings in the city core and elsewhere; and ensure development is sustainable and as "green" as possible to keep the city a healthy place to live. I'd love to see a successor build a convention centre in the downtown core.

The strategic plan called *Our Future Mississauga* outlines a path for the coming decades to achieve this vision, while retaining the commitment to providing quality services and infrastructure in a fiscally responsible manner. Council will need to continue paying attention to our city's evolving culture, especially the needs of our aging population.

In the short term, there are lots of things that will keep me busy around the house. There are literally thousands of photographs and slides that Sam took over the years that need to be sorted. He was a photographer by training, even if he became a newspaper publisher and a commercial printer. I have hundreds and hundreds of stamps that have to be organized in my collection. And I'd like to get back to better tending my roses and vegetable garden. As mayor, the hundred-hour work weeks meant I let things at home slide.

In the longer term, I will continue to fight for better, fairer funding and more autonomy for municipalities across Canada. Let me repeat: I will not be involved in Mississauga affairs specifically, but I will do my best to use my experience and my pulpit to convince the federal and provincial governments that municipalities need a better deal. I'd like to help revamp and modernize the antiquated Ontario Municipal Act to benefit future generations of municipal leaders.

I'd also like to work in some way—some meaningful way—to help ease the gridlock around the Greater Toronto Area so that people and goods can move more easily around the economic engine of Canada. I don't know exactly what role would be best for this former "Queen of Sprawl," but I'd like the powers that be to know that I'm passionate about finding solutions and I'm willing to serve.

Whether they like it or not, my family is going to see a lot more of me. I've already witnessed my beautiful granddaughter, Erika, become a smart young woman and I look forward to seeing what's next in store for her and the rest of the family.

I hope to continue to travel and talk to new and old friends in places like China, Japan, India, the United States and Europe. Quick story: in the mid-1980s, the Mississauga Chinese Centre brought over sixty artisans and tradespeople from the Jiangsu Province of China to build its authentic Chinese architecture, including its magnificent forty-six-foot high (14m) traditional Chinese Gate. Years later, on one of my trips to China, I bumped into one of the craftsmen who built the gate and he told me how much he had enjoyed his time in Mississauga twenty years earlier. Can you believe it? What a small world that I would meet him in China years later.

Lastly, I plan on joining the exclusive Centenarian Club in Canada, of which there are fewer than six thousand members today.

From farmland and villages only four decades ago, Mississauga is today a global urban centre by any measure. Our services are highly valued by residents and businesses and funded with one of the lowest tax rates in the Greater Toronto Area. And Mississauga is ranked first in the "Mid-Size Cities of the Future" category in *Foreign Direct Investment* magazine's ranking of cities across the American continents and second for economic potential and fourth for infrastructure.

As the *Globe and Mail* wrote on my eightieth birthday: "It took the old City of Toronto 200 years to build its economy to the level Mississauga achieved during the reign of one mayor, more or less."

The future looks bright. I'll miss my job and my people, but I'll be enjoying life in this great city we've built together. I'm so thankful for the trust placed in me in each of my twelve mayoral elections. It has been a great privilege serving as Mississauga's mayor. Even still, with all that has been built and all that's been done, it's not the chores, the meetings and the work, but the happy memories shared with family and friends that truly resonate. The wise person doesn't expect life to be worth living, he or she makes it that way.

Marcel Proust, the French novelist and essayist, once said, "We don't receive wisdom; we must discover it for ourselves after a journey that no one can take for us or spare us."

No one can live our lives for us. Our experiences, the challenges we face and the knowledge we gain from having lived are unique to each individual. It is up to each of us to decide whether we simply exist or whether we are going to live meaningful, noble and purpose-filled lives, hence the subtitle of my book: *A Life with Purpose*.

From an early age, I decided that I was going to lead a life of purpose; that I would not let my modest Depression-era background or lack of formal education define me or place limits on what I could achieve. Sure, I've made mistakes along the way—who hasn't? Mistakes are an important part of life and an integral part of our evolution as human beings. They help build character. I've always tried my fervent best to do the right thing, to stand out from the pack and be a leader, not a follower. As the old adage says, "It is always better to be an original than an imitation."

Throughout my life, I have always tried to adopt a positive outlook and I think my strong faith was the catalyst for this. We can choose to be happy or sad. We can condemn or we can forgive. We can complain or we can contribute. The choice is ours and our wrinkles should merely indicate where our smiles have been.

One of the important lessons I've learned is that a life of purpose is not lived in solitude. The relationships we build are what sustain us as human beings and nourish our souls. I have been abundantly blessed in this regard. First, with a wonderful family: kind and loving parents and siblings who provided me with a sense of security and tenderness. I grew up knowing there is love in the world. And I hope my own children know they are loved and that one of the greatest joys in my life has been being their mother and Erika's grandmother.

I've also been blessed with the most supportive, loving friends any woman could ever deserve. I am fortunate to have not had many fair-weather friends. Those closest to me have been in my life for thirty or forty or fifty years, and the friendships have been life affirming and supportive. I don't know what I would have done without them during the difficult times in my life, when Sam passed away or during the judicial inquiry.

One of my favourite expressions is, "The true meaning of life is to plant trees, under whose shade you do not expect to sit." I hope that my life's work and all that I have accomplished, not only as mayor of the City of Mississauga (and Streetsville before that) but as a human being, has in some small way improved the life of someone else and that when I am remembered years from now it will be with fondness and affection.

It's time to hand the reins to someone else and if my counsel and advice are needed from time to time, I will avail myself and share my knowledge and experience, but I had my run and it's time to turn over the future of our city to someone else.

In the latter part of life, you think about your legacy. I hope my legacy will be my role in helping to transform Mississauga into the wonderful, thriving city it is today.

As an elected official, you want to leave your mark on your city, and over the years I've been overwhelmed by the number of individuals—from citizens to journalists and academics—who have commented about the extent to which Mississauga's identity and image is so inextricably linked to me. It's often been said that "Mississauga is Hazel McCallion" and "Hazel McCallion is Mississauga." What greater tribute could there be? I am also so proud when residents traveling say they are from Mississauga, not simply Toronto. This shows their pride in their city!

I hope I am remembered for helping to uplift, inspire and elevate those around me and that I always put Mississauga first—but I'll leave it to others to decide.

Acknowledgements

For many years, numerous friends and loved ones, including my children, Peter, Linda and Paul, kept urging me to write a book and tell my story my way. I am grateful to all who thought my life significant enough to chronicle. For this particular project, I would like to thank Elliott Kerr for acting as my book agent. I'd also like to thank my executive assistant, Carol Horvat. Carol knows me so well after almost twenty-five years of working together that her help in telling my story as best possible was invaluable. Of course, I want to thank the people of Mississauga for trusting me as their mayor for thirty-six years and electing me twelve consecutive times. I simply cannot think of a better job, and I am humbled and appreciative of the support given me over the years.

—H.M.

Sometimes things are simply meant to be. My connections to Streetsville must be acknowledged and thanked—going all the way back to a 1969–70 Streetsville tyke hockey team, the

273

only squad to beat my tyke team from East York that season. Unfortunately, those Streetsville kids had to do it in two of the last three games of the year, costing us the greater Toronto area title. I'd never heard of Streetsville until that fateful season and wouldn't hear of it again until more than a decade later on a date, when my future wife proudly proclaimed she was from Streetsville. In married life, we would move from Toronto to Mississauga's Port Credit area, and Streetsville has long been like a second home.

During this project I am truly indebted to my wife, Cobi Ladner, for her input and editing, and to our children, Aidan and Charlotte, for putting up with me. And also to the other Streetsville Ladners—from the late Eric Ladner and his wife, Mary (who worked for Hazel McCallion on the Streetsville Planning Board in the 1960s), to Todd, Liz, Erica, Alex and Duncan Ladner. I'm also appreciative of the research help from Kim Jeffs and my sister Mary Katherine Whelan, who has a librarian-like eye for detail with a flair for finding good anecdotes. Speaking of research, thanks also to Nick van Rijn for help with the derailment, and to my cousin Steve Brehl in New York for help with details about his city.

I am grateful to the mayor's lawyers, Liz McIntyre and Freya Kristjanson, who saved me so much time when it came to issues surrounding the judicial inquiry. The mayor called Liz and Freya "fabulous" and I understand why. At the City of Mississauga, I'd like to thank legal counsel Mary Ellen Bench and Susan Amring, Director of Economic Development, for their valuable help. Like the mayor, I would also like to thank her staff, especially Carol, and agent Elliott Kerr; and I tip my hat to Hilary McMahon and Rick Broadhead for their advice and ideas.

At HarperCollins, I'd like to thank editor Jim Gifford for his direction and excellent input into the manuscript, copy editor Anne Holloway for her exacting and deft touch, and production editor Maria Golikova for her patience.

I'd also like to thank Ralph Hunter, Dave O'Brien, Jim Murray, Jake Dheer, Margaret Marland, Ron Duquette, Ron Lenyk, Jennifer Evans and other friends of the mayor who provided insight into her personality and shared many terrific stories about her. I'd like to thank several of my friends and colleagues for their support during this project with such a short time frame, including Bill Fanjoy, Adam Toth, Mark Coombs, Steve Elgee, Paul Barter, Jan Innes, Samer Bishay, Maged Bishara, Cameron Zubko, Nader Marzouk and Rob Bracey.

Most importantly, I'd like to thank Hazel McCallion for not only choosing me to help her with her incredible story, but for being such a pleasure to work with, answering every question and never ducking anything, something not altogether uncommon for most politicians. I think Mississauga's first mayor, Martin Dobkin, said it best when he said Hazel McCallion is "probably the most unique politician Canada has ever produced." After working with her on this project, I could not agree more. At 93 years young, her mind and memory are incredibly sharp and her energy level is higher than mine. Hazel is an inspiration to me. I'm sure I am not alone there, either.

—R.B.

Index